Free Church, Free State

Free Church, Free State

The Positive Baptist Vision

Nigel G. Wright

PATERNOSTER

British Library Cataloguing in Publication Data
A catalogue record for this book is available from
the British Library

ISBN   1-84227-353-1

Cover Design by fourninezero design.
Print Management by Adare Carwin

Dedicated with much
love and appreciation to
Ruth

Contents

Foreword

In this centennial year of the Baptist World Alliance (1905–2005), it is proper that we have a textbook for understanding who Baptists are, where they have been and where they need to go. Dr Nigel Wright has done a great service for Baptists and those interested in co-operative Christianity. In the best sense of the terms, this book is both sectarian and catholic, that is, it is written by a Baptist for Baptists, but also for the larger ecumenical church in the twenty-first century.

The modern Baptist movement had its origins in Great Britain and therefore it is good that a British Baptist write this significant study with pastors, church planters, evangelists, lay pastors and preachers in mind. But it is more than a book for Baptist leaders and laity. It is written for the whole church of God, giving a positive vision of who Baptists are and their contribution to the church universal. The Anglican bishop, historian and missiologist, Stephen Neill, once said that the ecumenical movement is like a treasure house to which each tradition brings its jewels as a larger contribution to the whole church. This comprehensive study of Baptist life brings the jewels of that tradition not only to the great spectrum of Baptist life, but to the Christian church worldwide.

This study is more than a history. It is a theological treatise comparing the baptist vision with that of the catholic vision. Note the use of the small 'b' for baptist. Early on Nigel Wright enlarges this historical and theological movement to include a whole host of other Protestants, Pentecostals, and evangelicals who would affirm a baptist vision of the church, but not call themselves Baptists or be part of their particular history. Using a small 'b' for a baptist vision of the church could at first be confusing for those who call themselves Baptists, as it was for my computer! But it is important to understand this distinction and the enlarging of the baptist vision to encompass all those Christian movements which affirm believers' baptism, autonomy and freedom of conscience.

This important study analyses two historical visions of the church, the catholic (note the small 'c') and the baptist. The distinctive characteristics of each underlie the thesis of this book. The catholic church vision does not consider itself a free church but sees itself in 'historic connectedness with the apostolic tradition flowing all the way back to the early church and centred in the common confession of the creeds and in the role of the bishops as agents of fellowship and relationship'. On the other hand, to show the contrast, those who follow the baptist vision 'find the essence of the church not in historic connectedness but in the living presence of Christ by the Spirit among those who believe, the life of Christ being free and diffused among believers as the living body of Christ' (p.xxiv). With this clear distinction in mind, the Baptist reader, as well as those from the larger baptist and catholic traditions, will be enlightened as to the origins of that historical movement called Baptist, its growth and influence today. But more than that, it will help Baptists gain a new vision of today's church and what our prophetic contribution to the larger movement can and should be. As such, it will help those from the catholic tradition to understand better that deep faith that we hold in common expressed in the trinitarian confession of Christ and his church.

Christians of all persuasions in the twenty-first century should rejoice in one of the greatest contributions that the Baptist movement has made to the church universal, that is, freedom of religion. This freedom demands a free church over against a state-supported church. This study provides background to the fact that the corollary to freedom of religion should therefore be a free state. At the beginning of the twenty-first century, which has been categorised by some as 'a clash of civilizations', this baptist vision of a free church in a free state is a solution for the pluralistic society in which we live. The tragic religious conflicts between countries such as Armenia and Azerbaijan, Serbia and Bosnia, following the fall of communism, and Israel and Palestine, are only a few examples of what happens when religion and the state are united and not separate. It is the baptist conviction that such wars can be avoided if religion is free from state control and the state is free from religious control. This is not to minimise the influence of religion in society, but on the contrary, such a vision would allow religion to rediscover and express its true nature and enable it to be a prophetic voice for peace and harmony in a world bent on destruction and violence. To hold to a free religion in a free state is not to encourage or allow the secular state to be atheist. Rather, this vision is 'a political strategy for pluralist societies' (p.217) which enlarges and corrects the definition of secularism, and contributes to peace among various religious traditions as they live together.

This study is a challenge both to the catholic tradition which is tempted by 'sacred power', and the baptist vision which tends towards 'fragmented sectarianism' (p.257), to recognise that both traditions are church. In this sense the book is a prophetic call for the baptist and catholic traditions to centre on Christ and his Lordship, to look beyond our historical and often man-made separations and seek a new unity for which Christ prayed, 'so that the world might believe'. In other words, the author challenges both traditions to recognise one another as authentic representations of biblical faith: 'If both the catholic and baptist foci in that ellipse we call Christianity could see the ways in which they could enrich each other, and draw from each other the good things that they bring, without sacrificing what really matters to either side, then it would become possible to imagine a new kind of unity within the body of Christ, the spiritual potential of which would be immense' (p.269).

This book is a challenge to Baptists as we enter a new century. It is not a comforting book, but a disturbing study of our history and theology that demands openness and a willingness to change and enlarge our vision. When Alexander Maclaren in 1905 called the first Baptist World Alliance to order and asked all to stand and recite the Apostle's Creed he was making a statement that the Baptist vision of the church did not begin in 1609 with Smyth and Helwys, but was rather a rediscovery of the church universal that went back to Christ and the apostles, as witnessed to in the New Testament. In order for a new vision of a free church and free state to become a reality we require men and women of courage, conviction and commitment. May the reading of this book begin such a pilgrimage for the many who are longing for a new beginning. Baptists and catholics are indebted to Nigel Wright for helping us to continue this pilgrimage together as brothers and sisters in Christ.

Dr Denton Lotz,
General Secretary, Baptist World Alliance

Introduction

Aims and Oddities

In this book I aim to set out in a systematic and contemporary way those convictions and practices which distinguish Baptist Christians. In short, my hope is that it may be a kind of textbook for any who are seeking a fuller understanding of what it means to be a Baptist or to belong to a Baptist church. At the same time it may well be that readers will encounter ideas and frameworks of thought that are distinctive. I weave together a number of elements: there must in particular be clear reference throughout the book to the Bible, the inspired and foundational text that Christians share in common and which differing traditions read in varying ways. This book must show how Baptists read the texts of Scripture and how their perceptions arise from the heart and the root of the Christian project contained there.

There must also be reference to the historical origins of Baptist movements and some account of what was believed to be at stake in the decisions and commitments that they made. I hope to show that although certain insights were born because of the pressure of historical circumstances, they were in some measure a recovery of something essential to Christian witness and the existence of the church. The book's subtitle has relevance here: Baptists were not simply reacting negatively against forms of the church or of society which they found it hard to accept as God's will; they were also discovering positive understandings of God's will for church and world which had been overlooked, neglected or suppressed in the church they inherited.

Added to the strands of Scripture and history there must also be a third strand, an engagement with some of the issues faced by the church today as it serves the coming of God's kingdom. If commentators are to be believed, that future is a complex one. Churches[1] of today and tomorrow may be distinguished according to whether they are traditional, contemporary or postmodern[2] and it would be a mistake to believe that in the complexities of post-modernity any of these styles is going to be consigned to the dustbin of history. Rather, each will exist side by side, if sometimes uneasily, with the others. The challenge is therefore to express the subject matter of this book in such a way as to let it have vitality for a variety of ways of being church; that means avoiding being too prescriptive, for the most part, about exactly how the values and principles described here can be worked out in particular practices. The declared goal is to shape the way Baptist Christians live out their lives today and in the future, and to offer an interpretation of Baptist identity for the generations to come. In doing this, I cannot claim that what is set out in this book is right, as if there were no complementary or competing perspectives to be set against it. I do believe, however, that what is here is responsible in negotiating some of the challenges we face, not least in improving on some of the weaknesses of this way of being church.

It is likely that this book will evoke the response from some that we live in a post-denominational age and so any writing that expounds the distinctives of any group of Christians is flirting with irrelevance. Whereas I agree with and welcome the fact that we are in some senses in post-denominational times I nonetheless regard this as a somewhat glib assessment. Weighty theological issues never go away and in one form or another we must always come back to them.[3] As Brian MacLaren has pointed out the prefix 'post' is best understood in the way it functions in a word such as 'post-pubescent'.[4]

Children who pass through puberty are never the same again but remain permanently changed by the experience. To be 'post' does not therefore mean that whatever we are 'post' no longer matters or affects us: quite the contrary. We need to understand it in order to grasp where we now are and how our history has changed us. We should not be bound by the past, but we are inevitably influenced by it and most of the time we are well advised to build upon its solid achievements.

At this point, a word is appropriate about those for whom this book is primarily designed. First, there are those who are offering themselves for recognised ministry among Baptist churches as pastors, church-planters, evangelists, lay pastors or local preachers. It makes sense that those who represent Baptist churches should have an adequate grasp of the distinctive doctrines of that tradition and their biblical base, and this book seeks to provide it. Secondly, there are members and leaders in Baptist congregations who ought to be aware of what they are a part of, why certain things are done in the way they are, how they can be done at their best and how they can be improved upon when they fall short of their best. The last thing we should desire is a mindless adherence to traditions, with no real grasp of the spirituality they are meant to express. Thirdly, there are interested observers or inquirers who may want to know what makes Baptists tick and who are engaging in comparative study (always profitable in my experience) for the sake of their own communions and traditions. The days have passed when any of us could claim that we have the monopoly on or even the highest expression of divine wisdom. At best, we are *a* tradition in the church rather than *the* Tradition of the church and in this newly modest age there is much to learn from each other.

Given the aims and the intended readership of this book it ought not to be surprising that there will be some repetition here of some quite basic material. Those who are well versed in this will no doubt quickly pass over what they know to find out what, if anything, is new. Occasionally, I have chosen to repeat arguments that can be found in similar form in other books and articles I have written. This is because I consider those arguments still to be cogent and worth recycling, and the works where they originally appeared are now out of print.[5] The last three chapters of this book also draw upon some of my newly published articles as indicated in the relevant footnotes. In recent years, and largely thanks to Paternoster Press, there has been a pleasing increase in the amount of material dealing with specifically Baptist concerns. Baptist studies, and Baptist ways of doing theology, are fair set to become a major field in their own right. Yet there remains, to my mind, a gap in what is available in accessible form when it comes to offering a sustained and broad interpretation of Baptist identity at a basic level. There are older books, such as those by Henry Cook[6] and H. Wheeler Robinson[7] which are still of value, but they belong to a former generation, as well as being long out of print. Stanley Grenz has written crisply and usefully, but for the North American scene.[8] His book has acted as a kind of model for this one, although without the particular forms of practice detailed by Grenz and which, in my experience, are more variable. Paul Beasley-Murray's officially sponsored book[9] has been widely used, but does not greatly concern itself with the social or political implications of Baptist identity and therefore cuts short its discussion. In many ways, the present volume could be seen as a more accessible version of my own book *Disavowing Constantine*,[10] but its focus is broader, more basic and more practical.

At this point, it will be helpful if I highlight and explain some of the distinctive, possibly unusual, perspectives which will be encountered in this book. First, a concept which will frequently appear is that of 'sacred power'. I contend that the Roman Catholic Church came to model itself upon the imperial state and conceived of the authority it had been given as sacred and legal power over its members. This is not an isolated judgment but is widely shared by Catholic historians as well as numerous Protestant critics.[11] In many ways, the Roman Catholic Church needs to be seen as the inheritor of the style and position of the Roman Empire in the Western world.[12] In understanding the positive Baptist vision, it helps to see that it was above all a reaction against the institutional church which had over a period of centuries become an immensely powerful and domineering institution. As we shall notice, this process is associated in particular with the legalisation of Christianity from 313 and continued apace well into the nineteenth century. The governing role of the bishops (particularly that of the Bishop of Rome), which had begun as a pastoral and servant ministry, became increasingly imperialistic, legalistic and juridical in character. They determined and enforced, often by the use of violence and intimidation, the prescribed orthodox line on the model of a monarchical authority. This is what I mean by 'sacred power'. Although increasingly gaining momentum in the church, and the cause of numerous conflicts with kings and rivals, this process did not come to a full and explicit expression until the nineteenth century, by which time the papacy had been transformed into an absolute monarchy with all the panoply which attaches to such institutions. The high point of this was the declaration of papal infallibility at the first Vatican Council in 1870, an act which profoundly alienated Orthodox, Protestant and, indeed, many Catholic Christians. For most of its history, the papacy has been a temporal as well as a spiritual power, and technically still is, although in a much reduced way.

As an example of the mentality of sacred power, Duffy cites the words of Pope Pius X (1903–1914):

> The Church is by its every nature an unequal society: it comprises two categories of person, the pastor and the flocks. The hierarchy alone moves and controls ... The duty of the multitude is to suffer itself to be governed and to carry out in a submissive spirit the orders of those in control.[13]

In the light of such comments, Baptist reactions against Roman Catholicism need to be seen as far more than religious prejudice.[14] They are reasoned and responsible responses to a religious system that up until the dramatic and welcome reversals of Vatican II (1962–1965) was characterised by papal authoritarianism and consistently opposed itself to religious liberty on the grounds that 'error has no rights', strenuously denying the doctrine of a free church in a free state.[15] This was fundamentally mistaken and is the element in the historic church that Baptists were above all reacting against, for the best of reasons. It is no accident that Lord Acton (1834–1902), the Catholic historian and ardent defender of liberty, was speaking of the papacy when he penned his famous words, 'Power tends to corrupt and absolute power to corrupt absolutely.'[16]

Traditionally, Protestants have probably seen their divergence from Roman Catholicism as primarily to do with soteriology (the doctrine of salvation) rather than with ecclesiology (the doctrine of the church). It is commonplace to hear argued that the divergence in traditions is over the doctrine of justification by faith. My contention is that this is only true in part. Ecclesiology and soteriology are of course intimately linked, since whom we deem to be a Christian brings us to the question of who belongs to the church. But here we see how the notion of sacred power can impinge upon salvation: if it is through the grace of baptism that eternal salvation is mediated by the Church and further sustained and completed by that same Church through other sacraments which it controls, such as the Eucharist and absolution, then the Church has power not only over this life but also over that which is to come. Infected by a belief in its own sacred power it can use its position to intimidate others to fall into line on pain of excommunication, and has done so frequently.[17] Entirely right though it may be to emphasise that justification by faith is one aspect of the gracious movement of God whereby God reclaims lost creatures and sanctifies them as God's own,[18] when this is made dependent upon the continuing approbation of an all-powerful Church, which has other goals and objectives, the corruption of sacred power is a short step away.

Secondly, in one clear respect this book literally re-presents an enduring perspective which I have frequently addressed in other writings and which is captured in the title, *Free Church, Free State*. It is my conviction that the positive Baptist vision implies a new conception of society arrived at by means of a particular understanding of the church. Sacred power sits easily with absolute power exercised in society at large, and its rejection in the church leads on logically to a corresponding rejection of overweening and authoritarian power as a desirable feature of social or political existence. If the church is called in Christ to be the first fruits of a new humanity, an expression of the way of living that both pleases God and promotes human flourishing, then the Christian community must in some way and in some measure display in its social existence a pattern for the rest of humanity. If it was true of Israel that God's call to her to be a holy nation was paradigmatic for other nations, this must be true all the more of the church. 'Their very existence and character as a society were to be a witness to God, a model or paradigm of his holiness expressed in the social life of a redeemed community.'[19] What is being attempted in the church therefore has relevance and transformative potential for the world. Of course, having made such astonishing claims they need to be moderated. The church is, after all, still a community of sinners and the world, as yet lacking redemption, can and will hardly rise to the greatest of moral heights. But despite all, God's Spirit is in the church. Analogies can be drawn and influence exerted between what the church is becoming and what the world could become.

Once put in these terms, it becomes important both to discuss how the church should have its existence in order to express its unique calling and how it should relate to the social order. This accounts for the Baptist preoccupation with church order. For Baptists freedom has been paramount, freedom in the first instance from 'sacred power', simply to be the church under the Lordship of Jesus Christ and to do those things its Lord asks of it as they are interpreted by a properly informed conscience. The corollary of this is a political one: it is wrong for princes and rulers to play God, to seek to determine what people believe and how they think, to enforce religion or ideology. So the notion of the free church requires a kind of counterpart in a free state. This is the insight the first Baptists stumbled across, however imperfectly they grasped it. It is truly revolutionary and has shaped political discourse ever since.

Another way of expressing this is in terms not of analogy but of contrast. The difference between being the church community and being the civil community requires the greatest care when advancing analogies between them and much hangs on the recognition that they are incommensurate. Church and 'state'[20] are radically different in that one is dependent upon spiritual persuasion and influence, the other upon its power to force and coerce. It is essential to maintain this distinction and to do so resolutely. Once the state clothes itself with religious and theological language it risks making itself into an idol, a matter of ultimate significance to which obedience is due as if it were divine. In doing this, it forsakes its limited, 'secular' vocation. Examples of this throughout history are commonplace. Conversely, once the church takes to itself or becomes involved in the state's power to coerce it betrays its essential nature and mission. Examples of this are equally commonplace in the history of the church. The early Baptists grasped that the 'separation of church and state' at these points was absolutely essential if either church or state was to maintain its integrity and fulfil its God-given mandate, the state to preserve and the church to redeem. If they were reacting negatively against the complicity of the church in state coercion, they were also arguing that it did not have to be this way and that a better, positive vision was both required by closer attention to Scripture and in greater conformity to the way of Jesus Christ. That positive vision concerns a free church existing in a free state. Closer attention will be paid to all these things in their due place but it is appropriate here to register the fact that the interaction of the ecclesial or 'churchly' and the social and political at this point constitutes both the heart and the burden of this book. If there is anything distinctive about it, this is it.

Thirdly, there are other distinctives in what follows, some might think them oddities, both in language and conception. It is important to explain them here because otherwise they may seem like mistakes or inconsistencies. It has become common in certain circles sometimes to use the term 'baptist' (with a small 'b') in preference to 'Baptist'.[21] It may be possible to read into this a more modest approach to one's own denominational identity. I welcome such modesty, but there are other reasons why I adopt the custom from this point on: I shall use the term 'Baptist' when referring more precisely to that tradition or community of believers which is self-consciously Baptist and designates itself by that title. But there is a much wider tradition which while not being denominationally Baptist stems from the radical wing of the Reformation, and whatever the other differences, nonetheless broadly shares some or all of those values associated with believers' baptism, the autonomy of the local congregation and freedom of conscience. Historically, this tradition includes Mennonites, Brethren, Pentecostals, Disciples of Christ and others, and in contemporary terms embraces the 'new churches' and many independents. In this book I am eager to maximise the sense of solidarity between all these groups. All of them are acknowledged as possessing a family resemblance and as being in the 'believers church' tradition at the radical end of Protestantism.[22] In contemporary and not always elegant language, they are described as 'baptistic', 'Baptist-friendly' or 'Baptist-compatible'. I shall use 'baptist' to refer to this broader tendency in the church of which 'Baptists' are a classic instance. I use this device intentionally so when readers encounter it they should assume that the particular usage is significant and not accidental. When the word occurs at the beginning of a sentence the reader will have to guess to whom I am referring. There is a limit!

Conceptually, and this constitutes a fourth unusual feature, I invite the reader to interpret the church today as roughly reflecting two tendencies: the catholic (note the small 'c')[23] and the baptist (also, note the small 'b'). This is not to say that other readings are invalid. Westerners are used to dividing the church into Catholics and Protestants, and for good cultural reasons. A wider perspective, increasingly unavoidable, acknowledges Catholics, Protestants and Orthodox. Long since, Lesslie Newbigin advanced the categories of Catholic, Protestant and Pentecostal to describe developments in the church, in view of the burgeoning Pentecostal movements that came to abound in the twentieth century.[24] My own preferred reading is to see catholic and baptist tendencies as being like the twin foci of an ellipse and as representing divergent tendencies in that phenomenon we call global Christianity. They are rough and far from tidy categories. In the catholic tendency are grouped Catholics and Orthodox and some of those historically associated with Protestantism, such as Anglicans and even Methodists, many of whom see their movement not as an historic free church but as a renewal impetus within Anglicanism, from which they have temporarily become detached. A key element in this approach, seen at its best, is the sense of historic connectedness with the apostolic tradition flowing all the way back to the early church and centred in the common confession of the creeds and in the role of the bishops as agents of fellowship and relationship. On the baptist side are those who find the essence of church not in historic connectedness but in the living presence of Christ by the Spirit among those who believe; the life of Christ being free and diffused among believers as the living body of Christ.

At the deepest levels of theology, Miroslav Volf, a Pentecostal and baptist, has argued that fundamental understandings of the divine Trinity are at stake in these differing construals of church. In his complex language, the Triune God exists not as an 'asymmetrical-monocentric' pattern of being, that is where the Father dominates the Son and the Spirit in a way that renders them subordinate, but as a 'symmetrical-polycentric' pattern of being. Consequently, God is imaged and reflected in the church not in a hierarchical ordering but in participative and affirming structures which recognise a fundamental equality between the various stakeholders.[25] It is this latter pattern to which baptists have borne witness in their church order. Yet, as the differing traditions come increasingly to share a common understanding of the Triune God there is potential to excite a reworking of both episcopal and baptist patterns in constructive directions which make rapprochement between catholic and baptist possible. Where the notions and practices of sacred power are abandoned in favour of understanding the church as a relational and pastoral community a new dialogue is inevitable. In parallel, where baptists realise how offensive to the body of Christ is their tendency to fragment and their false individualism, to be livingly connected to the whole body of Christ becomes an imperative. Shorn of their pathological distortions the catholic and the baptist concerns become mutually complementary.

My point in this interpretation is to argue that the health and the future of the church are in direct proportion to the ability of these broad models of church to interact and interpenetrate. For this to happen fruitfully, both tendencies will need to renounce sectarianism. The catholic tendency is at its sectarian worst when it denies to baptists the right to be regarded as truly church on the grounds that they are not properly 'connected' to the whole. The baptist tendency is sectarian when it fails to see the importance of the whole body of Christ and imagines that its own local expression of church is all that matters. Both tendencies at their best bear witness to key elements for the church. But neither tendency is often at its best and so both need to be redeemed from their respective versions of sectarianism to embrace the whole body of Christ and to bring their distinctive offerings into the commonwealth of the church which is yet to be. How this might be imagined and eventually brought to pass will be an underlying but persistent theme of this book and in particular a major burden of the last chapter. Some baptists will therefore find this book all too ecumenical. So be it. There will be, I trust, no sacrifice of essential baptist principle and probably quite the reverse; but hard questions need to be asked of ourselves. I could not agree more that, 'When faith no longer frees people to ask the hard questions, it becomes inhuman and dangerous.'[26]

One final point: Baptists are now a numerous and multi-farious community spread throughout the world,[27] and baptists greatly more so. Although there are values held in common across this spectrum there are also variations of style and theology. There is no doubt that context shapes theology. It is entirely foolish to imagine that any one cultural expression of baptist life can be normative for the whole since that leads to a kind of cultural imperialism. Fruitful dialogue and debate there might be between culturally influenced ways of interpreting Scripture, but domination by any certainly not.

This book is written by one who takes as his primary community of reference the Baptist churches of England and, in a parallel way, lives within the stable liberal democracy of the United Kingdom. As Baptists take their origin from England, the English experience is of particular interest in understanding how Baptist values have been shaped and expressed. All of this will be reflected in this book. But this expression is only one among many and can make no claim to precedence on the basis of age. My hope is that this book might prove useful in many parts of the world and that those who live in different places might nonetheless find many points of connection. A primary baptist commitment, along with many other parts of the church, is to the living and dynamic rule of Jesus Christ in the church as this is discerned by means of engagement with the canonical and normative authority of Scripture. This is where our journey begins.

Notes

[1] I prefer to use the word 'church' without a capital letter and this will be my custom in this book even when referring to the whole or universal church. When there is a capital it will be because I am referring to some institutional form of the church which counts as a proper rather than a common noun, e.g. the Roman Catholic or Anglican churches.

[2] Brian D. MacLaren, *A New Kind of Christian: A Tale of Two Friends on a Spiritual Journey* (San Francisco: Jossey-Bass, 2001), 147.

[3] See also on this Nigel G. Wright, *New Baptists, New Agenda* (Carlisle: Paternoster, 2002), chapter 4.

[4] MacLaren, *A New Kind of Christian*, 15.

[5] In particular see *The Radical Kingdom: Restoration in Theory and Practice* (Eastbourne: Kingsway, 1986) and *Challenge to Change: A Radical Agenda for Baptists* (Eastbourne: Kingsway, 1991).

[6] Henry Cook, *What Baptists Stand For* (London: Kingsgate Press 1947, 1964).

[7] H. Wheeler Robinson, *Baptist Principles* (London: Kingsgate Press 1945).

8 Stanley J. Grenz, *The Baptist Congregation: A Guide to Baptist Belief and Practice* (Vancouver, British Columbia: Regent College Publishing, 1985, 1998).

9 Paul Beasley-Murray, *Radical Believers: The Baptist Way of Being the Church* (Didcot: Baptist Union of Great Britain, 1992).

10 Nigel G. Wright, *Disavowing Constantine: Mission, Church and the Social Order in the Theologies of John Howard Yoder and Jürgen Moltmann* (Carlisle: Paternoster, 2000).

11 See for instance the excellent account of the history of the papacy by Eamon Duffy, *Saints and Sinners: A History of the Popes* (New Haven and London: Yale University Press, 1997, 2001), *passim* and 286–318. Duffy describes the power of the papacy at the end of the nineteenth century as 'absolutism' and cites Cardinal Henry Manning's approval of 'the beauty of inflexibility', 305.

12 'The reconciliation of the Roman Empire with Christianity under Constantine the Great (ca. 280–337) and the establishment of Christianity as the state religion altered the nature of churchly offices. Church officials received numerous privileges, some of them rising to the rank of senators. Civil and religious laws were now often identical. Canon law entered upon a boom period. After the partial breakdown of the Roman Empire, high church officials also took over political functions.': August Bernard Hasler, *How the Pope Became Infallible: Pius IX and the Politics of Persuasion* (New York: Doubleday, 1981), 35.

13 From R. Aubert (ed.), *The Church in a Secularised Society* (London, 1978), 129–43 as cited by Duffy, *Saints and Sinners*, 325. Leonardo Boff: 'Through the latter centuries, the church has acquired an organizational form with a heavily hierarchical framework and a juridical understanding of relationships among Christians, thus producing mechanical, reified inequalities and inequities. As Yves Congar has written: "Think of the church as a huge organization, controlled by a hierarchy, with subordinates whose only task it is to keep the rules and follow the practices. Would this be a caricature? Scarcely!".' See *Ecclesiogenesis: The base communities reinvent the church* (Glasgow: Collins, 1982), 1.

14 English Baptists were of course reacting against sacred power as they experienced it in the Church of England which they saw as perpetuating the errors and corruptions of Rome.

15 Duffy, *Saints and Sinners*, 295, 359, 363.

16 Letter to Bishop Mandell Creighton in Louise Creighton, *Life and Letters of Mandell Creighton* Volume 1 (Longmanns, Green & Co., 1904), 372.

[17] Even contemporary examples of this are not lacking.

[18] For marked convergence between Protestants and Catholics on justification see the *Joint Declaration on the Doctrine of Justification* agreed between the Lutheran World Federation and the Catholic Church, *http://www.ewtn.com/library/CURIA/pccujnt4.htm.*

[19] Christopher J.H. Wright, *Living as the People of God: The relevance of Old Testament ethics* (Leicester: Inter-Varsity Press, 1983), 43. Wright goes on to add: 'A paradigm is not so much imitated as applied. It is assumed that cases will differ but, when necessary adjustments have been made, they will conform to the observable pattern of the paradigm.'

[20] The word is really an abstraction for the sake of convenience but is used to refer to those people or forces in any given society that have the monopoly of the use of force. Chapters 10 and 11 deal more fully with this topic.

[21] E.g. James William McClendon Jr, *Systematic Theology Volume 1: Ethics* (Nashville: Abingdon 1986), 7–8.

[22] For more on this see Donald F. Durnbaugh, *The Believers' Church: The History and Character of Radical Protestantism* (London: Macmillan, 1968).

[23] When 'Catholic' occurs this will be a specific reference to the Roman Catholic Church; 'catholic' embraces other traditions.

[24] Lesslie Newbigin, *The Household of God: Lectures on the Nature of the Church* (London: SCM, 1953), 9.

[25] Miroslav Volf, *After Our Likeness: The Church as the Image of the Trinity* (Grand Rapids and Cambridge: Eerdmans, 1998), 234–39.

[26] Daniel L. Migliore, *Faith Seeking Understanding: An Introduction to Christian Theology* (Grand Rapids: Eerdmans, 1991), 5.

[27] Estimates of community strength often range between 80 and 100 million.

1. On This Rock

Biblical and Theological Foundations for the Church

Introduction

It should come as no surprise that a book on the church begins with the Bible. The Bible is the foundational text for the church and is regarded by baptists along with all other Christians as inspired by God to be the liberating and enlivening source of authority for Christian belief and practice. To be sure, this common claim is then interpreted in different ways. For the Roman Catholic Scripture is interpreted through the lens of tradition. In the belief that tradition represents a consistent, Spirit-guided unfolding of the truth of Scripture (after all, what is the point of an infallible Scripture without an infallible interpretation?), scriptural teaching is held to be of a piece with what the Roman Church has taught ever since. By contrast, and by observation, baptists hold that just as it was at the time of Jesus,[1] tradition can err and make void the Word of God. This does not mean that tradition is of no value since of itself it simply means a 'handing on'[2] of the faith and none of us would be where we are without somebody having 'handed on' the faith to us. Tradition is essentially good. But aberration is always a possibility and individual traditions need to be tested against their point of origin to see whether they are a legitimate unfolding of the apostolic witness or illegitimate deviations from it. The baptist conviction is that when it comes to the church, deviations of considerable proportion have taken place and that a corrective return is necessary to the Bible's teaching.

A Radical Way

The New Testament in particular is our point of orientation. If baptists belong to the *radical* end of the church[3] it is a *conservative* kind of radicalism which believes that the will of God for the church has been revealed in Christ and through the apostles, and that we need frequently to go back to those roots to be sure that what grows from them is truly a healthy part of the tree and not some extraneous or malignant growth. The 'baptist way of being the church' has its origins in the time of the Reformation, when for the first time the Bible became widely available to people. Reading Scripture for themselves, faithful believers began to question whether the church they had inherited was really what Christ had ever intended. Many concluded it was not. They are our forebears.

Here is another crucial feature: if the Bible does not lay down a blueprint valid for all times, it certainly does supply us with an enduring vision of the church and a whole host of images and metaphors by which we can navigate. Some Protestants have taken the view that all that really matters in our reading of the New Testament is how we can be made right with God. Personal salvation and justification by grace through faith are the essence of it all and anything else is a matter of indifference or, worse still, law. By contrast, baptists have assumed that the whole counsel of God merits our attention and that the New Testament says much, even if it does not say everything, about how the life of Christian communities is to be ordered under the rule of Christ. *How* to be the church is not a matter of indifference but of discipleship. We rightly look to Scripture to understand the will of God for the ordering of the Christian community. More than that, if the church is the community of the redeemed and if we are called to be a 'chosen race, a royal priesthood, a holy nation, God's own people, in order that you may proclaim the mighty acts of him who called you out of darkness into his marvellous light,'[4] how we share a common life as the church may actually be quite crucial.

What is the Church? Where is the Church?

How we go about answering these questions is important. In any age there is no shortage of people or agencies who have their own agenda for the churches. They are not slow to suggest what they should do and be. Sometimes it is governments who are keen to co-opt generic 'faith communities' into their programmes for social regeneration. At other times it is ideologues keen to hear their own preferred theories played back to them in a religious key in order to assert their dominance over the culture. The issues of identity and relevance belong together. The church will not truly be relevant until and unless it is faithfully what it is called to be; and the identity of the church must be defined not out of contemporary culture but out of its own story as narrated through the Scriptures, history and theology. The church is relevant when it is being what it is with integrity. What it is called to be is the church of Jesus Christ.

The English word for church, and its equivalent in a number of other languages, is actually derived from the Greek word *kyriakon* which means a 'house' or 'household' of the Lord. This can be misleading since it perpetuates the common misunderstanding, perpetuated even among free-church believers, that the church is a building. Despite the fact that this is routinely and correctly denied by numerous preachers we still have trouble removing this notion from our heads, let alone our notice boards. Early Baptists had it right when they called their simple buildings 'meeting houses'. New church baptists have a sure instinct when they refer to their worship or pastoral facilities as 'Christian centres'. Even the word 'chapel' is better than the word 'church' when referring to a building. The point is that it is all about people not about places, although people certainly need to make use of places. The distinction in German between *Kirche* (the building or the institution) and *Gemeinde* (the community or the congregation) is what is at stake. Biblically speaking, the church is the people and translates the Hebrew *qahal*[5] and the Greek *ekklesia*,[6] both of which words have the sense of the congregation or assembly that is *called together* or gathered by God's summons. God calls people together by the Word of the Lord to exist for and under that Word.

Images of the church abound in the New Testament, one scholar[7] managing to detect ninety-six of them including: salt,[8] light,[9] ambassadors,[10] witnesses,[11] the household,[12] a city,[13] the New Jerusalem,[14] exiles,[15] vine branches,[16] the poor,[17] a bride,[18] fishers,[19] and a letter.[20] However, three clear and primary images of the church emerge from among the plethora on offer and these are: the church as *the people of God*, as *the body of Christ* and as *the temple of the Holy Spirit*. These will be examined in some detail but before this is done it is appropriate, as they themselves suggest, to place even these images within a broader theological context.

The Church as the Image of the Trinity

It is no accident that the three primary images to which I have referred point us immediately towards the Holy Trinity: Father, Son and Spirit. As the people of God the church is called together by the Father; as the body of Christ the church exists in, for and through the Son who is its head; as the temple of the Holy Spirit the church is indwelt by the Spirit of God who gives life to all. The church is to be seen therefore as existing for and within the life of the living Triune God. It is through Christ that we have access by one Spirit to the Father.[21] According to John, Jesus prayed that just as the Son was in the Father and the Father in the Son so the whole church might indwell both Father and Son and be indwelt by them in a complete unity.[22] The church is called to reflect God and to embody the life of God within its own communities. If

God is understood to be Triune, that is to say a community of persons indwelling each other in indivisible unity, this immediately suggests a pattern for the church. Before the church ever takes form as an institution, and before we factor in any place for buildings and 'sacred places', the church is a community, a communion, a fellowship of persons in relationship. This is suggested by the very life of God. According to Colin Gunton, 'the manifest inadequacy of the theology of the Church derives from the fact that it has never seriously and consistently been rooted in a conception of the being of God as triune'.[23]

> It is remarkable how often Paul, for example, uses the word *koinonia*, communion or community, when speaking of the church and its way of being in the world. The church is the human institution which is called in Christ and the Spirit to reflect or echo…on earth the communion that God is eternally. The church is therefore called to be a being of persons-in-relation which receives its character as communion by virtue of its relation to God, and so is enabled to reflect something of that being in the world.[24]

Father, Son and Spirit have their life together in the communion of relatedness. The personal identity of each is the product of relationship with the others and of mutual interdependence so that the Father is the Father of the Son, the Son is the Son of the Father, the Spirit is the Spirit of the Father and the Son. This is more than metaphysics or impenetrable mystery: it is the essence of God and therefore the essence of the universe, the fundamental theme underlying the symphony of created existence. The church participates in this divine communion,[25] and believers participate in fellowship with each other as a consequence of it. The church therefore must be seen as a community of persons in relationship with God and with each other, participating on an equal basis in the life of God.

Crucial decisions need to be made at this point concerning how we understand the Trinity. If the church is really to be understood as *imaging* the Trinity then a hierarchical view of the Trinity will lead inevitably to a hierarchical view of the church. To see the Father *over* the Son who is in turn understood to be *over* the Holy Spirit in the inner life of God might lead to a corresponding structure for the church on the model of 'sacred power' delegated downwards through a priestly system. By contrast, to understand, as the church has long wished to do, that the divine life is essentially a communion of love (the technical word is *perichoresis*) among those who share equally in divine nature, a mutual reciprocity, leads to a model of church which is strong on fellowship and mutuality, where power is equally owned and distributed by common consent. This is the approach adopted by baptists. [26]

The Church of Jesus Christ

Of course, Christians believe in God as Trinity only because of Christ. It is the belief that God was incarnate in Christ that has led them to a re-imagining of who and what God must be in the light of Christ's coming. The Trinity is not finally a kind of abstract and abstruse mathematics but an attempt to tell a story, the unfolding story of redemption which involves the coming of God to us in the Son and then in the Spirit. The one whom we encounter in these ways is the same God, whom we acknowledge as the Father. Jesus comes to us out from the life of the Trinity as the Son of the Father and the gift of the Spirit. We take seriously therefore the fact that the church is the church of Jesus Christ.

At such points books on the church frequently quote the famous saying by Alfred Loisy: 'Jesus preached the Kingdom and what came was the Church.'[27] It was meant to be provocative and that it is so often referred to shows it has succeeded. At one level the saying must be true. It is hard to imagine that Jesus intended to found that immensely wealthy and elaborate organisation which we now know as the Roman Catholic Church, or, indeed, any other such organisation. These are in many ways the antithesis of the carpenter from Nazareth who was at odds with the Jewish establishment of his day. But did Jesus intend to found or gather any kind of community? The answer to this must surely be yes and the arguments to support this are as follows:[28]

- Jesus gathered a group of twelve disciples to be with him.[29] This is clearly meant to symbolise the formation of a renewed community within Israel, by reflecting the twelve patriarchs who were the founders of the nation.
- Jesus instructed his followers in a characteristic ethical code which was meant to distinguish them as an alternative community within Israel.[30]
- Jesus understood himself to be the Messiah, anointed to announce and to realise the kingdom of God and saw his disciples as a community of those who gave allegiance to him in this way.[31]
- Jesus entrusted this community of disciples with a mission and a message and authorised them to represent him and to extend and continue his work.[32]

Jesus preached the kingdom of God which although it is not only a community implies the gathering of a community in its service.[33] At the very least it must be said that Jesus *laid the foundations* of the church which came into being after the resurrection and Pentecost.[34] However, on two occasions the word 'church' is specifically said to occur on Jesus' lips, in Matthew 16:13–20 and Matthew 18:15–20 and these occasions are worth closer examination. It is commonplace for scholars to question the authenticity of these sayings. They are often seen as later interpolations into the ministry of Jesus deriving from the early church. Even were this true these verses still represent the canonical witness of the first Christians who were closer to Jesus than we are and might be thought to have a better idea of what he intended than we do.

Matthew 16:13–20

> Now when Jesus came into the district of Caesarea Philippi, he asked his disciples, 'Who do people say that the Son of Man is?' And they said, 'Some say John the Baptist, but others Elijah, and

still others Jeremiah or one of the prophets.' He said to them, 'But who do you say that I am?' Simon Peter answered, 'You are the Messiah, the Son of the Living God.' And Jesus answered him, 'Blessed are you, Simon son of Jonah! For flesh and blood has not revealed this to you, but my Father in heaven. And I tell you, you are Peter, and on this rock I will build my church, and the gates of Hades will not prevail against it. I will give you the keys of the kingdom of heaven, and whatever you bind on earth will be bound in heaven, and whatever you loose on earth will be loosed in heaven.' Then he sternly ordered his disciples not to tell anyone that he was the Messiah.

If ever there were a foundational text for the church it is this one. How the text should be interpreted is at the heart of some of the major disagreements in the church and it is instructive to show the distinctions.[35]

- *The Roman interpretation.* For Catholic Christians there is no doubt that Peter himself is to be seen as the rock on which the church is built. Jesus is playing on Peter's Aramaic name which is 'Cephas' and means 'rock'. In Greek this becomes *petros*, or 'stone'. As the leader of the disciples Peter is singled out for a leading role. But, according to the interpretation, it is more than this: here we see Jesus enunciating what has come to be called the 'Petrine principle', or 'Petrine office', the need for there to be in succession to Peter one who will take his office in the church in each generation. This succession came to be associated with the bishops of Rome and with the papacy. Papal power is therefore essential for the integrity of the church and the popes have the 'power of the keys' over the church, to permit or to prohibit in guiding and administering it. This reading of the text is strengthened by John 21:15–19, where Peter is commissioned to feed Christ's sheep, by 1 Corinthians 15:5 where 'Cephas' is listed as the first (male?) witness to the resurrection, and by Luke 22:32 where he is told by Jesus, 'once you have turned back, strengthen your brothers'. The weak point in the argument however concerns the transmission of the role of primacy to the next generation, which cannot be found in the text and rests on other assumptions. So we have, alternatively,

- *The Reformation interpretation*, which focuses not on Peter personally, but on Peter's confession of Christ as Messiah and Son of the living God, a confession which Jesus identified as coming by revelation from the Father, not by human insight. This confession is truly a turning point in the Gospel narrative and the foundational insight which constitutes the Christian church. When Jesus then says 'on this rock I will build my church', he is, according to the Reformation alternative to the Roman approach, speaking both *doctrinally* so that the church will be built upon this revealed truth, and *reflexively* in that he is referring to himself: he is the rock. This clearly corresponds with other biblical texts which speak of Christ as the foundation,[36] or as the cornerstone.[37] Consequently it is hard to dissent from this interpretation. But before we settle upon it a third is worthy of consideration and that is,

- *The Radical interpretation*. Without disagreeing with the last understanding, this approach points out that Jesus was indeed speaking to Peter. Peter here is a disciple who confesses Jesus Christ by revelation from the Father. As such he is the first of many and this is the point where building a church, a community of disciples, becomes possible. The rock on which the church is built is the rock of confessing discipleship. Where there are people like Peter who confess Jesus as Messiah, the new messianic community which is centred upon Christ and transmits his message and his life becomes a reality. The keys of spiritual responsibility, authority and competence are not therefore given to Peter in an exclusive way but to all who see what he saw and confess what he confessed.[38]

It can be seen that these three interpretations correspond in general with the Catholic, Protestant and free-church strands in the history of the church and the one advocated here is the third, which quite properly takes the second up into itself.

Matthew 18:15–20

> If another member of the church sins against you, go and point
> out the fault when the two of you are alone. If the member listens
> to you, you have regained that one. But if you are not listened to,
> take one or two others along with you, so that every word may be
> confirmed by the evidence of two or three witnesses. If the
> member refuses to listen to them, tell it to the church; and if the
> offender refuses to listen even to the church, let such a one be to
> you as a Gentile and tax collector. Truly I tell you, whatever you
> bind on earth will be bound in heaven, and whatever you loose
> on earth will be loosed in heaven. Again, truly I tell you, if two of
> you agree on earth about anything you ask, it will be done for you
> by my Father in heaven. For where two or three are gathered in
> my name, I am there among them.

Here is another foundational text. For free church and baptist
believers in particular it has played a key role in determining
what the church is and where it is to be found. The church is
found where two or three are gathered in the name of Jesus. By
contrast with the Jewish synagogue, which relied upon a
quorum of ten men before it could be formed, a church can be
formed where there are two or three believers, be they men or
women. What is crucial is that they gather in the name of
Christ, recognising him as the reason for their being together
and meeting intentionally for his sake. Such a gathering
becomes competent and capable of praying and acting
because Christ is in the midst and enables such prayer. It can
'bind and loose', allow or disallow on the basis of the
Scriptures. Authority apparently emanates not hierarchically
from the approval or legitimation of a bishop or other
authority, but from below and from within, from Christ who is
in the midst and around whom we gather. This community
has power, but not to impose. Rather, it enacts discipline
among its members by a careful and pastoral process of
admonition which can if not heeded escalate to the point
where the church acting together and as a whole excludes
someone from its fellowship who has chosen to remain in sin.
It is significant here that the highest level of appeal is not to

elders, or bishops or even to a primate but to the church (v. 17). This is, once more, a radically egalitarian vision of a community where spiritual authority arises within and among its members.

Attention will be given elsewhere to the nature and practice of discipline within the church. The authenticity of these verses has been questioned, perhaps understandably, because everywhere else in Matthew's Gospel Jesus is presented as the friend of Gentiles and tax collectors. This text seems therefore to jar with that consistent picture. The implication is that disobedient disciples are to be considered as being on the outside of the Christian community. Two solutions are possible to this: one is to argue that Jesus is referring, in an admittedly shocking way – but purposefully so – to the way the *Jews* treated the Gentiles and tax collectors, and so underlining the need to take obedience seriously in the church: treat disobedient disciples in the way the Jews treat Gentiles and others. The other is to say that even when they have been disciplined, the disobedient should be treated in the way that *Jesus* treated the Gentiles and tax collectors, in other words, by befriending them and seeking to re-include them within the community. These verses can then be seen to occupy a credible place within the teaching of Jesus and give essential pointers to the kind of church Jesus envisaged.

Primary Images of the Church

Having offered some trinitarian and christological perspectives we can now return to the three primary biblical metaphors for the church. These ought to confirm for us that the theological grounding we have given accords with the wider New Testament teaching.

The people of God

This image takes us back into the Hebrew Scriptures. Its origin is in the calling of Abraham described first of all in Genesis 12:1–3. The wider context is the story of the human predicament. Genesis, which means 'origins', depicts the beginnings of the world in God's creative purpose, the emergence of life and of humanity and then the dislocation of the world through human resistance towards and rebellion against God. Other 'origins' follow – of violence and conflict, of human civilisations and languages, of oppression and crime. The choice of Abraham is God's response to all of this and the beginnings of his redeeming purpose. Abraham is chosen with the promise that God would bless him and make a great nation of him, that he would be a blessing and in him all the families of the earth would be blessed.

This is not a selection for elite status among the nations. It is rather an election to a distinctive role with a view to imparting blessing to all. Yet the theme of election is foundational: God has chosen one people to be the means of blessing to all peoples. Other verses make it plain that God's choice is not based upon Israel's achievement but on God's grace alone. Election is not a sign of their worthiness but of God's free grace. He chooses an insignificant rather than a numerous people in order that it may be clear to all that whatever is accomplished through them is God's doing.[39] The story of Israel is not, as has often been supposed, a story of salvation through obedience to the law. It is as much to do with grace as is the New Testament and the response to grace is an obedient life under the rule of Yahweh, a life of holiness before the Lord expressed in ways which distinguish Israel from the nations. So it is that law,[40] circumcision,[41] sabbath,[42] temple worship and sacrifice are all to be seen as concrete ways in which Israel is to be distinguished from the 'nations', bulwarks against the continual threat of assimilation to the environment and its idolatries.

Israel's calling by Yahweh comes to be seen as a vocation to be a light to the nations,[43] to be God's witnesses.[44] The theme of the people of God is extended into the New Testament in which Jesus' calling of the twelve is symbolic of the renewal of Israel from within. As the church moves out from its Jewish point of origin it takes the momentous step of including Gentiles within its ranks without insisting that they become Jews in the process.[45] This marks a huge and very radical transition from being an ethnically defined religion to becoming an inclusive, international movement. In the light of the coming of Christ and the gift of the Holy Spirit without distinction, outward and concrete practices of Judaism assume an optional status with the stress now falling upon inward reality not outward conformity. Those are children of Abraham who share his faith, not his genes.[46] Circumcision is now a matter of the heart not the outer flesh.[47] Membership of the covenant people is now not by birth but by new birth.[48] Neither foods nor peoples are any longer to be regarded as unclean.[49] The old regulations are now seen as outward forms which were intended to prepare the way for the coming of the reality.[50] This does not mean that Israel has been abolished or replaced as the people of God, but Israel has been expanded to include people from all nations and in this new work of God's grace Israel has no less a place than any other nation in the divine favour.[51] God will be true to his ancient promises.

The whole church, which embraces Jews and Gentiles, is now the royal priesthood, the holy nation, the covenant people.[52] The distinctiveness of the church does not primarily consist in its adherence to concrete laws and rituals concerning which, with some clear exceptions such as baptism and Eucharist, there remains a great freedom and flexibility in the church.[53] Instead, conformity to Christ and imitation of his way is consistently laid down as the distinguishing mark of those who acknowledge the Messiah and belong to his community.[54] Because of this the people of God are pilgrims, never fully at home in the present order of things and pursuing a vision of future glory and fulfilment in the kingdom of God.[55]

The body of Christ

The church is to be seen as the people of God. It is also the body of Christ and here we encounter an image of the church replete with possibilities. In Christ the Son of God took to himself a body so that the invisible might become visible. In the resurrection that same body was glorified and then Christ ascended into heaven. While it would be wrong to claim an identity between the glorified body of Christ and the church, the metaphor suggests that in some sense the church must be a continuing locus or extension of the presence and action of Christ in the world by the Spirit. First, however, the image of the body suggests some more straightforward ideas.

Christ is, for instance, the head,[56] from whom the body draws its life and its direction. Christ governs the church, and this place belongs to no other. As members of the body believers are deeply rooted both in Christ and in each other, they belong together and are connected. All parts of the body have functions.[57] The body is charismatically ordered in the sense that the Spirit of God bestows and dispenses gifts for the common good.[58] Yet within this dynamic freedom there is also a structure and an order which serves to co-ordinate and integrate the gifts of all into a harmonious whole.[59] The images here are organic, dynamic, relational and participatory, suggesting a variety in unity. There is both equality and diversity among the members of the body. The body is both local and universal in expression and as a human body is activated by spirit and breath, so the Spirit of Christ is the life-giving principle within the body of believers.

In what sense may we say then that Christ is present in his body? On the one hand, we can be affirming and believe that Christ continues to take form through the flesh and blood members of his church. The church may be seen as a sacrament in that Christ by the Spirit chooses to mediate his presence through the church just as he does through the water of baptism or the bread and wine of communion. But the church is not itself Christ, however closely it may be joined to him by the Spirit. This means that the church should not be seen as a 'prolongation' or 'extension' of the incarnation. Hans Küng, writing as a Catholic, explains why this is the case:

> It is extremely misleading to speak of the Church as the 'continuing life of Christ' or as a 'permanent incarnation'. In such views the Church is identified with Christ, so that Christ as its Lord and head takes second place to his Church, which pretends to be the Christ of the present in constantly new incarnation. Christ is seen as therefore having abdicated in favour of a Church

which has taken his place and become his autonomous representative in everything, and so has gone a long way towards making him superfluous.[60]

It can be seen from this that to identify the Church as Christ can provide a foundation for a doctrine of sacred power. But the 'body of Christ' is a *metaphor* for the church rather than a literal description. At the same time as affirming the presence of Christ in and among its members we do well also to recognise the continuing distinction between Christ and ourselves and our church community. The perils of obscuring this distinction should be obvious.

The temple of the Holy Spirit

Jesus said that he would 'build' his church and in so doing suggested the image of the temple. When Yahweh brought the children of Israel out of Egypt they were instructed to build a tabernacle or tent which would be God's dwelling place in the midst of the people.[61] After many centuries the tabernacle was replaced by a temple, and this then became the dwelling place of Yahweh.[62] Events took yet a different turn when the Word became flesh and Jesus of Nazareth became the dwelling place of God among human beings, whose glory was seen by his disciples.[63] When he had been crucified and had risen and ascended, this same Christ poured out the Holy Spirit on his disciples and they then became the dwelling place of God, the temple of the Holy Spirit.[64] All of this is a stage on the journey towards the vision of all creation being the temple of God, the immediate dwelling place of the Lord.[65] It should be clear from this both that the church in its many communities occupies a unique role in human history and that it is, in God's perspective at least, central to the divine purpose. The church is characterised by the Spirit, by the reception of the abiding power and presence of God which is seen by the prophets as the fulfilment of the age to come.[66] It is the messianic community, anointed with the Spirit of Christ and distinguished from the saints of former ages by the fact that these are the latter days in which the Spirit is being poured out to bring God's purposes to pass. Even so the Spirit is yet a foretaste of a greater fulfilment still which is yet to come.[67] As the church awaits that day, its mission is to bear witness to Jesus the Messiah to the ends of the earth.[68]

The Priority of Mission

Reference here to the Spirit of God leads to some further theological reflections which are bound to shape our thinking about the church. The church must be seen as a missionary community participating in God's saving outreach to the world. This is implied in our former reflections on the church as the image of the Trinity. As the church participates in the life of God it is caught up in God's outreach to the world. The God whose vision we catch in the worship of the Trinity is the God who in the power of the Spirit sends the Son into the world and then in the name of the Son sends the Spirit to extend and apply the redemption that has been gained through the Son. This outward movement is referred to as the *missio Dei,* the mission of God. The church exists within this dynamic movement to such an extent that mission has to be seen not as an added activity but as the defining essence of the church.[69]

> A trinitarian ecclesiology would take its basic clue from the fact that the most fundamental Christian affirmation about the God who has been revealed in Jesus Christ through the continuing activity of the Holy Spirit is that God is extravagant, outreaching love. The triune God is a missionary God, and the mission of the church is rooted in the trinitarian missions. Furthermore, according to trinitarian doctrine, the very nature of God is communal, and the end for which God created and reconciled the world is depth of communion between God and creatures. The church is the community called into being, built up, and sent into the world to serve in the name and power of the triune God. When the church is true to its own being and mission, it offers an earthly correspondence to God's own unity in diversity, to the inclusive and welcoming love of the other that characterizes the communion of the triune God.[70]

Mission is clearly implied in each of the three primary images of the church we have identified. The people of God exist in the world to represent the Lord and to declare the works of God. They are distinctive in their Christ-orientated lifestyle and yet are scattered through all the nations, acting as salt and light. As salt they are all but invisible because they are scattered and dispersed, but their presence is effective in resisting corruption on the one hand while encouraging that which is good and fruitful on the other. As light they are seen to be present and shine by contrast with the darkness of ignorance and emptiness. As the body of Christ, the church is that community in which activated by the Spirit Christ takes shape and form through flesh and blood and may be encountered in the worship and witness of real-life communities. As the temple of the Holy Spirit, the church is the place to which the earth's tribes may go up to know and worship the living God. Although God is always to be found by those who call upon the name of the Lord,[71] God is especially to be found in God's temple. Mission is the essence of the messianic community.

The Church and the Kingdom of God

However, another important distinction is to be made here. Although the church serves the kingdom of God and may rightly be described as the community of the kingdom, the church and the kingdom cannot be wholly identified. The kingdom of God is seen in the New Testament as both a present reality and a future one. Jesus preached the good news that the time of fulfilment had come, the kingdom of God was near and his hearers should respond with repentance and faith.[72] The signs of this were that the demonised were set free, the sick were healed and the outcasts were included within the community once again. The kingdom of God meant a powerful conflict with the prevailing order within Israel as Jesus opened up God's alternative. At the same time, Jesus looked for a kingdom which was still to come[73] and taught his disciples to pray for its coming.[74] If the church is that community which comes into being because of the present experience of the kingdom it also awaits the consummation of the kingdom in the future. It may be a sign and an instrument of the kingdom but is not itself the kingdom. To identify the two would risk making the kingdom a pattern of delegated authority expressed through the church such that to be in the authority structure is to be in the kingdom. This then loses the dynamic nature of the kingdom of God and imprisons God within the form of an ecclesiastical structure. The church may be the product of the kingdom but it is not itself the kingdom of God and is always being called into question as to whether it is truly serving it. Its forms and institutions remain open to change and reformation at all points in order that it may serve the kingdom more completely.

The 'Ecclesial Minimum'

So far we have attempted to answer the question 'what is the church?' and to do so by reference to Scripture and theology. We have not yet fully answered the question 'where is the church?' and we need to do so. This is a practical question: how do we know if the church we lead, or are thinking of joining, or are contemplating starting as an experiment in 'postmodern' or 'emerging' church is *really* church? Is there a minimal set of requirements, an 'ecclesial minimum' that we need to fulfil? The answer to the question is plainly yes; not everything that claims the name of church is really church.

On the face of it the answer might seem straightforward. It was expressed many centuries ago by Cyprian (ca. 200–258), Bishop of Carthage: *ubi Christus ibi ecclesia*: 'where Christ is there the church is'. When we gather in the name of Christ and he is truly present, there is the church. We might describe this as the *internal* reality of the church. But this does not answer every question: we must go on to ask, how do we know that it is truly *Christ* who is in the midst? To the internal mark of the church we must add *external* signs by means of which we may recognise the internal reality of Christ. Cyprian's answer to this was that where there is a bishop of the Catholic Church you can be sure that Christ is truly present. Baptists have not been so confident about this answer, but they have had their own.

Here we return to Jesus' teaching about two or three gathering in his name (Mt. 18:20).[75] Of course, this specifically requires a gathering, a coming together of flesh and blood people and it is hard to imagine how it is possible to be church without this. It also implies faith in Christ on their part since to meet 'in Christ's name' means to do so intentionally and because of some quality of belief in him and devotion to him. These in their turn cannot be separated from the content of that belief, the doctrine of Christ which underlies them and must be in accord with the apostolic testimony. The prescribed ways of making this confession, which the New Testament traces back to Christ himself, are the practices of baptism[76] and the Lord's Supper.[77] When we have identified these elements we have come near to clarifying the minimum requirements for being church. Some approaches, which we shall later identify, wish to go further and to argue, with Cyprian for instance, that a relationship with a properly constituted bishop is also necessary, or that some kind of pastoral oversight is an essential part of a proper church. By contrast, the Reformers argued that the marks of a true Christian community are the right proclamation of the Word of God and the administration of the sacraments, a definition which comes close to the ecclesial minimum outlined. Baptists have wanted to add to this the idea of a covenanted community of disciples. Even in these definitions it is implied that there is someone who preaches the Word and administers the sacraments so some sense of an order of oversight within the church is functionally implied. But what we have uncovered here indicates that much that we do as church is not strictly necessary to our existence, whereas without other elements we have no existence at all. The church is able to take many forms and to display great adaptability across time and cultures while maintaining its essential being. This is one of its great strengths and is one of the reasons for its universal growth.

If Acts is taken not only as a history of the early church but as setting before the church certain ideals and standards, it is clear that Acts 2:41–42 is significant:

> So those who welcomed [Peter's] message were baptized and that day about three thousand persons were added. They devoted themselves to the apostle's teaching and fellowship, to the breaking of bread and the prayers.

It is of the essence of being church to believe the message of the gospel which asks for repentance and faith, to demonstrate this through being baptised, and then to be devoted to the community of the church which is informed by the apostles' teaching (now contained in the New Testament), enriched by continuing fellowship, and sustained by the breaking of bread and prayer. These elements surely belong to the very existence of the church and whatever may be added to the 'ecclesial minimum' remain at its heart.

It is instructive to distinguish between what belongs to the *esse* (or essence) of the church, what belongs to its *bene esse* (its well-being) and what might pertain to its *plene esse* (its fullness of being). These are distinctions that the following chapters will employ from time to time. In this chapter we have laid some biblical and theological foundations which will enable us to understand and apply these categories in the sometimes complex discussions that await us.

Notes

1 Matthew 15:3.
2 1 Corinthians 15:1–11.
3 George H. Williams, *The Radical Reformation* (Philadelphia: Westminster Press, 1962).
4 1 Peter 2:9.
5 E.g. Exodus 12:3, 6, 19 and *passim* thereafter.
6 E.g. Matthew 16:18; 18:17; 1 Corinthians 1:2; Galatians 1:2.
7 Paul S. Minear, *Images of the Church in the New Testament* (Philadelphia: Westminster Press 1960).

8 Matthew 5:13.
9 Matthew 5:14.
10 2 Corinthians 5:20.
11 Acts 1:8.
12 Ephesians 2:19.
13 Hebrews 12:22.
14 Revelation 21:2.
15 1 Peter 1:17.
16 John 15:1–11.
17 Matthew 5:3.
18 Revelation 21:2.
19 Matthew 4:19.
20 2 Corinthians 3:2–3.
21 Ephesians 2:18.
22 John 17:20–23.
23 Colin E. Gunton and Daniel W. Hardy (eds.), *On Being the Church: Essays on the Christian Community* (Edinburgh: T&T Clark, 1989), 48.
24 Colin E. Gunton, *The Promise of Trinitarian Theology* (Edinburgh: T&T Clark, 1991), 12. There are also excellent expositions of this in Paul S. Fiddes, *Participating in God: A Pastoral Doctrine of the Trinity* (London: Darton, Longman & Todd, 2000), 11–61, and *Tracks and Traces: Baptist Identity in Church and Theology* (Carlisle: Paternoster Press, 2003), 65–82.
25 2 Peter 1:4.
26 As we have previously noted, these issues are widely explored by Miroslav Volf in *After Our Likeness*, especially chapters 5 and 6.
27 E.g. Hans Küng, *The Church* (London: Burns & Oates, 1968), 43.
28 Here I am following in particular R. Newton Flew, *Jesus and his Church: A Study of the Idea of the Ecclesia in the New Testament* (London: Epworth Press, 1938), 35–88.
29 Mark 3:13–19.
30 Matthew 5–7, and *passim* including Matthew 20:20–28.
31 Matthew 16:13–38.
32 Luke 10:1–24.
33 Flew, *Jesus and his Church*, 87.
34 Küng, *Church*, 74.
35 For similar expositions of this passage see Cook, *What Baptists Stand For*, 46–56 and Walfred J. Fahrer, *Building on the Rock: A Biblical Vision of Being Church Together from an Anabaptist-Mennonite Perspective* (Scottdale, PA: Herald Press, 1995), 19–23.
36 1 Corinthians 3:11.

37 1 Peter 2:6–7.
38 Notably, in John 20:21–22 the risen Lord breathes on the disciples present with him and empowers them to forgive and retain sins.
39 Deuteronomy 7:7–10.
40 Deuteronomy 6:1–3; 10:12–22.
41 Genesis 17:9–14.
42 Exodus 31:12–17.
43 Isaiah 42:6.
44 Isaiah 43:12.
45 Acts 15:12–21.
46 Romans 4:9–12, 16–25.
47 Romans 2:28–29.
48 John 3:1–10.
49 Acts 10:1–16; 11:1–18.
50 Galatians 3:19–29.
51 Romans 11:11–16, 25–36.
52 1 Peter 2:9–10.
53 Romans 14:1–9.
54 Romans 12:1–2; Hebrews 12:1–3; 1 Peter 2:23–25.
55 Hebrews 11:8–40.
56 Ephesians 4:15–16; Colossians 1:18.
57 1 Corinthians 12:12–31.
58 1 Corinthians 12:1–11.
59 Ephesians 4:15–16.
60 Küng, *Church*, 237.
61 Exodus 40:34–38.
62 2 Chronicles 7:1–3.
63 John 1:14.
64 Acts 2:32–33; 1 Corinthians 3:16–17; 6:19; Ephesians 2:22.
65 Revelation 21:9–27.
66 Acts 2:17–21.
67 Ephesians 1:13–14; Hebrews 6:4–5.
68 Matthew 28:18–20; Acts 1:8.
69 Jürgen Moltmann, *The Church in the Power of the Spirit: A Contribution to Messianic Ecclesiology* (London: SCM, 1977, 1992), 33–7.
70 Migliore, *Faith Seeking Understanding*, 200–201.
71 Matthew 7:7–11; Acts 2:21.
72 Mark 1:14–15.
73 Matthew 8:10–12; 26:29.
74 Matthew 6:9–10.
75 In this section, I follow Volf, *After Our Likeness*, 128–54.

[76] Matthew 28:19.

[77] 1 Corinthians 11:23–26. This raises the question as to whether, for instance, a Quaker meeting and a Salvation Army assembly qualify as 'church'. This is a matter of debate within those movements themselves.

2. Genesis and Genius

Types, Traditions and Baptist Origins

Introduction

We have said enough so far to indicate there is potential for great variety in the church of Christ. The Bible offers a wealth of images which may be developed in different directions. Former generations of Christians, especially of baptist persuasion, were less tolerant of diversity than we now find ourselves to be. It was clear to some of them that there was only one pattern for the church in the New Testament and, just as the construction of the tabernacle was to be precisely 'according to the plan for it that you were shown on the mountain'[1] and 'according to all that the LORD has commanded'[2], so they expected that the details of church order could be spelled out and adhered to. By contrast, I have suggested that, although there is an ecclesial minimum for the church, without which we are no longer church, considerable variation is possible beyond that. This does not mean that any variation should be seen as wise, helpful or even scriptural since as well as the *esse* of the church we are concerned about its *bene esse* or well-being: not everything makes for the church's well-being. However, there are differing and legitimate ways of being the church and difference should not lead us to deny to others the status of church if the marks of a true church, the ecclesial minimum, are in place.

In recent years it has become common for Baptists to speak of their 'way of being the church' and this certainly represents a new and welcome degree of modesty. It does not necessarily signify a lack of conviction. It is possible to believe that some things are good and that others are even better, which in this case means being closer to God's will as we understand it. It is possible to see strengths in other patterns of church while also believing that the weaknesses outweigh them; or to acknowledge weaknesses in one's own way of being church without needing to abandon it. A baptist vision of the church claims to be not only a possible way of interpreting the New Testament evidence but probably the most faithful. Yet all such claims are 'chastened'. This is not only because we should all be aware of our many failures to live up to our own ideals but also because we recognise that our practices are derivative: they cannot claim to correspond directly with the way it was in the New Testament church, only to be our responsible attempt to derive from the New Testament a form of obedience and response.

The aim of this chapter is to show how various models and patterns of church life have emerged and to identify the genesis and the genius of the baptist way of being church among them.

Unity and Diversity

There has been a growing recognition in the world of biblical scholarship that the New Testament contains both unity and diversity. Beneath the surface of the text closer examination reveals a series of competing models of theology and practice. In relation to the church this means variety in forms of ministry, of worship and sacraments and of confessional statements.[3] Eduard Schweizer was long since able to demonstrate that models and traditions of church made their appeal to the differing theological perspectives of the New Testament writers. So, so-called 'early catholicism' with its preoccupation with the orderly transition of ministerial

authority was continuing alone a trajectory to do with the
pastoral offices already in motion in the Pastoral Epistles.[4] The
Protestant and baptist concerns for the church as community
clearly extend from Paul's teaching on the body of Christ.[5] The
individualised and anti-clerical spiritualities of groups such as
the Quakers are inclined to draw upon references to the
anointing of the Spirit in the Johannine writings.[6] There is no
'law' of the church in the New Testament such that what
applies in Jerusalem must also be the law in, say, Corinth. But
there are theological concerns behind the different ways of
being church and it is these which constitute an authority for
the church today, however they come to be expressed in
practice.[7] Granted that in the New Testament such tendencies
might seem reconcilable and that the unity can be discerned
beyond the diversity, it might also be seen how once
extrapolated throughout later history differences are apt to
become divergences.

Divergent Views of the Church

A highly significant attempt to chart these divergences was
made at the beginning of the twentieth century and has
shaped the discussion ever since, and sometimes distorted it.
In *The Social Teaching of the Christian Churches* Ernst Troeltsch
undertook to survey the ways in which the churches
understood themselves and their relationship to the social
order. From his analysis there emerged a 'typology' in which
he traced the existence of three main approaches.[8] These are
called 'ideal types' because they are not claimed necessarily to
cover every angle or variation in what is, after all, a complex
field. Instead, they are an intellectual device designed to
enable comparisons and contrasts along the way. Troeltsch
identifies:

- *The church-type*, by which he means that form of church life
  which has sought to lay direct claim to the whole of life, the
  social as well as the spiritual, and to provide an

all-embracing canopy by means of which it might be both interpreted and determined. This type therefore is characterised by both *universality* and *comprehension* and represents a majority tradition in the history of the faith in that it has been exemplified both by the Roman Catholic Church and by the more nationally defined state churches of Europe. The urge of this type is to encompass whole populations and all the orders of life which it has sought not only to interpret but also, very often, to control. This is the point of its particular weakness: in wanting to be comprehensive it both dilutes its own distinctive message by being assimilated to the natural and general religiosity of humankind and makes compromises with power for the sake of its own continued dominance. By way of contrast is:

• *The sect-type*, which aspires not to universality but to *intensity* and *faithfulness*. Its concern is to remain close to the source of faith in Jesus of Nazareth and to be true to the gospel. This means accepting, in all probability, minority rather than majority status since embracing the way of Christ in this way is not popular. In turn, this means accepting that the Christian community will live with some degree of discomfort within its wider social setting, will not be in a position to control the social order and for the sake of Christ probably should not attempt to do so, although influence by means of persuasion is acceptable. It will in all likelihood be at variance with the form of religion represented by the church-type which it sees as encouraging nominal rather than true religion and as compromising the faith. Contrasted with this again is:

• *The mystic type*, for which the watchwords are *inwardness* and *privacy*. Although the mystic-type may have some form of communal existence, it is apt to be more comfortable with private, non-credal spiritual experiences and will as a consequence shade off into unorthodox beliefs and moralities. Mystics by definition are highly orientated towards experience rather than doctrinal standards. They have often been located within the mainstream of the church but there is a significant fringe presence throughout church history of such types. While we here acknowledge the mystic type it does not readily fall within the concerns of this book and so not much more will be said about it.

This has been an immensely influential typology. It is at its best when functioning not as a straightjacket or a series of convenient pigeonholes by which to dismiss people but as an analytical tool to illuminate the actual phenomena of the church's existence. Above all it should be seen as a *sociological* device, not a *theological* analysis. Sociologically speaking, to call a group 'sectarian' is to describe the nature of its social existence. To do the same theologically is to accuse it of a spiritual crime against the church. Wrongly used therefore, the typology can disadvantage those who belong in the minority traditions by prejudicing the way sectarian groups are perceived. The word 'church' carries immense prestige; with the word 'sect' it is the opposite. The typology misused in this way might be thought to imply that there is a normal, respectable and proper way to be the church, a way which values nominal religion; then there is an improper way to be the church, which is when people are serious about what they believe. The potential misuse of the typology can be applied both ways round. A moment's thought leads us to recognise that there are many lively 'sect-type' congregations within 'church-type' structures, and conversely some 'sect-type' denominations or movements which have not been averse to wanting to exercise political power. Despite these cautionary words the typology is still an illuminating one.

The Genesis of the Church

The origins of the Christian church clearly belong within the camp of the sociological sect-type. It was certainly a move-ment of great spiritual intensity and without profound experiences first of the risen Lord and then of the Spirit would never have begun. Originally, the followers of Jesus, or of 'the Way',[9] were a sect within Judaism, at variance both with the prevailing religious establishment and the imperial power.

They were thus in double jeopardy and any thought of embracing all of the social order was beyond them. Instead, they were acutely aware of the difference between themselves and the 'world'.[10] This did not make them apolitical. Whatever mystical qualities Jesus may have had, he was directly engaged in challenging the way in which his society was ordered and the way in which it made victims, religious victims even, of the poor and the excluded.[11] Christianity began then as a counter-culture, a movement of dissent both from the majority religion (Judaism) and from the majority ideology (Roman domination). A counter-culture experiences some alienation from the dominant culture and sets itself against it to a lesser or greater degree.[12] This was certainly true for the first Christians who attracted persecution to themselves precisely because they would not conform to the religious and political ideology of Rome in which the emperor was understood as a Lord, a divine figure due both worship and political allegiance. Christians owned only one Lord, the Christ. They would pray for the emperor and honour him; they would not pray to him, but instead would fear God.[13]

The reversal in the church's fortunes under Emperor Constantine (306–337)[14] effectively brought about a shift from a sect-type to a church-type existence and, in time, from being a counter-culture to being the established religion of the empire. It was also true that as the Christian church had been growing in numbers it had already been positioning itself for a new and influential role before Constantine and it would take some years after his reign before the shift was completed. In 380, under Emperor Theodosius I (379–395), Christianity was proclaimed in the 'Theodosian Code' as the official and only orthodox religion of the empire and was in a firm position to penalise any who did not submit to its dominance.[15] This change from persecuted sect to persecuting religion has been seen by many as the proper triumph of Christianity as an all-embracing system of truth and by others as a fundamental betrayal of Christianity's true nature. These divergent interpretations quite clearly mirror the church-type/sect-type distinction and more will be said about them in other places. The synthesis of church and state made possible by

Constantine's conversion and systematically carried through by Theodosius was to remain intact for over a thousand years and even after that would continue to shape the relation between the two. In some senses it is here that our story begins to take wings.

The Persistence of the Sect-Type

Once the church-type was established as the dominant form of Christian presence we begin to find the sect-type persistently re-emerging as a minority presence in the church. This is seen first in the rapid growth of monasticism. The monastic movement was already underway by this time as a response to the lukewarm commitment of many within Christianity as it grew in popularity. It was also given impetus by the lifting of persecution from the church. Christian heroism, previously diverted into the extremes of martyrdom, now looked for new forms of expression. This impetus continued into and beyond the mediaeval period. Monasticism was characterised by spiritual rigour, an intensity of devotion to the Christ whom it sought to imitate, and a reaffirmation of the qualities of evangelical poverty, chastity and obedience classically expressed in the Rule of St Benedict. If such devotion was not possible for all it certainly was seen as a possibility for some and had the power to attract some of the most outstanding figures of the period. At times this devotion was seen by way of contrast with the growing wealth and power of the Roman Church, as with the Franciscans. At others it was placed specifically at the service of the institutions of the church, as with the Dominicans and the Jesuits. The histories of these movements demonstrate that they were all capable of their own kinds of corruption and compromise; but equally the constant movements for reform show the vitality of the sectarian tendency and the ability of the memory of Jesus and the early church to go on inspiring and motivating people.[16]

All of this constitutes a highly significant minority history on the underside of the church with a constant capacity for new energy and initiatives. The same might be said about a variety of reform movements in the late mediaeval period which were to challenge the religious monopoly of the Roman Church and majority formulations of Christian doctrine, such as those associated in England with John Wycliffe (ca. 1329–1384), in Czechoslovakia with Jan Hus (1373–1415) and in Italy with the Waldensians. These were seen to threaten the status quo and were pursued and persecuted as heretical and unorthodox. The pre-Reformation period seethed with religious and political debate. Issues of theology were closely entwined with those of national identity and social reform, and with aspirations towards new forms of the social order. Ideas do not spring out of a vacuum. They emerge from the struggles of human beings in societies; and theological ideas are rarely simply theological: they have implications for the wider social enterprise and for political systems. So it is that religious visions and hopes can serve as a means of social progress and change, or by contrast as a means of social reaction and conservatism. When the dominant language and metaphors of societies are themselves religious it should not be surprising if social change is imagined in terms of religious imagery and expectation. At the Reformation, and for the century after it, we encounter this phenomenon in spades. Out of this ferment the baptist witness emerged clearly, if not without controversy.

The Reformation and its Aftermath

The effect of the Reformation of the early sixteenth century – ostensibly initiated in 1517 when the Augustinian monk Martin Luther nailed his Ninety-Five Theses for debate onto the north door of the town church in Wittenberg – was to break open the fragile crust of European Christendom. Up until that time a semblance of unity had been maintained and whatever the religious debate beneath the surface, it had not come to final rupture. From then on religious and national disagreements were in the open and people would take sides. What

Luther had not bargained for was that there were many who were more advanced (or extreme) than he in their pursuit of social and religious change. This assumed tragic proportions in the uprising known as the German Peasants' War when an army of ill-equipped peasants under the charismatic pastor and leader Thomas Müntzer was easily destroyed at Frankenhausen in 1525 by an alliance of Protestant princes urged on by Luther himself. In retrospect, the twelve articles for change demanded by the peasants seem reasonable and progressive, but the fact that they were prepared to take up arms in their cause was clearly provocative. Throughout this period religious radicalism had dangerous overtones of violence and many were spurred on to revolutionary acts not only by the poverty of their circumstance but by apocalyptic religious fervour. This was to culminate in the takeover of the German city of Münster and its re-designation as the New Jerusalem by 'Anabaptists' until the rebellion was brutally overcome in 1535.

None of this makes for an easy or unproblematic narrative. Clearly people at this time were coming to new convictions about baptism; some of them were implicated in the violent events. It is also clear that in parallel, and then in the wake of such events, as people became disillusioned with violence, there were those of non-violent conviction, peaceful disposition and discernible baptist convictions emerging from the Reformation. Here we encounter those Anabaptists who can credibly claim, certainly in spirit and possibly also by ancestry, to be the forerunners of Baptists. The term 'anabaptist' means a 're-baptiser' and refers to the activity of baptising as adults those who had previously been baptised as infants. The Anabaptists themselves (for the sake of argument we shall continue with the name) simply referred to themselves either as 'baptists' (Täufer) or 'brethren'. They did not understand themselves to be re-baptising but simply administering for the first time the true Christian baptism concerning which they had become persuaded through reading the Scriptures.

Anabaptism[17]

Anabaptists have come to be seen as the classic instance of the sect-type of Christianity and this explains the context into which they have been placed in this chapter. They are not to be seen as a new invention but as a definitive emergence into the light of a type of Christianity which has been present from the beginning and which, indeed, represents the kind of movement the Christian church was in its origins. Anabaptism was a diverse movement originating in many places across Europe and embracing those with violent and non-violent tendencies as well as some of unorthodox and heretical views.[18] However, it was the peaceful strands of Anabaptism[19] often associated with the Swiss Brethren who emerged in Zurich in 1525, along with Menno Simons, the Dutch Anabaptist apostle, who were to outlast many others and become the majority voice. They are sometimes called 'evangelical Anabaptists'. Not surprisingly, they and their direct descendants, the Mennonites, have wanted to disassociate themselves from the violent memories of Müntzer and Münster, and have established themselves as an historic peace church. The nature and identity of Anabaptism has often been tied up with the question of origins and it is instructive to review the theories that have been advanced. We note five:

- *Anabaptists as the 'left-wing of the Reformation'*: The famous historian Roland Bainton argued, for instance,[20] that Anabaptists should be seen as Protestants who were prepared to carry the reformation of the church according to Scripture further than Luther, and slightly later, Calvin were prepared to do. As such, they were further to the reforming left than either of them. For whereas both of these teachers were exponents of the doctrine of justification by faith, neither was prepared to go on (as the Anabaptists saw it) to reform the church's practice of infant baptism or to set the church free from its bondage to state control. Indeed, each in his own way was dependent upon the state authorities for protection, Luther upon the Elector of Saxony and Calvin upon the city authorities in Geneva.

The Reformers therefore were 'half-way men' who needed to carry through their reforming principles to their logical conclusion. In their turn, the Anabaptists are portrayed not as wild-eyed fanatics but as consistent Protestants.

- *Anabaptists as the Radical Reformers.* The characterisation here is parallel to the first and reflects the magisterial work of George H. Williams.[21] Once more the Anabaptists are to be seen as part of the Reformation but as seeking a more radical reform than their mainstream counterparts. The magisterial Reformers (so-called because they looked to the magistrates, or the civil authority, to enforce their reforms) were seeking to reform the church from within the structures they had inherited. By contrast, the Anabaptists took the more radical way of 'restitution', abandoning the inherited structure in order to restore a New Testament pattern of the church from the roots up. They wished to break with the churches of Christendom, which they saw as fallen and beyond reform, in order to return to an apostolic order of the church. Moreover, by (re)baptising people they were in effect declaring that they were not already true Christians and so needed to be gathered into the true church for the first time.

- *Anabaptists as the 'stepchildren of the Reformers'.* This interpretation, which follows the approach of Leonard Verduin,[22] is out of line with the previous two. In place of the assumption that Anabaptists were of a piece with the Reformation, they should really be seen only as their stepchildren. Their true parents were the movements of reform that took place in the centuries before the Reformation but which on being suppressed went underground. When Christendom was fractured all the suppressed energies which had never gone away then rose to the surface, sometimes in chaotic fashion. Anabaptists then are more than Protestants and have a wider and more diverse set of origins. Most of all, going back beyond the churches of their day to re-read the New Testament with new eyes means that Anabaptism can be seen as neither Catholic nor Protestant, a sign of which (at least in their 'evangelical' form) is their rejection of violence.[23]

- *Anabaptism as 'laicised monasticism'*. It is a matter of record that a significant number of the early Anabaptist leaders were, like Luther, former monks and friars, some of them having occupied senior positions. Either prior to or because of their contact with Anabaptism they forsook their monasteries in search of a fuller expression of their devotion to Christ and found it within the Anabaptist movement. This interpretation, developed by Kenneth Davis,[24] finds in Anabaptism striking parallels with the monastic Rule of St Benedict. Its concerns are with the purification of the church in holiness and righteousness and include, like monasticism, emphasis on the centrality of Christ, the concept of discipleship as the imitation of Christ, the understanding that belonging to a Christian community is a commitment to a disciplined life in which one's way of living is observed by others, and the idea that baptism, on analogy with the monastic vow, involves an oath of obedience and dedication by which one is bound. The difference here is that the disciplined monastic life is 'laicised', it becomes the normal pattern of life for the whole community of believers and not only for a heroic minority.

- *Anabaptism as spontaneously generated under biblical influence*. It may be that all of the above interpretations are true and there is no reason in this area as in others why a complex movement should not be seen as having a complexity of origins. It is also true that the Bible has an amazing capacity to go on re-asserting itself and its message generation after generation, and that when people dedicate themselves to studying it they are apt to come to roughly similar conclusions. The Bible keeps alive the subversive memory of a radical Christ. The Swiss brand of Anabaptism originated in the home Bible studies that were encouraged by Ulrich Zwingli, the Swiss Reformer. If the Bible can speak for itself this factor must be set against all the rest as helping to provoke the movement.

The Genius of Anabaptism

The likelihood is that all of the above factors played some part in the genesis of the Anabaptist movement and in forming its developing genius. Summarising that genius, its distinctive beliefs, is no easy task, given the complex and diverse nature of Anabaptism. The following convictions seem to have been clear to most of them:

- Anabaptists believed that the church had fallen from its original condition and was no longer what Christ had intended. The fall of the church was associated with its legalisation under Constantine and its subsequent involvement in coercive power.
- Given the fallen condition of the church, Catholic and Protestant, reform was not enough. Anabaptists believed that the more radical strategy of restoration or 'restitution' of the true and original church was necessary and saw themselves as engaged in this task.
- The church accordingly was to be restored as a disciplined community of willing and faithful disciples who signified their acceptance of Christ's lordship by accepting baptism. Infant baptism was regarded as invalid and the baptism of disciples was carried out by the pouring of water. The new churches met in homes and placed a value on simple worship rooted in Bible study.
- Baptism into Christ involved a life of discipleship, of imitation of the way of Jesus Christ. This could be imitation unto death and large numbers of Anabaptists were martyred for their faith by both Catholics and Protestants. This was seen as the ultimate act of obedience and witness.
- Since the identification of church and state was now being questioned, Anabaptists appealed for freedom of worship and liberty for people to pursue their own consciences. They did not reject the role of the civil rulers and authorities in keeping the peace but denied that this extended to enforcing religious conformity.

- Generally, non-violent Anabaptists did not accept that disciples should serve as magistrates in the coercive functions of the civil authorities. This was partly because the magistrates still had a role of religious coercion, but more generally because the power of the 'sword' was considered to be at variance with the way of Christ.

The Genesis of the English Baptists

English Baptists emerged just less than a century after the Anabaptists and the extent to which, knowingly or otherwise, they were influenced by the Anabaptists is a matter of debate. The first English Baptist congregation was formed in 1609 in Amsterdam under the leadership of John Smyth (d. 1612), an Anglican priest. Smyth became convinced about believers baptism and took the unusual and controversial step of first baptising himself, and then his congregation. A few years afterwards this church joined with a Dutch Mennonite congregation and, as a result of disagreements, divided, one part of it returning to England under Thomas Helwys (ca. 1550–1616) to establish in 1612 in London the first Baptist congregation on English soil. In the same year, Helwys was to publish his book, *A Short Declaration of The Mistery of Iniquity*, which was the first appeal in the English language for religious freedom.[25] He was imprisoned for this and died in gaol shortly after.

Smyth and Helwys were 'General Baptists', which meant that they were Arminian in theology. They believed Christ had died for all, not just for the elect, and that a general appeal to all people to be saved was a consequence of this. Like the Anabaptists, they baptised by pouring, not immersion. A second and distinct Baptist denomination emerged in London in the 1630s, this time with Calvinist convictions about particular redemption. They were called Particular Baptists and practised baptism by immersion. The first joint Baptist confession of faith was produced by a group of these churches in 1644 in London and in this we can see the beginnings of an association of churches.[26] Both groupings grew strongly in the period of the English Civil War in which many Baptists were engaged on the side of Parliament and in the New Model Army. In fact, early church growth throughout the British Isles was greatly aided by the fact that as the Army travelled on campaign Baptist chaplains, officers and soldiers would establish new churches.

That English Baptists were willing to take up arms in the cause of liberty as they understood it strongly suggests that they were not entirely in line with evangelical Anabaptism. Generally, opinion points to Baptists being a development from within English Puritans and Separatists.[27] But it is impossible to exclude the possibility that there were Anabaptist influences upon them. This is suggested in that Smyth's congregation began in a bake-house belonging to a Dutch Mennonite and that many of the earliest English Baptist congregations were formed in eastern areas of England where Dutch influence was strong. Whereas the formal line of descent is most demonstrably from separatist Puritanism, it seems likely that Anabaptist ideas were circulating at the time when Baptists were emerging and were influential upon them.[28] The early disagreement between Smyth and Helwys does point to theological differences concerning the role of the state and the matter of whether believers should serve as magistrates. Smyth was against this and Helwys for it, suggesting that whereas both traditions argued with one voice for religious liberty, the Baptists who took root in England took a more positive view of the role of civil government and of the magistrate.[29] This remains a point of difference between contemporary Baptists and Mennonites.

After the restoration of the monarchy in 1661 both Baptist groups found themselves on the receiving end of fierce persecution and were consistently penalised for their faith. This lifted with the Edict of Toleration in 1689 but civil discrimination continued against them well into the nineteenth century. Over this whole period the Baptist message had been spreading into America and across the English-speaking world, and then across the world through the great missionary movements inspired in part by the Baptist pioneer, William Carey (1761–1834). The General Baptists tended in the eighteenth century to drift into Unitarianism but a vigorous New Connexion of General Baptists was formed in 1770 by Dan Taylor (1738–1813). The Baptist Union was formed in London in 1813 (and reorganised in 1831) and as Particular and General Baptists grew together over the century they came to unite under its umbrella in 1891. Distinct unions came to be formed in Wales (1866), Scotland (1869) and Ireland (1895), with the Baptist World Alliance being established in 1905 and the European Baptist Federation in 1949. Beyond these developments, there continue to be in the UK considerable numbers of independent Baptist churches and smaller groupings of Reformed, Strict or Grace Baptists.

Baptist Beliefs

Despite a common label, Baptist (and baptist) churches across the globe are very diverse, reflecting the varieties of culture and religious context in which they have emerged and their varying responses to spiritual movements and trends in the wider church. It is often claimed that baptists are non-creedal, accepting only the Bible as their authority and declining to adopt binding doctrinal statements which come between believers and the Scriptures. If this is true at all, it is only true in the sense that there is both a deep commitment to the priority of Scripture over creeds and an aversion to imposed doctrinal formulas being used to enforce ideological positions. Baptists are orthodox Christians, more than willing to affirm the faith of the church expressed in, for instance, the Apostles' and Nicene Creeds, and frequently the producers themselves of doctrinal confessions which both explain their beliefs to others and act as expressions of faith around which churches may gather. As with other traditions in the church, those who wished to join a Baptist body would have to demonstrate that they satisfy the basis of faith, explicit or implicit, with which that body works; this might be described as a creedal test.[30] However, this is to be understood within a context of free choice and not of the exercise of sacred power. Properly understood, baptists are catholic Christians, embracing the historic faith of the church. Where they differ from other traditions is in the realm of ecclesiology, the doctrine and practice of the church, and the inferences they derive from this for the nature of human society and government.

Even in their understanding of the church Baptists share many of their individual doctrines with others in the wider baptist stream, believers baptism[31] in particular. Distinctive Baptist identity might best be understood as a *combination of beliefs* by analogy with the genetic code underlying particular human identities. Each doctrine on its own may be shared with others, but the peculiar cluster of beliefs accounts for the recognisable identity of this specific group. Several scholars (including Stanley Grenz and myself, among others) have attempted to unravel the genetic code. There is considerable overlap between Grenz's account and mine, which serves to underline their content.

Grenz's attempt to do this is in the form of an acrostic around the world 'Baptist'[32] and looks like this:

- B – *believers baptism* is the mark that people most readily identify and reflects the conviction that baptism does not receive its proper meaning, and some would say *any* meaning, unless it is preceded by repentance and faith and gives expression to them. For the baptist, any religious action which does not spring out of voluntary choice (although this choice is only possible because of the grace of God that precedes and enables it) and is not accompanied by faith is an empty symbol.
- A – *the autonomy of the local church,* by which is meant not the freedom of the local church to do anything it wants, to change the basic doctrine of the faith for instance, but its competence and ability because of Christ in its midst and the gift of the Spirit to discern for itself and within the boundaries of Christian orthodoxy how to govern its own affairs and to undertake its own mission. It can do this without seeking permission or legitimation from an external authority (although this may not apply in the same

way to precise matters of civil or property law by which it is bound).

- P – *the primacy of Scripture*: the normative authority of Scripture is, in theory at least, shared by all believers and especially by evangelical Christians. What may be distinctive among baptists is their insistence that this authority speaks also to the ordering of congregations and that matters of church life are not secondary to primary issues of faith and salvation but bound up with them. Compare this with a widespread indifference among many about matters of church order.

- T – *true believers only in the church*: this is the principle of *the believers church* and is based on the belief that people need to be incorporated into Christ by the Spirit through faith and baptism before they can properly be seen as members of the body of Christ. Church membership is not a nominal status based upon infant baptism or any other ritual not accompanied by faith. It is not a component of national identity but a choice for discipleship.

- I – *individual competency and believer priesthood*: the way this is expressed by Grenz reflects the strong individualism of North American Baptists. What lies behind it is the belief that through the Holy Spirit believers are given the 'mind of Christ'[33] and that 'his anointing teaches you about all things, and is true and is not a lie'.[34] Taken to an extreme this could be a recipe for anarchy, but held in tension within a discerning Christian community it is an affirmation of all believers in their ability and responsibility to discern the mind of God.

- S – *separation of church and state* is the recognition that church and state are expressions of two different kinds of power, the one based upon spiritual persuasion and the other on coercion. The distinction between the two remains crucial in order to avoid the state clothing itself with religious symbolism and over-reaching itself, especially through any claim to govern the church. Equally, the church is to avoid any use of coercive power for its own ends since this corrupts and destroys true spirituality.

- T – *two ordinances*: these are baptism and the Lord's Supper which were ordained by Christ as visible expressions of the gospel to be practised within the church as focal rites and dramatic enactments of the meaning of faith.

Grenz's acrostic offers a handy way of identifying the Baptist 'genetic code'. Each of the items listed will receive further and sustained treatment in later chapters. My own summary is not dissimilar and is as follows:[35]

- *The Scriptures have supreme authority for all matters of faith and conduct* including church order. Of course, authority properly belongs to God and to Christ but is mediated by the Spirit through the primary and inescapable authority of Scripture. The instinct to go on returning to the primary documents of the faith is sometimes referred to as 'primitivism' or 'restorationism'. Hans Küng expressed this well when he wrote: '(T)he Church is headed in the right direction when, whatever the age in which it lives, the Gospel of Jesus Christ is its criterion, the Gospel which Jesus proclaimed and to which the Church of the apostles witnessed.' [36] I have already described this as the point of orientation by which we are enabled to navigate since what is in view here is not a legalistic attempt to reproduce the church of the first century but a free search for authoritative guidance and inspiration for responsible decisions the church must make in whatever time and culture it finds itself.
- *The church is to be composed of believers* since church member-ship is not a mere formality or an aspect of national culture but living incorporation by the Spirit into the people of God; and therefore:
- *Baptism is the sign of freely chosen faith*, and not of an inherited or second-hand religious allegiance passed on from the family or tribal group to which a person belongs.
- *The priesthood of all believers* emerges from this as an acknowledgement that all believers have equal shares in the grace of God, that there are no classes or gradations of membership or privilege and there is access to God both in

worship and the seeking of wisdom without the need for any mediator other than the one mediator with the Father, Christ himself.

- *The autonomy of the local church* follows from this in recognition that believers together have a God-given competence to discern the way of Christ for their congregation and that free congregations cannot be compelled into conformity in matters by denominational groups or representatives.
- *Freedom of conscience* also follows from the belief that all believers may discern for themselves the will of God and means that great respect must be shown not for people's prejudices, which are often founded upon ignorance, but for their opinions and decisions arrived at through the active exercise of conscience.
- *Separation of church and state* is the classic formula for expressing both the freedom of the church from state interference and the freedom of the state from religious ideology in a way which enables each to stay true to its distinct responsibilities under God.

These two attempts to unravel the code of Baptist identity set an agenda for the rest of this book which is a closer exposition of the issues involved.

The Wave of the Future

In this chapter we have been looking back into the long history of the Christian church and taking note of the divergent tendencies we see within it concerning the church and its social teaching. We have in particular drawn attention to the sociological (not theological) categories of church-type and sect-type and have located the baptist way of being church clearly in the second of these. When baptists emerged at the radical edges of the Reformation they were not a competely new phenomenon. Their inclinations had long been present in a variety of forms as a minority tradition within the church.

Moreover, whereas the sect-type was often a protest against the abuses and aberrations of the church-type, it was also a recovery in some degree of the life and style of the first Christians. A negative reaction therefore gave rise to a positive recovery.

This tradition has been a minority one in the church's history, but things are now changing. The conditions that allowed the church-type to dominate have retreated. What is likely to be the wave of the future? My prediction is that the baptist model has the vitality to become the majority expression of church and to do so in two ways. First, it has the potential to continue growing in the way that it has been doing for several centuries. It is fundamentally a missionary model of church because it calls people to personal commitment and faith and has demonstrated its effectiveness in many parts of the world. Secondly, its impact is also seen in the way the values of the believers church are influencing some at least of the majority traditions of Christianity both in their stated policies and in their style of church life. Examples of the former include the abandonment at Vatican II by the Roman Catholic Church of the doctrine that 'error has no rights' and its commitment for the first time to full religious liberty.[37] Examples of the second include the emergence in South America of so-called 'basic Christian communities',[38] along the lines of the sect-type, and the increasing willingness of episcopal churches to see their hierarchies no longer as structures of sacred power but as forms of connectedness and of nurturing relationship. Miroslav Volf is an acute observer of this trend:

> The various Free Churches are growing most rapidly among Protestants, particularly among the Pentecostals and the charismatic groups, who are characterized not only by the notion of religious immediacy, but also by a high degree of participation and flexibility with respect to filling leadership roles...Just as significant as the rapid growth of these Free Churches, however, are the incipient structural transformations within the traditional Protestant and Catholic churches, which are undergoing a process of 'congregationalization,' even where this process has

not yet been accommodated ecclesiologically. The life of the church is becoming increasingly less the exclusive prerogative of pastors and priests...this 'process of congregationalization' is clearly evident even in the Catholic Church which is (still?) committed to a hierarchical structure.[39]

All forms of church have their strengths and weaknesses with the latter being the shadow side of the former. If the pendulum seems to be swinging globally in the direction of baptist ways of being church, we have already recorded that there is that in the catholic, church-type traditions which, suitably re-imagined, needs to correct the inadequacies of the sect-type. This applies not least to the sense of being part of the whole church which can often be a deficiency of the 'localist', baptist tendency as also to the need for a stance towards culture, the social order and the state which bears witness to the universal significance of the gospel, albeit in a way which avoids any kind of coercive powers. The catholic and the baptist, when the genius of each is understood, re-appropriated and re-imagined, have much to contribute to each other in the movement towards becoming the church in all its fullness.

Notes

[1] Exodus 26:30.
[2] Exodus 36:1 and often repeated.
[3] James D.G. Dunn, *Unity and Diversity in the New Testament* (London: SCM Press, 1977, 1990), 33–59, 102–73.
[4] E.g. 1 Timothy 3:1–13.
[5] E.g. 1 Corinthians 12.
[6] E.g. 1 John 2:27.
[7] Eduard Schweizer, *Church Order in the New Testament* (London: SCM Press, 1961), 13–14.
[8] Ernst Troeltsch, *The Social Teaching of the Christian Churches* Volume I (London: George Allen & Unwin, 1932), 335–37.
[9] Acts 9:2; 19:9, 23; 22:4.
[10] 1 John 2:5–17.

11 For a fuller exploration of this see Ched Myers, *Binding the Strong Man: A Political Reading of Mark's Story of Jesus* (Maryknoll, New York: Orbis Books, 1998).

12 A counter-culture is 'a social construction set up as an objective reality within society, but which is quite distinct from that society, from which it experiences some degree of alienation': R.S. Giles, 'The Church as a Counter-Culture Before Constantine' (M.Litt Dissertation, University of Newcastle-upon-Tyne, 1987), 3.

13 1 Peter 2:13–17.

14 In 313 Constantine promulgated the Edict of Milan which contains the provisions, 'We therefore announce that, notwithstanding any previous provisions, concerning the Christians in our former instructions, all who choose that religion are to be permitted to continue therein, without any let or hindrance, and are not to be in any way troubled or molester…Note that at the same time all others are to be allowed the free and unrestricted practice of their religions; for it accords with the good order of the realm and the peacefulness of our times that each should have freedom to worship God after his own choice; and we do not intend to detract from the honour due to any religion or its followers': H.R. Bettenson (ed.), *Documents of the Christian Church* (Oxford: Oxford University Press, 1967), 16.

15 'It is our desire that all the various nations which are subject to our Clemency and Moderation, should continue in the profession of that religion which was delivered to the Romans by the divine Apostle Peter, as it has been preserved by the faithful tradition; and which is now professed by the Pontiff Damascus and by Peter, Bishop of Alexandria, a man of apostolic holiness. According to the apostolic teaching and the doctrine of the Gospel, let us believe the one deity of the Father, Son and Holy Spirit, in equal majesty and in a holy Trinity. We authorize the followers of this law to assume the title of Catholic Christians; but as for the others, since, in our judgement, they are foolish madmen, we decree that they be branded with the ignominious name of heretics': Bettenson, *Documents*, 22.

16 J.G.G. Norman, 'The Relevance and Vitality of the Sect-Idea', *Baptist Quarterly* 26.6 (1979), 248–58.

17 Standard and accessible introductions to the Anabaptists are William R. Estep, *The Anabaptist Story* (Grand Rapids: Eerdmans, 1975) and Franklin H. Littell, *The Origins of Sectarian Protestantism: A Study of the Anabaptist View of the Church* (London/New York: Macmillan, 1964).

[18] Nigel G. Wright, '"The Sword": An Example of Anabaptist Diversity', *Baptist Quarterly* 36.6 (1996), 264–79.

[19] In a letter to Thomas Müntzer dated 1524 this group, led by Conrad Grebel, was to write, 'Moreover, the gospel and its adherents are not to be protected by the sword, nor are they thus to protect themselves...True Christian believers are sheep among wolves, sheep for the slaughter...No more of this.': 'Letters to Thomas Müntzer by Conrad Grebel and Friends', in George H. Williams and Angel M. Mergal, *Spiritual and Anabaptist Writers* (Philadelphia: Westminster Press, 1962), 80.

[20] Roland H. Bainton, 'The Left Wing of the Reformation', in *Studies on the Reformation* (London: Hodder & Stoughton, 1964), 119–29.

[21] Williams, *Radical Reformation*.

[22] Leonard Verduin, *The Reformers and their Stepchildren* (Exeter: Paternoster, 1966), 13.

[23] Walter Klaassen, *Anabaptism: Neither Catholic nor Protestant* (Waterloo, Ontario: Conrad Press, 1973), 10.

[24] Kenneth R. Davis, *Anabaptism and Asceticism: A Study in Intellectual Origins* (Scottdale, PA: Herald Press, 1974), 296.

[25] Extracts can be found in H. Leon McBeth, *A Sourcebook for Baptist Heritage* (Nashville: Broadman Press, 1990), 70–72.

[26] 'The London Confession, 1644', in William L. Lumpkin, *Baptist Confessions of Faith* (Valley Forge: Judson Press, 1969), 144–71. It is of interest here that the churches behind the 1644 Confession describe themselves as 'commonly (though falsely) called Anabaptists'.

[27] B.R. White, *The English Separatist Tradition* (Oxford: Oxford University Press, 1971); Kenneth R. Manley, 'Origins of the Baptists: The Case for Development from Puritanism-Separatism', in William H. Brackney (ed.), *Faith, Life and Witness: The Papers of the Study and Research Division of the Baptist World Alliance – 1986–1990* (Birmingham, AL: Samford University Press, 1990), 56–69.

[28] E.A. Payne, 'Contacts between Mennonites and Baptists', *Foundations* 4.1 (1961), 3–19.

[29] Nigel G. Wright, 'Baptist and Anabaptist Attitudes to the State: A Contrast', *Baptist Quarterly* 36.7 (1996), 349–57.

[30] There are some interesting comments on this in Mark Hopkins, *Nonconformity's Romantic Generation: Evangelical and Liberal Theologies in Victorian England* (Carlisle: Paternoster, 2004), 241–8.

[31] As nobody seems to be sure whether this should be believer's or believers' baptism I have decided to dispense with the apostrophe both here and with the term 'believers church'.

[32] Grenz, *Baptist Congregation*, 82.

[33] 1 Corinthians 2:14–16.

[34] 1 John 2:27.

[35] Wright, *Challenge to Change*, 22–35.

[36] Küng, *Church*, x.

[37] *Dignitatis Humane: On the Right of the Person and of Communities to Social and Religious Freedom in Matters Religious*, promulgated by His Holiness, Pope Paul VI on December 7, 1965: *http:// www.vatican.va/archive/hist_councils/ii_vatican_council/documents/ vaticanii_decl_19651207_dignitatis-humanae_en.html.*

[38] E.g. Leonardo Boff, *Ecclesiogenesis*, and *Trinity and Society* (Tunbridge Wells; Burns & Oates, 1988).

[39] Volf, *After Our Likeness*, 12. Volf goes on to cite Joseph Cardinal Ratzinger who said in interview: 'My impression is that the authentically Catholic meaning of the reality of "Church" is tacitly disappearing, without being expressly rejected…In other words, in many ways a conception of Church is spreading in Catholic thought and even in Catholic theology, that cannot even be called Protestant in a "classic" sense. Many current ecclesiological ideas, rather, correspond more to the model of certain North American "Free Churches."'

3. The Gathering Church

A Community of Disciples

Introduction

So far we have used with little explanation a variety of terms to describe the baptist or Baptist way of being the church. They have overlapping meanings with subtle distinctions between them. Before going on to describe in fuller detail the vision of the church with which this book deals, it is helpful to review the varied terms being used and to explain them more fully.

We have already done this in relation to the terms 'Baptist' and 'baptist'. The first of these refers to that historic tradition which describes itself with this word and whose most obvious distinguishing mark is believers baptism. The word baptist refers to a wider swathe of churches in the same general tradition or family which may not call themselves Baptist or share all the features of the Baptist genetic code. The term 'gathered church' is also used to embrace this spectrum and refers to churches which emphasise fellowship and community, and understand Christ to be among the two or three who gather in his name, as described in Matthew 18:20. Churches which practice infant baptism are also called gathered churches when they put the emphasis on the church being the community of believers along with their children who are being nurtured in the faith. These usually belong to the 'Congregationalist' tradition, so-called because they affirm the ability of each congregation to govern itself locally through the participation of its members. Baptists are congregationalists as far as the government of the church goes and probably developed out of the early Congregational or Independent churches as they became persuaded of believers baptism.

Two historic terms were once also common to describe the tradition: Dissenters and Nonconformists. These belong very much to the English experience and so tend not to be used, or to feel appropriate, in other contexts. They refer to the refusal of many to assent to the dictates of the Church of England at a time when Elizabeth I was seeking to impose religious uniformity on the nation, or to conform to the prescribed forms and orders when the *Book of Common Prayer* was re-imposed on churches in 1662. In that year a 'Great Ejection' took place as large numbers of nonconforming clergy were removed from their livings, heralding a period of intense persecution. The effect of this was firmly to institutionalise within English society the religious divisions between Catholics, Anglicans and Nonconformists, and between church and chapel. Historically, Dissent has included Congregationalists, Presbyterians and Baptists who together are sometimes called 'Old Dissent'. As some of these denominations underwent doctrinal decline and became Unitarian, this emerging denomination, although largely theologically unorthodox and committed to 'free thought', associated itself with them in its particular resistance to imposed creedal or doctrinal formulas. As new denominations came into being these would sometimes lean towards Dissent without having gone through the formative experiences that lay behind the word.

In the nineteenth century both these words were largely replaced in England by the term 'free church' which was held to represent a more positive focus upon the values of this tradition rather than its history as a negative reaction. Even this term is problematic, however, since a denomination may be formally free from government by the state as a matter of contingent practice rather than coherent principle. As examples of this, in Scotland the Episcopalian Church (essentially the Anglican Church in Scotland) is formally a free church since the Church of Scotland (which is Presbyterian) is the nationally recognised church.[1] By contrast, in England the Presbyterians (now subsumed into the United Reformed Church) are a free church. Both denominations are happy in principle to have some kind of established status when it is on offer. Other traditions, such as the Baptists, have deep-seated objections to giving up any freedom or to ever violating the principle of separation of church and state. To be a free church is for them a theologically necessary position and giving it up in any place at any time would be seen as radical compromise.[2] The term 'free church' appears in the title of this book and will go on doing so as a reference to this principled position, but 'believers church' is also a preferred term originating in Mennonite circles which has come into usage more recently as a positive and bridge-building expression of the baptist tradition in its broadest aspects.[3] The language of 'radical' or 'sectarian Protestantism'[4] tends to be used in the academic sphere with sociological overtones by and for those who are acquainted with the church and sect typology or the wider historical debates about Anabaptist origins.

This chapter introduces two relatively new terms: the 'gathering church' and the 'community of disciples'. Both are used here to chart the way ahead for the baptist and free-church tradition by subtly nuancing existing language. The 'gathered church' suggests a static image which 'gathering church' is keen to overcome.[5] The churches of Christ go on gathering. They gather and scatter continually as they make their way through life and live in the very dynamic of life together and witness dispersed. This is being light (concentrated, intense and obvious) and salt (invisible, scattered and yet tasty). In this dynamic they are also gathering in the sense of 'gathering in', drawing into their own fellowship those who are being befriended and influenced, harvesting people for Christ,[6] seeking lost sheep and bringing them home.[7] The gathering church therefore exists as an open community of disciples, a fellowship of those who have made it their intention to lose their lives for Christ's sake, to take up their cross and follow after him.[8] This is a vision of a regenerate and committed church. It is composed of those who have come to new birth in Christ by the Spirit and have made the commitment in baptism to be declared and witnessing servants of the Messiah.[9] It is a fellowship of believers, of companions on the way, of children of God who know in whom they have believed. One authoritative Baptist document, having asserted that the origin of the church is in the gospel, goes on to say:

> It is in membership of a local church in one place that the fellowship of the one holy catholic Church becomes significant. Indeed, such gathered companies of believers are the local manifestation of the one Church of God on earth and in heaven ... Such churches are gathered by the will of Christ and live by the indwelling of His Spirit. They do not have their origin, primarily, in human resolution. Thus the *Baptist Confession of 1677*, which deals at length with doctrine and church order, uses phrases which indicate that local churches are formed by the response of believing (people) to the Lord's command. Out of many such phrases we may quote the following: 'Therefore they do willingly consent to walk together according to the appointment of Christ.' 'Churches are gathered according to His mind, declared in His word.' Membership was not regarded as a private option, for the *Confession* continues: 'All believers are bound to join themselves to particular churches when and where they have opportunity to do'...The basis of our membership in the church is a conscious and deliberate acceptance of Christ as Saviour and Lord by each individual.[10]

The *Corpus Christianum*

To highlight the positive values of the gathering church it helps to grasp that it arose in the first instance, as we have already noted several times, as a negative reaction against an alternative, namely, a church which was territorial, institutionalised, nominal and oppressive.

It was *territorial* in that it claimed that all were Christians who were in the geographical boundaries over which it had sway. Prior to Constantine, to be a disciple of Christ involved a choice and a commitment, one which was likely to set those who made it against the pagan culture in which they were living. People thought twice before doing this and to be baptised was to be marked out as being different, possibly deviant, certainly oddities. With Constantine, being a Christian became first acceptable and, as the church grew in scope and influence, then advantageous and finally indispensable. Once the church was made into the orthodox religion of the empire, being a good Roman citizen and being a Christian were so closely entwined that to be one was also to be the other. This arrangement is sometimes called the *corpus christianum*, the Christianised body in which church and state are but two sides of one coin. Christianity was now no longer a choice for discipleship: it was an aspect of national or imperial identity, bestowed by virtue of birth. Moreover, Rome's conflicts with other nations were now religious conflicts, with victory in battle leading to the imposition of the dominant spirituality. Christianity moved for most people from being a form of discipleship to being a tribal religious loyalty based on birth and geography.

Even the Reformation left this religious nationalism unchallenged. For the Reformation to survive it had to depend upon the protection and the interests of the civil rulers. The principle at work in this is known as *cuius regio eius religio*: whoever is the prince determines the religion of the people. The Reformers' strategy therefore continued to be a territorial one, working towards the conversion of the rulers to the Protestant cause in order to gain territory. Within all of this there was ample room for genuine faith, but the whole enterprise was entwined with allegiances of a different kind so that geography was more of a determining factor in religion than inward faith. So it is that Richard Hooker, the formative theologian and theorist for the Anglican Church, could claim that a person was a member of the Church of England by outward profession rather than inward transformation and that therefore the church existed as a 'mixed multitude' and would do so until at the judgment Christ sorted the sheep from the goats.[11]

The church was *institutional* in that it was conceived of in terms of ecclesiastical power and jurisdiction rather than fellowship. A territorial church is integrated into the social and political structures of its society with its chief pastors being understood as an ecclesiastical civil service. The effect of the Constantinian shift upon the church was to provide an imperial model for the church's government, a model that was reinforced as the institutions of the Roman Empire weakened or were overcome by invading powers and the responsibility for carrying on Roman life and government passed by default to the church. The church as a community and a fellowship of believers was overcome by the church as a system of delegated imperial authority in which the key note was the administration of sacred power. Through all of this the nature of what it means to be a Christian changes. No longer is it a choice to be a disciple of Christ. Instead, it becomes a process of incorporation by default into a tribal religion and a sacred institution. This leads to a membership which is largely *nominal* and formal rather than a product of spiritual rebirth. The baptism of disciples becomes a rite of passage for infants as they are welcomed at birth into the national and religious community. It is received passively rather than embraced actively and the assumption is made that being a Christian is a matter of inheritance not of personal conversion. Increasingly baptism is deprived of its biblical meanings and is seen as an act of naming, of reception both into the religious and political communities.

Furthermore, this becomes *oppressive*. In that religion is here being used to define and cement national identity, any departure from or challenge to the national religion is subversive and dangerous, a loosening of the social ties that hold a society together. Deviants are persecuted as heretics and traitors since the assumption is made that a cohesive society requires a uniformity of religious belief and practice. People may indeed have their doubts and their private views but once these intrude upon the public discourse they are deemed to be a challenge to the well-being of society. This uniform religious and political system begins to fall apart once people can read the Bible for themselves and make up their own minds concerning its meaning. Up until the widespread public availability of the Bible made possible by the advent of printing, people were given the officially filtered interpretations determined as much by the vested interests of the sacred and temporal power systems as any concern for truth. But these are subverted once people can read the Bible for themselves and come to different conclusions.[12]

The Church as the Community of the Regenerate

The reaction against the 'system' I have described came both from below as for religious and political reasons people become dissatisfied, and from teachers within the church whose studies called it increasingly into question. At the heart of the debate is the deceptively simple question, who is a Christian? The received answer would be that to be a Christian is to have been born into the Christian religion and to have been incorporated as an infant by means of the sacramental grace of baptism into the church. There are still those who believe that this is the appropriate answer. By contrast, believers church Christians have responded that those are Christians who on repentance and faith experience the new birth and as a consequence take up the challenge of holy living. The doctrine of salvation defines the doctrine of the church.[13] Merely formal reception of the church's sacraments is not enough but leads to the creation of 'name Christians' or 'professors' who have not experienced for themselves the reality of saving faith. This does not mean that the sacraments of baptism or the Lord's Supper are despised but that they are made effective through faith and are powerless without it. This is a fundamental Reformation principle which the Reformers themselves failed to follow through consistently, probably because to have done so would have jeopardised the social position of Christianity: without faith it is impossible to please God.[14] Faith for the Christian is the inward reception of God's saving grace by means of assent to what God has promised and personal trust in Jesus Christ and his saving work leading to a transformation of the heart. Without this the sacraments of the faith remain outward rituals rather than saving actions. The church is the community of those who are experiencing this regenerating and renewing work.

The writings of the first Baptists put this clearly: For instance, John Smyth:

> (T)he outward church consists of penitent persons only, and of such as believing in Christ bring forth fruits worthy (of) amendment of life.[15]

> (A)ll penitent and faithful Christians are brethren in the communion of the outward life, wheresoever they live, by what name soever they are known.[16]

Or Thomas Helwys,

> (T)he Church of Christ is a company of faithful people, separated from the world by the word and Spirit of God, being knit unto the Lord and one unto another, by baptism, upon their own confession of the faith and sins.[17]

This is the 'voluntary principle' or 'voluntarism' according to which spiritual and religious acts are meaningful only if they come out of sincere hearts and are the product of freely chosen obedience to God. The emphasis on heart religion is characteristic of this whole tradition and resonates with the teaching of Jesus on the emptiness of merely outward observance and the spiritual and transformative nature of true worship.[18]

The approach described attracts criticisms. Among these is the assertion that we are in no position to judge the condition of a person's heart and so should not attempt to do so. It is certainly true that Christians are forbidden to stand in judgment upon anybody.[19] But standing in judgment is not the same thing as exercising responsible pastoral discernment. In this sense Christians 'discern all things' because through the Spirit they have the mind of Christ.[20] Nowhere is this more vital than in the life of the congregation with a view to maintaining its health and well-being.[21] A further criticism is that the church is reduced to the status of a sectarian ghetto. But this ignores the fact that the early church was precisely a community of regenerate disciples and that far from being a ghetto it succeeded in turning the world upside down. Moreover, it is churches of the gathering church type who have been and are at the forefront of evangelism and social transformation across the world. A more serious criticism is that on this account the church becomes a society formed by the will and choice of those individuals who constitute it, a merely human assembly. But this is to see things the wrong way round. The church is not created by individuals: it pre-exists them all and is the very community through which the Spirit gathers them into itself and therefore into the communion of God's own life. Faith is not therefore simply a matter of human decision: it is a response to the gracious work of God which always goes before it and which is mediated to human beings by the Spirit through the church.

Territorial churches exist not to change the *status quo* but to preserve it. They mislead people into believing that they are already Christians by reason of ethnic identity or nominal membership of the church. They also place people in positions of formal leadership within the church who, whatever their social distinctions or qualifications, do not possess the spiritual qualities needed to be stewards of the grace of God. Territorial churches can of course be turned to good, but only insofar as they adopt the values of the believers church approach and fashion themselves into communities of disciples. They can play a role in inclining people nominally towards the Christian faith but it requires those of the believers church inclination, many of which are indeed formally part of territorial churches, to transform this into a religion of the heart.

Membership of the Body of Christ

Each of the three primary images of the church to which I have drawn attention implies the kind of commitment envisaged by the believers or gathering church. To be a member of the people of God requires a birth, not this time into an ethnic group as was the case in Judaism but by the Spirit into the spiritual family which is comprised of sons and daughters of God.[22] To belong to the body of Christ involves being joined organically, relationally and spiritually to the other members of that same body.[23] To be the temple of the Holy Spirit requires that same Spirit to take up residence in one's own life and to fuse the temple together as though it were made of living stones.[24] This therefore is no loose affiliation to a religious institution but lively participation in the life of God and of God's church.

The question of church membership is widely discussed today and various attempts are being made to redefine what is meant by it. Baptists are not alone in rethinking their stance.[25] Baptists have always practiced a formal discipline of church membership, conceiving the way in which we belong to each other in the church as a covenantal relationship. As God has made covenant relationship with us so we are drawn into explicit and expressed commitment to each other in the church.[26] The congregational form of church government practiced by Baptists also requires some form of membership since, if a church is to govern its own life, how do we know who has the right to participate in that process of government? The effect of this is to introduce into the affairs of the church a subtle but important distinction which has the power to distort. In other places I have described this as the difference between *organic* and *organisational* membership or between a *constitutional* and a *covenantal* or *consensual* order.[27]

Churches have a dual existence. They are communities of friends and disciples who work together in the service of the kingdom of God and where the bonds that bind them are love, affectionate trust and shared experience. But in order to transact business and endure through time they usually have to adopt an institutional form. Institutions can be useful. Without people nothing happens but without institutions nothing lasts. Some churches, fearing institutionalisation, opt to stay together solely on a relational basis and this can be done successfully. But often such churches encounter difficulties and transitions along the way and find that they have no institutional wisdom or substructure to see them through. What procedures should be followed, for instance, when one group of leaders moves on or gets into difficulty? An analogy here is marriage. Marriages work best when they are sustained by love and trust. But most people who stay together for a long time also go through troubled periods when the undergirding structure of the marriage relationship helps to see them through. Institutional forms can help churches to endure. Church membership as Baptists have practiced it has had these two coinciding dimensions: membership of a community by reason of strong and supportive relationships and membership of a formal organisation for purposes of church government and good order. Problems arise when people are members in the latter sense but not in the former, when they have formal power in the church but are not part of the spiritual life of the community. These problems are sometimes of a church's own making for failing to exercise proper discipline of its formal membership list, retaining those on it who have long since ceased meaningful commitment. Formal organisational membership should remain closely related to actual organic membership by means of regular revisions and clear policies.

Current trends suggest people are increasingly reluctant to be members in the organisational sense. They wish to belong to a Christian community, are prepared to offer service to it and support it financially but do not wish to be 'tied down'. By contrast, a strong and well-established current of opinion refuses to baptise those unwilling to become formal church members on the grounds that baptism is about participation in the life of the community of disciples. This is surely absolutely right in principle since 'those who welcomed [Peter's] message were baptised…and they devoted themselves to the apostles' teaching and fellowship, to the breaking of bread and the prayers.'[28] But there is also unease about making formal membership a condition of baptism since this could make a man-made institutional form a condition for an act of grace.

People qualify for baptism through repentance and faith not works of the law.[29] Yet each church is dependent upon its ability to foster the kind of discipleship which is prepared to shoulder burdens and work hard for the sake of the kingdom. Churches are built by sacrifice, by workers, by confessing disciples. How is this to be resolved?

Church membership and process

In other areas of reflection on Christian initiation, the way in which people become Christians, it has become normative to think in terms of process. Not everything that belongs to initiation into the kingdom of God happens all at once, but it is important to be aware of the overall process so that at the right time all the necessary elements are built in. It is reasonable to expect that those seeking baptism will give evidence of wanting to share in the church community since this belongs to the nature of discipleship. It may not be necessary at that point to insist on formal church membership; indeed, to do so may obstruct the right timing for baptism. In a process, however, each part should prepare for and give rise to what is to follow. It is crucial to insist that the process is one coherent whole and that belonging to the Christian community is not a privilege to be enjoyed without responsibilities. In practice this means that whereas people should first be prepared for baptism, baptism itself should lead into further nurture and preparation for what is then to follow. Baptism is only a beginning.

In another place[30] I have argued that the current Baptist practice of membership is not adequate for the actual communities we are nurturing: it recognises only one way of belonging to a church whereas some belong as children, others as seekers, and yet others as temporary sojourners. If a local church is seen as a series of concentric circles with a very definite core both of beliefs, values and committed people, the outer circles may allow people to belong to a community while they test out their own faith commitments. As they are drawn in through a process of nurture and education, baptism marks new birth and provides a threshold into deeper engagement. Alongside this and beyond it is the declaration of enduring commitment within a particular community of disciples. As with all other aspects of the voluntarist approach to religious faith, the important dimension is that of helping people make genuinely spiritual, personally owned and lasting commitments to Christ and his people. There is value therefore in a wider *community membership* of a local congregation allowing people in various conditions of faith and growth to know that they belong to a Christian community, with at the core a *covenant membership* of those who are ready to take full responsibility for the government and mission of the church. Community membership is designed to help people pursue a journey of faith at their own pace while being under the pastoral care of the congregation and its pastors;[31] covenant membership is intended to be demanding of people's discipleship while only ever being based upon their own willing commitment. The covenant membership of a church will be smaller in number on this model than its community membership and must always be portrayed as an open possibility for everyone who is willing to take on board its expectations. It will not be regarded as synonymous with membership of the body of Christ as such since this embraces all who have been born of the Spirit. It will be seen as a responsible way in which discipleship and community may be expressed at the local level, a conscious response to the need to build strong, resilient and durable communities which are not there only to meet the needs of the membership but to fulfil with patience the purposes of God. A variety of roles and ministries within the church will be open only to those who are covenant members. This is to ensure that the values, convictions and practices of the church are properly adhered to. However, many other ways of serving and functioning may be open to community members according to their gifts and capacity.

The Church as an Ordered and Disciplined Community

The model described is far from being the only one possible. It may be discerned that it moves in two directions at once. In one direction it affirms the diverse ways in which people belong in the belief that a sense of belonging helps people to grow in their capacity to believe. Its desire is to include people and to exist as an open community. In the other direction it moves towards making covenant membership more demanding and expecting here higher levels of understanding, commitment and dedication. Whereas community membership should be available by means of a general welcome, covenant membership would require more systematic training to induct people into what the church stands for. This could be caricatured as a 'two-tier' system of membership by those who want to insist that we are 'all the same'. But the point is we are not 'all the same'. We may all have equal access to God's grace through Christ but we have not all explored that grace to the same measure. Understandings of membership are needed which are flexible enough to affirm where people really are. The better model is not two-tier but concentric. It is a healthy dynamic which draws people from the circumference to the centre and which is open to everyone who wishes to make the journey.

Here we address a complex issue. Within the baptist and believers church tradition discipline has gone hand in hand with discipleship. Church members have understood themselves to be under a church's discipline. This sense is greatly reduced in contemporary Christianity. When people are baptised and become church members this is usually without any reference to the church as a disciplined community. There are several reasons for this. One is that culturally we prize freedom and autonomy and resist anybody's right to 'tell us what to do'. We have also become, and rightly so, very sensitised towards abuse and are well aware that there are many historical and contemporary examples of *religious* abuse.[32] People, rightly, avoid becoming locked in to any system, even church systems, where they would lose legitimate control. Equally, many are impatient with issues of order and lose interest when they come into consideration. The gospel is about life and vitality, joy and vigour! This is true. But 'God is a God not of disorder but of peace', and so 'all things should be done decently and in order'.[33]

Order enables life and freedom rather than stifling it. The supreme example of this, relevant if we are to see the church as the image of the Trinity, concerns the ordering of the divine life. The Trinity has its life in mutual communion and indwelling, but it is also clear, to use the traditional language of the church's creeds, that the Father has begotten the Son from all eternity by the Spirit and that the Spirit proceeds from the Father through the Son. This is communion arising out of an order of divine life not in contradiction to it. By analogy, the communion of the church is also rooted in a sense of order arising from the sovereign rule of God over and in the congregation. We have already considered one basis for this in the teachings of Jesus in Matthew 18:15–20 which lays down a pattern of what we would call 'conflict resolution', or 'caring confrontation'. It is highly instructive. We should note:

- The expectation to confront seems to be laid upon all members of the church and not only upon the responsible leaders.
- Some ancient manuscripts omit the words 'against you' in verse 15 implying that it is not only in matters of personal offence that action should be taken but any form of sin. This is a wider level of responsibility therefore.
- The process starts at the lowest and most private level with a confidential broaching of the issue between two people. Most matters would probably be resolved at this level.
- In case of lack of response the process escalates with the involvement of a few others who can guarantee objectivity, act as mediators and add seriousness. No doubt this brings a further level of resolution.
- If this fails the most serious level of escalation is to 'tell' the whole church, which appears to function as the final human court of appeal.

- If everything fails then the most extreme action is to return the church member to the status of an outsider, which in effect is the status that the person has chosen for themselves.
- Interpretations vary, as previously noted, as to whether being treated as 'a Gentile and tax collector' means treating someone as the Jews would do this, with distance, or as Jesus did, with friendship.

That the early church saw itself as a disciplined community is clear. Acts 5:1–11 contains the disturbing incident of Ananias and Sapphira. In 1 Corinthians 5:1–6 Paul refers to a shocking case of sexual immorality and urges that the perpetrator should be handed 'over to Satan for the destruction of the flesh, so that his spirit may be saved in the day of the Lord'. This presumably refers to being put out of the church to learn repentance. Paul goes on to liken the man's sin to yeast that affects the whole loaf (vv. 6–8). Although the Christian message is one of forgiveness, it is in fact immoral to gloss lightly over sin as though it did not matter. Sin needs to be taken seriously, not minimised and trivialised. One intention of church discipline is to let the truth be seen and affirmed since sincerity and truth are paramount.[34] But another intention is to face people up with their wrongdoing in a spirit of gentleness and vulnerability in order that they may repent and be restored.[35]

Discipline and discipleship

Although gathering churches have taken discipline seriously, perhaps too seriously, in the past there are large questions about this process today. In the past people lived and worked side by side and in near proximity to each other, so inevitably their lives were observed and examined in ways that could be regarded as intrusive and out of place in today's more private and anonymous society. In the contemporary church it usually only emerges that a church member has a serious problem when this is made known in some other way, such as through a court action or press revelation. Churches are often the last place for a problem to become known and are left dealing with damage limitation exercises rather than proper discipline. Moreover, there is a greater awareness of the demand for confidentiality than in previous generations and so more reluctance to 'tell it to the church' even if the church ought to know. Litigation against supposed breaches of confidentiality and alleged professional malpractice on the part of ministers is not unknown. In any case, most cases of church discipline end up with people withdrawing their membership from a church and going down the road to another one which, glad to recruit new members, asks no questions. It is difficult to see how church discipline can be shaped to meet today's needs. Yet if we exist as communities of disciples it must have some place.

This brings us back to church membership. To be a church member involves belonging to a community committed to the 'observed life' in which we work to keep each other up to the mark as disciples. To enter into membership involves giving to other members a mandate to challenge us when we do wrong. Yet it is quite true that no one has the right to do this unless we willingly assent to it. In the process of initiation it is virtually impossible to broach this issue adequately (along with so many others) as part of baptismal preparation unless that part of the process of initiation is considerably lengthened. This is another reason for distinguishing covenant membership within community membership. Foundations can be laid as people are prepared for baptism. But covenant members can be instructed in this aspect of formal membership, and others likewise, so that they fully understand its implications. They can also be trained to practise more competently the mediation skills required to fulfil this ministry in a spirit of gentleness and humility, skills which are profoundly in tune with God's work of reconciliation in the cross and will stand them in good stead in many other areas of life.

Free commitment is the precondition of both discipleship and discipline and also the safeguard against any potential abusiveness in religious systems. The decision to be a disciple of Christ and a member of a local church is and remains a free one. The New Testament issues strong warnings against allowing anyone to deprive us of our freedom: 'For freedom

Christ has set us free. Stand firm therefore and do not submit again to a yoke of slavery.'[36] Churches are called to enhance this freedom in Christ not to remove it and this means acknowledging the full right and responsibility of each believer to be a steward of her or his own life. This is foundational. Having squarely addressed the issue of discipline it is possible to put the issue in proper context.

The Community of Disciples

That proper context is the life of discipleship. A disciple is one who learns from a teacher and is open to his or her instruction and formation. Christian disciples are followers of their teacher Jesus Christ and make it their aim that he should form them in his own image. This is done by means of the Spirit and the Word. By receiving the continuing energy and power of the words of Jesus and by beholding the risen Lord we are changed.[37] It also comes through the church which is the body of Christ, the community in which he takes form. We are engaged with each other in such a way that we receive from each other aspects of the manifold grace of God, setting an example to each other. It is not church leaders alone who do this but the whole body. This is the continual activity of the church of Christ, to be a discipling community. The word 'discipling' is sometimes used to refer to the intentional instruction of one person by another in the things of God, a form of mentoring. But essentially it is a community project since no one person has everything that we need to learn. Each of us possesses only a fragment and the shaping of lives does not necessarily work from above to below, from leaders to led, from older to younger. Since Christ is in the midst and in each one it works in all directions. This is a different model of church life from that of being a place of preaching or of the drama of the sacraments, as though the church were first of all a lecture room or a theatre. Crucial as teaching and the sacraments are, they acquire their greatest potency when they are central aspects of a learning and dedicated community of disciples.

Seen against the backdrop of discipleship, church discipline is simply an occasional if precise tool that needs to be used reluctantly, sparingly and always kindly. It allows significant issues and failures to be confronted in the hope of something better. It will be exercised in a pastoral style which approaches people caringly with full respect for the struggles of life and proper confidentiality. It will not be an exercise of power but of vulnerability. On those rare occasions when such an approach does not yield fruit and exclusion from membership becomes necessary this will be a last step in a longer process and it will be seen simply as a recognition that this is where the person concerned has placed her- or himself, outside the community of committed disciples who gather together in the name of the Christ, but always with the possibility by the grace of the Christ-like God of being restored.

Notes

[1] It also needs to be said that the Church of Scotland has full self-government and would deny that it is any way governed by the state. It can also with justification claim to practice the separation of church and state for this same reason.

[2] This does not stop Baptists in some countries becoming very 'cosy' in their relations to the governing party.

[3] Durnbaugh's, *The Believers' Church* has been very influential in this regard.

[4] Littell, *Origins of Sectarian Protestantism*.

[5] Wright, *New Baptists, New Agenda*, 75–77. A similar 'make-over' can be detected in Keith G. Jones, *A Believing Church: Learning from some contemporary Anabaptist and Baptist Perspectives* (Didcot: Baptist Union of Great Britain, 1998).

[6] Matthew 9:37–38.

[7] Luke 15:1–7.

[8] Matthew 16:24–28.

[9] John 3:1–10.

[10] 'The Baptist Doctrine of the Church' (1948) in Roger Hayden(ed.), *Baptist Union Documents 1948–1977* (London: Baptist Historical Society, 1980), 5–6. For the Confession of 1677, otherwise known as the 'Second London Confession', see Lumpkin, *Baptist Confessions of Faith*, 235–95.

11 Richard Hooker, *Laws of Ecclesiastical Polity*, Vol. III.i.7–8, in John Keble (ed.), *Richard Hooker: Works*, Vol. 1 (Oxford: Oxford University Press, 1845), 342–43.

12 NB Conrad Grebel: 'But after we took Scripture in hand too, and consulted it on many points, we have been instructed somewhat and have discovered the great and harmful error of the shepherds, of ours too, namely that we do not daily beseech God earnestly with constant groaning to be brought...to attain to the true faith and divine practice': Williams and Mergal (eds.), *Spiritual and Anabaptist Writers*, 74.

13 A robust statement of this was from John Owen, '(T)he Scripture doth in general represent the kingdom or church of Christ to consist of persons called *saints*, separated from the world... regeneration is expressly required in the gospel to give a right and privilege unto an entrance into the church or kingdom of Christ, John iii.3, Tit. iii.3-5': 'The True Nature of a Gospel Church and its Government', in William H. Gould (ed.), *The Works of John Owen*, Volume XVI (Edinburgh: Banner of Truth Trust, 1968), 11–12.

14 Hebrews 11:6.

15 Article 64 'Propositions and Conclusions concerning the True Christian Religion, 1612–1614', in Lumpkin, *Baptist Confessions of Faith*, 136.

16 Ibid., Article 69.

17 Article 10 'A Declaration of English People remaining at Amsterdam in Holland': Lumpkin, *Baptist Confessions of Faith*, 119.

18 Matthew 6:5–8; John 4:23.

19 Matthew 7:1–5; Romans 2:1.

20 1 Corinthians 2:14.

21 1 Thessalonians 5:21.

22 Titus 3:4–7; 1 Peter 2:1–10.

23 1 Corinthians 12:12–13.

24 1 Peter 2:5.

25 The Church of England, for instance, is undecided whether to estimate its membership on the basis of infant baptism, which would be a large but mainly nominal number; on the basis of those who have confirmed their baptism, which would be considerably fewer; on the basis of those who receive Easter communion, which would be even fewer; or on the basis of the collective electoral rolls of the parishes which might include those who have neither been baptised or confirmed: The Archbishops' Council, *Statistics: A Tool for Mission* (London: Church House Publishing, 2000), 12–13.

26 Fiddes, *Tracks and Traces*, 21–47.

[27] Wright, *Challenge to Change*, 62–66, 101–103.
[28] Acts 2:41–42.
[29] Acts 2:38.
[30] Wright, *New Baptists New Agenda*, 64–80.
[31] American churches sometimes call this 'watch-care' membership.
[32] Nigel G. Wright, 'Religious Abuse: The Precarious Potential of Religious Believing', *Journal of European Baptist Studies*, 3.2 (January, 2003), 5–14.
[33] 1 Corinthians 14:33, 40.
[34] 1 Corinthians 5:8.
[35] Galatians 6:1.
[36] Galatians 5:1.
[37] 2 Corinthians 3:12–18.

4. The Baptism of Disciples

The Nature of Christian Initiation

Introduction

Baptists are distinguished from the majority traditions of the church by the fact that they practice exclusively the baptism of believers and not infant baptism. From this distinctive practice, shared as we have noted with the majority in the baptist and believers church tradition, they have derived their name. It is the most public and most obvious difference from other churches, but it would be wrong to see this as the main issue at stake. The baptism of believers follows directly and secondarily from the nature of the church as we discussed it in the previous chapter. If the church is a community of the voluntarily committed, of confessing disciples, then the sign of entry into this community must reflect this. It must be something to which people come as an aspect of their discovery of faith rather than to which they are brought without the element of choice. Infant baptism was the logically consistent sign of the territorial church according to which ethnic and religious identities were entwined: people are Christians by virtue of birth and inheritance; they are Christians for passive reasons based on someone else's choice whether that of parents or of some past ruler. By contrast, in the community of disciples, commitment is the product of new birth and costly choice symbolised in the present age, as it was in the New Testament, by believers baptism.

Once more a word is necessary about terminology. Reference is often made to 'adult baptism'. It may be the case that many believers are baptised as adults. It may also be that there is a case for encouraging baptism only when people are of age. However, most baptists would agree that the decisive issue in making baptism authentic is not age but repentance and faith, making 'adult' baptism a misnomer. 'Credobaptist' is the more technical term for believer baptists corresponding to 'paedobaptist' for infant baptists. Jürgen Moltmann uses the term 'vocational baptism' to indicate that it is rooted first in the call of God to those who can respond or 'give an answer' on their own account.[1] The heading to this chapter introduces the term 'baptism of disciples', implying that faith is not the only relevant issue; the will to accept the demands of discipleship also belongs to the question of readiness for baptism.

The Initiatory Rite

As a way of overcoming historic disputes about baptism it has become customary to speak of 'Christian initiation' to refer to the whole process or the 'continuing character of Christian nurture' through which people enter the kingdom of God and the church.[2] In this is the recognition that baptism is part of a wider complex of practices and prerequisites that give it meaning: for instance, the need to understand the elements of Christian conversion, the place of catechism and preparation of the understanding of the meaning of faith, of life within the church. Baptism receives meaning because of the things that go before it and follow on afterwards. Ecumenical discussion has also come to agree that baptism on profession of faith is the form of baptism most clearly attested in the New Testament, which gives no unambiguous examples of infant baptism; the theology of baptism should therefore work on the assumption that those baptised are choosing baptism for themselves in response to the liberating call of God. Infant baptism is then to be seen as derivative from this rather than normative over it. It should be understood that paedobaptist traditions have no problems at all with the practice of believers baptism as such and in some countries probably baptise more people as believers than do believer baptists. The debate over this issue is not reciprocal since believers baptism, clearly attested in the New Testament, is not subject to the same kind of criticism as infant baptism. For infant baptists the problem is not with believers baptism but with anything that might be considered 're-baptism'. [3]

Baptism is meant to happen once and is intended as the definitive rite of entry into the kingdom of God and the church. It belongs to the very beginnings of the Christian life. On the day of Pentecost those seeking salvation were told to, 'Repent and be baptised every one of you in the name of Jesus Christ, so that your sins will be forgiven; and you will receive the gift of the Holy Spirit.'[4] Baptism belongs to the elementary or foundational teachings of the faith.[5] It is noteworthy that, issues of believers or infant baptism apart, some form of baptism constitutes the indispensable rite of initiation for virtually the whole of the Christian church.[6] It is a universal practice carried through almost always, everywhere and by all. The New Testament gives divergent accounts of the exact verbal forms by means of which baptism is administered. Acts makes frequent reference to baptism 'in the name of Jesus'[7] whereas in Matthew 28:19 Jesus is said to commission the disciples to baptise 'in the name of the Father and of the Son and of the Holy Spirit'. It seems probable that this latter formula reflects the emerging and then settled practice of the early church. To baptise in the name of a person means with their authority, on their behalf and in such a way as to bring the baptised person into closer relationship with the one who is named. If there is a minimum requirement to the rite of baptism it is associated with the use of the divine name and of water. Any baptismal liturgy would be considered basically flawed without them.

All religions do, of course, cater for rites of passage in their religious practices as ways in which people may be socialised into the practice of their religion and recognised as valid members of the religious community. It is very frequent for the fundamental element of water to figure in these ceremonies.

The Jewish tradition made use of washing in a number of its practices including the practice of so-called 'proselyte' baptism. When Gentiles wished to convert to Judaism, males would have to accept circumcision as a sign of the covenant and whole families could be ritually washed to symbolise their passage into the people of God.[8] John the Baptist preached 'a baptism for the repentance of sins', and he baptised those who received his message in the River Jordan.[9] The location is significant. It might be inferred from John's baptism that Jews were being exhorted to become part of a renewed Israel within Israel and this is strengthened by their being baptised in the Jordan since Israel entered the Promised Land through the Jordan.[10] Contemporary Jews were being asked to make an inward transition through repentance and faith into the prepared people of God. Christian baptism builds upon John's baptism by proclaiming not just a time of preparation but of fulfilment. Jesus is the Messiah who baptises with the Holy Spirit and with fire.[11]

The Meaning of Baptism

Baptism is a form of drama, a way of acting out what it means internally. With other Christian practices it may be seen as a 'visible word', as distinct from a spoken word, in that the very drama of baptism communicates. However, the visible word should be accompanied by the spoken word in order to interpret the meaning appropriately. Taking believers baptism as the norm, the following particular images can be seen to be expressed through baptism:

Being born: John 3:5–6 speaks of the need to be 'born of water and the spirit' in order to see the kingdom of God and amplifies this: 'What is born of the flesh is flesh, and what is born of the Spirit is spirit.' Being 'born of water' could be a reference to natural birth in that before a child is born the sack of water which contains it in its mother's womb must burst. Jesus would therefore be saying that just as we are born physically so must we be born spiritually: both births are necessary for fullness of life. Alternatively, being born of water and the Spirit could be two ways of saying the same thing. Water is a frequent symbol of the Holy Spirit,[12] and birth of water and Spirit is a parallel in spiritual terms with physical birth. When a person is baptised and passes through the water this is a symbol of passing into new life through the work of the Spirit who is the mother of their life in Christ. The Spirit gives birth to believers in a way parallel to the work of the Spirit in the womb of Mary the Virgin.[13] Arguably here Mary acts as a sign of the motherly and life-giving work of the Spirit of which she is the instrument. What is impossible for humans is abundantly possible for God and we are 'born from above' to share in the life of Jesus Christ. A potent symbol of this is the church which did not possess a baptismal pool; instead the members borrowed and assembled within their building a birthing pool in which to conduct their baptisms. This is highly appropriate drama. Baptism is the sign of new life and new birth into the life of God in such a way as to renew and transform us, incorporating us into the living community which is Christ's body.[14]

Being washed: Inevitably, the drama of baptism should also be read as being like a bath. Titus 3:5 refers to the '[washing] of rebirth and renewal by the Holy Spirit'. New birth therefore carries the implication of being washed and made clean from the polluting effects of the sinful life. Cleansing is related to the blood of Christ which is seen as a powerful agent for removing sin.[15] Christ has purged us of our sins by his sacrificial and atoning work.[16] As believers are brought into relationship with Christ so the benefits of Christ's work on behalf of human beings are imparted to them and they experience their powerful impact. Baptism is a public demonstration of the way in which on confession of repentance towards God and faith in Christ past and present sins are washed away and a new way of living begins. Baptism is more than an outward washing of dirt from the body: it is 'an appeal to God for a good conscience' on the basis of all that Christ has accomplished on our behalf.[17]

Being buried and raised: Slightly more demanding in its dramatic imagery is the idea that baptism is like being laid in the grave. The precise physical mode of baptism is open to debate and no one mode of baptism should be seen as essential in the way that the use of the Triune name is. However, some ways of being baptised are more complete than others in terms of imagery. To be baptised by being laid backwards in total immersion captures most completely the symbolism of burial. According to Paul in Romans 6:3–4, believers are baptised into the death of Christ: 'Therefore we have been buried with him by baptism into death, so that, just as Christ was raised from the dead by the glory of the Father, so we too might walk in newness of life' (v. 7). Christ's own baptism might be seen as a precursor of the later baptism of death which he was to undergo on our behalf.[18] To be baptised then is to have the old life put to death, to show that we have been crucified with Christ.[19] As with circumcision, there is a life-threatening quality to baptism. When a male child is circumcised the knife comes close and could slip. Baptism symbolises a circumcision of the heart, the stripping away of the flesh inwardly so that the life of the Spirit may prevail.[20] When people are baptised they might just, with careless handling, be drowned since they are making themselves vulnerable. Baptism signifies death to the old ways of living and those parts of ourselves that cling to them. This is part of its power. Joyfully this burial is accompanied by a resurrection signified by coming up out of the water.[21]

Being immersed in the Holy Spirit: There are different modes of baptism. It is possible to perform the act by pouring water onto somebody's head; it is perhaps more usual to baptise by immersing totally in water. Both of these forms have reference to the Holy Spirit. On the one hand, the Spirit descends upon those baptised as the dove alighted on Jesus at his baptism.[22] On the other hand, the Spirit is the medium into which we are immersed as we enter into spiritual life.[23] The word itself means to 'plunge' or to 'dip'. Baptism in water therefore signifies a baptism into the realm of the Holy Spirit with all that means for our regeneration, sanctification and empowering. It is not surprising that baptism in this way is closely associated with the enduing of the church with the power of the messianic age at Pentecost;[24] or that significant visitations of the Spirit upon the emerging church awakened the memory of Pentecost in the minds of the apostles.[25] Baptism in the Spirit implies that just as Jesus was anointed with the Spirit at his baptism to be the agent of the messianic age of fulfilment, so now that age breaks upon the community of disciples which has been gathered to carry forward the work which he has initiated. This is the age in which the Spirit is poured out upon all flesh and the sons and daughters of the new Israel will prophesy, see visions and dream dreams.[26]

Collectively, these dramatic images help us see the way in which Christian baptism completes and goes beyond the baptism of John the Baptist. John preached a baptism of preparation, the church a baptism of fulfilment. John exhorted his hearers to get ready for the one who was to come, Christian baptism refers to the Christ who has come and whose living, dying and rising transform our situation and our very selves. Baptism recapitulates the story of our salvation and mediates the benefits of that salvation to us through its dramatic imagery in the power of the Spirit. It speaks of being buried and raised with Christ and so of the cleansing and life-changing impact of Christ's work upon those who embrace it in repentance and faith. Baptism is the Jordan by means of which we enter the Promised Land of God's rest. More strictly: by means of what baptism signifies we enter into God's promises as they are proclaimed over us and applied to us by the Spirit in the baptismal act. On one occasion Paul encountered a group of 'disciples' who had been baptised according to John's baptism. His immediate response was to baptise them in the name of Jesus since these clear elements of fulfilment make a qualitative difference to what baptism is. In consequence, these disciples entered into the benefits of the messianic age as the Spirit came upon them.[27]

Baptism becomes the point at which we make our personal confession of faith and take our stand for Christ, not being ashamed to own him as Lord.[28] It is often pointed out that although people may be secret believers in Jesus Christ, it is only at the point of baptism that this becomes a public and open commitment. Consequently, it is here, as they openly declare their break with past loyalties and own Christ as Lord over all, that they become the objects of persecution. Within Christianised cultures this element can be lost and even believers baptism can be seen as a benign rite of passage into conformity with the prevailing values. In many other places it is the point of no return, the cost of which has to be counted in advance.[29] This is truly a baptism of disciples.

The Normal Christian Birth[30]

As the designated rite of Christian initiation, an analogy may be made here with physical human birth. There is a normal way of being born: children for instance are normally born head first. Some, however, depart from the norm and prefer to come out of the womb the other way round. Others are given no choice and are born by Caesarean section. The end product is the same: a living and, hopefully, healthy child. In Acts the normal Christian birth is set out in Acts 2:37–42 and follows the following pattern:

- conviction of sin, followed by
- repentance (and presumably faith), followed by
- baptism in the name of Jesus Christ (or Father, Son and Spirit), resulting in
- the gift of the Holy Spirit, leading to
- incorporation into the community of disciples, and then
- steadfast participation in the church, its disciplines and its mission.

Alternatively stated we have here:

- *What we do*: We respond to the message about Jesus Christ. Any response we make is itself a product of the Holy Spirit already at work upon and within us since none can come to the Father unless they be drawn.[31] The appropriate response awakened within us is that of repentance and faith, turning from our old ways of thinking and behaving and placing our whole faith in Jesus Christ. In this spirit we come to baptism and make request for it in the way the Ethiopian eunuch did.[32] Baptism is to be willingly received and earnestly desired and is the opportunity for the confession that 'Jesus is Lord!'[33] Then there is:

- *What the church does*: The church administers the rite of baptism which has been entrusted to it, making sure to do so with the correct use of the baptismal formula. Baptism is administered at the church's discretion, not our own and in coming to baptism we demonstrate that we are in a dependent situation. We cannot absolve or save ourselves: this comes to us from outside, through Christ who is our Saviour. That we must ask the church to baptise us is a sign of our dependence at this point. In a commonly used form of words, candidates for baptism are baptised on their 'confession of repentance towards God and faith in our Lord Jesus Christ' and having promised to 'serve him forever in the fellowship of his church'.

- *What God does*: God grants the gift of the Holy Spirit as the divine response to our request. This does not imply that the Spirit has so far been absent in the process since we cannot sincerely come to this point without the influence of the Spirit within us. But there are different aspects to the Spirit's work: first we are awakened to our need of God and convicted concerning our sins, then we are regenerated and enabled to repent and believe as the Spirit draws us out of ourselves and into relationship with God's self, then we are empowered by the Spirit to live as members of the messianic community. Baptism captures all these elements in its symbolism and leads to their being embedded within us.

We need to be healthily born and effectively initiated into the kingdom of God and the church. We might imagine that deficiencies in our later Christian discipleship will emerge if the proper foundations are not laid. For this reason, work done at the beginning of the Christian life with a view to a well-rounded initiation into the life of Christ is highly valuable. Although there may well be the exact point at which we cross the line from the realm of unbelief to that of belief, this will be part of a process that first prepares for it and then builds upon it. The pattern of the normal Christian birth is not intended to dictate that every person's experience must follow it exactly. Acts demonstrates that the Spirit of God does not always stay within the pattern. The Samaritans, for instance, believed and were duly baptised but did not receive the gift of the Spirit until considerably later, when Peter and John made a special apostolic visit from Jerusalem.[34] This was probably because, given the ancient hostilities between Jews and Samaritans, some special way of embodying the unity of the church was needed in this case. By contrast, the Holy Spirit fell on Cornelius and his household before Peter had even finished preaching. Peter had hurriedly to instruct that they be baptised in order to catch up with the Spirit's enthusiasm to embrace these Gentiles.[35] Later on Paul encounters a group of apparent disciples in Ephesus only to discover on questioning them that they need a crash course in proper Christian initiation, which he effectively provides.[36] God's Spirit must always be free; but that does not give us the freedom to depart from the patterns laid down for our instruction. These help us discern what elements may yet be lacking in a person's initiation into the kingdom and to supply what is needed.

Infant Versus Believers Baptism

If Christian initiation is seen as a process within which there are variations, to what extent does it matter if people are baptised before they come to repentance and faith? Or is baptism organically dependent upon the prior presence of faith? If the Spirit may be given prior to baptism, does it follow also that baptism may be given prior to the personal exercise of faith? The majority of the church has answered these questions by affirming the validity of the baptism of infants. Seen this way, as people grow to maturity they are able to claim as their own promises that have been made on their behalf previously. Baptism therefore does not need to be preceded by the faith of those baptised, provided that in its administration the church and parents are exercising faith on their behalf. This commitment is then confirmed by the baptised person in more mature years. Believer baptists disagree with the logic of this account arguing that although God is free to bestow the Spirit at any point, that does not constitute a freedom on the church's part to vary its part in the pattern as laid down. This follows an ancient principle that although *God* is not bound even to the sacraments divinely appointed, *we are* since we are not God.

Can a credible case for infant baptism be made? There is a difference between the baptism of an infant and that of a child. A child, growing into consciousness, may well have a sincere faith in Christ and the appropriateness of baptism here is open to further discussion on believer baptist premises. An infant is not of an age where such faith can be exercised. There are no clear-cut instances in the New Testament of the baptism of either infants or children. A case has been made for the baptism of infants within those of whole households, as in the case of the Philippian jailer.[37] But here it explicitly says that the word was spoken to all who were in his household and that they all rejoiced that he had become a believer.[38] Similarly with the household of Cornelius, in which those were baptised who were heard 'speaking in tongues and extolling God'.[39] It has also been argued that when Jesus welcomed the little children and said, 'Let the little children come to me; do not stop them',[40] he was demonstrating how we should welcome children also to be baptised. Yet, notably Jesus did not himself baptise the children but simply took them in his arms and blessed them. Often, behind these arguments is the conviction that families must be seen as having a solidarity with each other and that the conversion of parents entitles their children also to belong to the Christian community and so to receive the 'mark of belonging'.[41] This perspective also leads to the criticism that baptists are too individualistic about their approach to baptism.

Wise commentators across the spectrum on this topic recognise that we look to the New Testament in vain for any unambiguous mandate for infant baptism. But this ought not to surprise us. In the New Testament we are introduced to the first generation of Christians who would not yet have encountered with full force the question of how to nurture the faith of the second generation or beyond. A space is left here for later questions which must be filled with theological rather than directly biblical wisdom. It has been widely felt that infant baptism is a legitimate way of occupying this space since the children of the church can hardly be regarded as pagans and must have some kind of relation to the community of disciples into which they have been born. As it is, there is clear evidence for infant baptism from the late second century and it seems first to have emerged for reasons of pastoral care rather than theology.[42] When the children of believers were dying, as they must frequently have done in that as in later ages, should they not be baptised as a sign that they are beloved of God and as a comfort to their parents that they are in the faith? So-called 'emergency baptism' is still a natural recourse for parents who feel that it is the last thing they can do for their child. With the practice of infant baptism thus established it then went in search of a theology, and as after Constantine it became increasingly advantageous to be part of the church, at least nominally, infant baptism and citizenship went hand in hand. It became important to justify it theologically.

The Case for Infant Baptism

While the practice of infant baptism has remained constant theological arguments to support it have varied considerably.

Augustine developed an argument from *original guilt*.[43] According to this, the whole human race was already included seminally within Adam and Eve when they sinned. The whole of humankind therefore sinned in them and became guilty and so worthy of condemnation. This sin and guilt was passed down generation to generation through sexual activity and procreation. Infant baptism involved the washing away of the guilt of original sin so that those baptised were thereafter left to deal only with the sin they themselves incurred, and to do this through penitence, faith and a holy life. Those infants who died without the grace of baptism were at best suspended in a condition known as 'limbo'.

There are difficulties of biblical interpretation in this approach since Augustine (who did not know Greek) seems to have misunderstood the Greek text of Romans 5:12 to imply that all sinned 'in Adam', whereas it rather means that all followed on the pattern set by Adam and sinned on their own account; sin is not counted if there is no law or personal culpability before the law (v. 13). Whereas it is possible to argue from Paul that there is a solidarity in sin which all human beings share as a primordial, disordered condition, this is not the same as original guilt attributed to us before we are born for acts not our own. The notion that newborn children are already irredeemably polluted and condemned and need to be cleansed at an early moment in their lives is surely problematic, and not just for sentimental reasons. As a way of thinking it conflicts with the vision of God revealed in the Christ who welcomed children and blessed them. Few paedobaptists would consider this as an argument for infant baptism today and most would repudiate it entirely.

A highly influential alternative with a noble pedigree is to see infant baptism as the New Testament equivalent of Old Testament circumcision, as a sign of the *covenant of grace* which extends to the children of believers.[44] According to this the children of believers are part of the covenant people of God and members of the body of Christ. They are not little pagans to be evangelised but fellow members of the people of God by reason of their solidarity within a Christian family. The new covenant is scarcely likely to be more restrictive than the old and so should be seen to embrace within itself the children of those who believe. Moreover, Paul taught that the children of believers are holy.[45] Jesus welcomed children to himself and spoke of the kingdom of God as belonging to them.[46] Put these considerations together and infant baptism, the reception of children into the covenant community, begins to look like a theologically responsible practice which answers the question of where children fit within the Christian community: they belong as true members in their own right. More than this, infant baptism can actually be seen to magnify the grace of God in that even before there is any kind of response, the prevenient grace of God, the grace that goes before us and makes possible any response to God on our part, is applied to a child's life. Later on, of course, it remains for each person to respond to this through their own growth in faith and discipleship and this may be expressed in a rite such as confirmation, which was newly created for this purpose. This is the point at which promises made on an infant's behalf in baptism are owned and embraced as their own. Neither would it be true to say that this is not in its own way a form of *believers* baptism since it is undertaken in a context of faith, the faith of parents who bring their children for baptism and of the church which administers baptism.

This is possibly the strongest theological defence of infant baptism available.[47] Even so, it is flawed in its fundamental logic and in particular fails to reckon with the essential discontinuity between the old and the new covenants. It proceeds on the assumption that there is a continuous flow in the administration of the covenant so that infant baptism could be seen as directly equivalent to circumcision. Membership of the people of God under the old covenant was a matter of birth and this was expressed for male children through the rite of circumcision. But, by contrast, under the new covenant membership of the renewed people of God comes about by means of new birth which is appropriately signified in baptism. To return to natural birth and inheritance as the criterion of membership in the church is to slip back into ethnic and biological categories which are no longer appropriate, however understandable it may be to want to find a place for one's own children among the redeemed. They do indeed have a place since 'the promise is for you, for your children, and for all who are far away, everyone whom the Lord our God calls to him'.[48] But that place is taken up by means of faith, not natural birth. In fact, Jesus made a decisive break with the politics of kinship loyalties and solidarity when, in an incident quite shocking to those who see Christianity as a religion of 'family values', he repudiated his own family and taught, 'Whoever does the will of God is my brother and sister and mother.'[49] The kinship of faith takes precedence over that of blood, and the two circles do not necessarily overlap. Indeed the whole argument from the covenant somewhat resembles the attempt to screw a lid on to a jar which it does not quite fit. The Old Testament cannot be read as though it were the New, and vice versa. Between the two there is a discontinuity at the point of how we enter the people of God, whether by birth or new birth which decisively alters the point at which circumcision and baptism can be seen in parallel.[50] Furthermore, to claim that infant baptism is a superior expression of the grace of God is both to believe that we know how to improve upon the sacraments that have been given to us and to neglect the fact that the grace of God engages us in relationship and draws out from us the response of faith of which on our own we are incapable. We have nothing that we did not first receive from God.[51] We shall return to the very important question of the place of children within the Christian community in a later chapter.

A less theological but still influential defence sees infant baptism as a *sign of welcome and inclusion* for children into the Christian community. In this way, children are affirmed and valued by the church which administers God's blessing not to the children of believers only but to all who are brought to it. Whereas the previous argument from the covenant leads to a more restrictive baptismal discipline and inquires extensively concerning the faith of the parents, this approach values inclusivity and generosity and regards an open baptismal policy as part of the church's mission. If it is indeed the case that baptism itself is the means of salvation this would not only make sense, it would be morally necessary to baptise as many as possible. However, this position does not begin here, since those who hold it are unlikely to believe that infants are spiritually lost. Rather, they are already included in the saving grace of God and infant baptism marks this. The church freely dispenses such grace as it has at its disposal. Children are marked with the sign of the cross.

It is hard to argue with the impulse towards generosity and liberality here. But it is questionable as to why baptism needs to be adapted, and in the process distorted, to be the means through which this is expressed. When Jesus welcomed children he took them in his arms and blessed them and this should be seen as a perfectly adequate way of expressing the prevenient and all-embracing love of God. To adapt baptism for this purpose inevitably neglects an aspect of the meaning of baptism which is that it is an 'appeal to God for a good conscience'.[52] It has a God-ward aspect which also belongs to its intrinsic meaning. To omit this is to distort the sign. There are better ways of expressing, liturgically and otherwise, the generosity and openness of the church towards God's world which do not require this distortion and these are prefigured in precisely the incident to which reference is made, the reception by Jesus of the children.

Criticisms of Infant Baptism

Generally speaking, believer baptists are not sufficiently aware of the strength of some of the theological justifications of infant baptism and are too inclined to dismiss it on the grounds that it is not 'biblical'. However, the justifications I have summarised do lay themselves open to criticism. For instance, whatever the intention, the practice and often the liturgies of infant baptism inevitably suggest we become Christians by birth not new birth. This creates room for a sense of illusion or false security, implying that the decision to believe can be made for us, so weakening the emphasis on repentance and faith. This is certainly not the baptism of disciples. Not is it enough to say that the elements of the process of Christian initiation can happen in any order. As already argued, *God*, who is free, is not bound by baptism and can bestow the Spirit in varying ways. But *we* are bound to baptism and to respect the order within the process. With a birth there has to be gestation beforehand and if baptism is meant to express response towards God on the basis of God's prevenient grace revealed supremely in the cross, spiritual regeneration has to be in a person's heart before it is a fully meaningful sign. Believers baptism affirms we all need to make our personal response.

The re-emergence of believers baptism has been seen by some as a consequence of Western individualism and therefore as inferior to the more communal assumptions of biblical and catholic Christianity. Certainly, believers baptism can play into the hands of a wrong form of individualism. But there is a *kind* of individualism implied in the gospel. When Jesus spoke of the need to enter through the 'narrow gate' and the 'hard way' that lead to life,[53] he surely intended to imply that we do not enter God's kingdom by virtue of membership in a family, or clan, or religious group. A narrow gate can be entered only one at a time, and so it is with the kingdom. In facing this decision we are all finally on our own before God, whatever the communal processes that have brought us to that point. Moreover, it is wrong to argue that a strength of infant baptism is exactly that it does neglect the dimension of response and so magnifies the unconditioned nature of God's grace. This is a truncated view of the grace that draws out our response to God in relationship.

Frequently Asked Questions

Having laid out a basic understanding of the baptism of disciples we now take up some of the questions that are most frequently asked.

Is baptism necessary? The issue here is, necessary for what? Few believer baptists would see it as necessary for eternal salvation since the saints of the Old Testament and the dying thief on the cross clearly indicate otherwise.[54] Moreover, we are justified by grace through faith, so trust in Christ is the moment when salvation comes to the individual. But for disciples baptism is not merely advisory or optional: it is commanded and should be seen as foundational.[55] It is necessary for *discipleship* therefore if we wish to follow after Christ in the way he asks of us. It is also necessary for the *church* in that it is one of the 'norming norms' that safeguard its identity and mission, continually holding in front of us in dramatic form the key events of the history of salvation in the

cross and resurrection. This is why when baptism is administered it is essential to baptise in the name of the Trinity and to
use a form of words which give to the baptismal act its
properly Christian interpretation.

Is baptism only in the name of Jesus valid? There are churches
which practice 'Jesus only' baptism and follow the formula
described in Acts of baptising 'in the name of the Lord Jesus'.[56]
It cannot be said that this is wrong or invalid since it is clearly
set out in Acts as an effective form of baptism. However,
baptism 'in the name of the Father, and of the Son and of the
Holy Spirit' seems to be the mature practice of the early church
which Matthew identifies with Jesus himself.[57] This should be
the preferred form of baptism.

Does baptism have to be by total immersion? Some baptist
churches stipulate that baptism should be by total immersion,[58] but the amount of water is secondary to the name in
which baptism takes place. Total immersion better captures
some of the imagery of baptism, particularly that of dying and
rising in Christ and of being plunged into the realm of the
Spirit. In addition, the word itself means to 'dip' or 'soak'.
Accordingly, when Jesus was baptised we read that he 'came
up from the water'. However, baptism by effusion (pouring)
captures the imagery of the Spirit coming upon believers in
anointing as upon Jesus in his baptism.[59] This form of baptism
may be necessary in certain climates and circumstances or in
the case of illness and infirmity.

Is there a minimum age for baptism? There is no formal
minimum age and the challenge is to discern the right time for
each person and the ways in which God is working within
them. A later chapter deals more fully with the 'age of
discretion'. Although reference is often made to 'adult
baptism' and a case could be made for postponing the rite
until adult years, this is not the logic of 'believers baptism' as
such which looks for the presence of sincere saving faith.
However, the title to this chapter refers to the baptism of
disciples in order to add to this the need for an awareness of
what it means to follow after Christ in costly discipleship and
not just to receive Christ's benefits. Any candidate for baptism
therefore should show some grasp of what it means to choose

Christ in preference to other lords and of the cost involved in following him.

Can infant baptism ever be seen as valid baptism? Baptist churches, with some exceptions when they are also involved in ecumenical partnerships, would only ever practice the baptism of disciples. Many, especially in Britain, would be willing to recognise that believers from other traditions have often travelled by different routes and yet have a clear heart faith and experience. They may be willing therefore to let the mode and timing of baptism be a secondary issue out of respect for individual conscience and background. Applicants for covenant membership would be seen as transferring their membership from another church. In this case the receiving churches might still need to be persuaded that all the individual elements that belong to the process of initiation have been respected. This policy does imply that infant baptism plus conversion plus confirmation, although it may not be the preferred route, is not the same as being unbaptised and therefore constitutes an irregular but still spiritually valid way of incorporating people into kingdom and church. Some churches receive new members solely upon 'confession of faith' leading to the anomaly of Baptist churches with members who have never been baptised in any way. In discussions like this it is possible to become overly concerned with the details of how something has happened rather than to inquire as to whether the desired outcome has indeed come to pass through whatever order of baptismal practice.[60] If people have been truly and effectively incorporated into the church, to ask them to go through it again, this time the proper way, can sound like legalism. On the other hand, if people who have come from other traditions find that through study, prayer and the application of informed conscience they come to a change of conviction about baptism then they should be encouraged to follow this through, not as a way of denying what has gone before but of completing it. This whole discussion is an area of sharp disagreement in ecumenical discussions with some infant baptists taking great offence at what is thought to be 're-baptism' on the grounds that it denies a person's previous status as a Christian and implies that the church from which they have come is not really Christian. Baptists do not see their witness like that but rather as, with Apollos, a way of explaining the Way of God 'more accurately' to those who may already be well acquainted with the things concerning Jesus.[61] A fruitful compromise for the future may be found in a refusal by Baptists to insist on the baptism of believers of those who are full members of other traditions mirrored by a corresponding acceptance by infant baptists that people do sometimes come in good conscience to a change of conviction and should be supported in following this through.[62]

Does baptism achieve anything? The answer is yes. In the next chapter the question of sacramental action will be more fully discussed. However, baptism is only effective where there is the faith to receive. It is a means of grace to the individual but also to the whole church which experiences renewal each time a baptism takes place. It is also a highly effective witness to the world. In all these ways baptism is not just a sign: it is an effective sign.[63]

The Grace of Baptism

The baptism of disciples is one of the great strengths of the gathering church tradition and has contributed to its penetration of many cultures. It signifies that following after Christ begins with a personal and responsible act. This makes sense to people, not least in an environment which prizes personal autonomy and choice, whatever the other delusions of these particular cultural values. No churches are immune from decay and decline, this being a natural human tendency. But those which practise believer baptism have at least one way of resisting those currents and maintaining healthy church life. As the minority tradition of the church has grown in size and influence it has become possible to imagine its values and practices being transmitted to the majority traditions. It would be hard to imagine infant baptism being dispensed with altogether; but as those traditions begin to adopt believers baptism as the norm for the way we think of baptism, it is possible that they will go beyond this first to incorporate it as a possibility within their general practice and then to adopt it as the preferred mode.

Notes

[1] Moltmann, *Church in the Power of the Spirit*, 242: The word (German: *Wort*) of God's call receives an answer (*Antwort*) from the believer.

[2] This clearly emerged in the World Council of Churches ecumenical study document *Baptism, Eucharist and Ministry*, Faith and Order Paper No. 111 (Geneva: WCC, 1982), 2–7.

[3] *Baptism, Eucharist and Ministry*, 4.

[4] Acts 2:38.

[5] Hebrews 6:1–2.

[6] The exceptions to this are the Society of Friends (Quakers) and the Salvation Army who look to an inward experience of baptism in the Spirit rather than outward ceremonies.

[7] Acts 19:3–5.

[8] 'The children of a proselyte shared the benefit of what their father had done and were forthwith circumcised and baptized. They retained the privilege, however, of reconsidering the matter when they came of age': W.F. Flemington, *The New Testament Doctrine of Baptism* (London: SPCK, 1948), 7–8.

[9] Mark 1:4–5.

[10] Joshua 3.

[11] Matthew 3:11–12; John 1:23–34.

[12] John 7:37–39.

[13] Luke 1:35–37.

[14] 1 Corinthians 12:13.

[15] 1 John 2:5–10.

[16] Hebrews 1:3.

[17] 1 Peter 3:21–22.

[18] Mark 10:38–40; Luke 12:50.

[19] Galatians 2:19–20.

[20] Philippians 3:3; Colossians 2:11.

[21] Colossians 2:12.

[22] Luke 3:22.

[23] John 1:33.

[24] Acts 1:4–5.

[25] Acts 10:44–48; 11:15–18.

[26] Acts 2:14–21.

[27] Acts 19:1–7.

[28] Matthew 10:32–33.

[29] Luke 14:28.

[30] J. David Pawson, *The Normal Christian Birth: How to give new believers a proper start in life* (London: Hodder & Stoughton, 1989). Pawson identifies four crucial elements: repenting towards God, believing in the Lord Jesus, being baptised in water and receiving the Holy Spirit, 11.

[31] John 6:65.

[32] Acts 8:36.

[33] 1 Corinthians 12:3.

[34] Acts 8:4–25.

[35] Acts 10:44–48.

[36] Acts 19:1–7.

[37] Acts 16:33.

[38] Acts 16:32–34.

[39] Acts 10:44–48.

[40] Mark 10:13–15.

[41] As an informed example of all these arguments see Michael Green, *Baptism: Its Purpose, Practice and Power* (London: Hodder & Stoughton, 1986), 59–80. The standard and unsurpassed Baptist work on the subject is George R. Beasley-Murray, *Baptism in the New Testament* (London: Macmillan, 1962) in which see 306–86 on infant baptism and particularly, 385: 'It seems that a small amount of water is bestowed on a small infant with a very small result.'

[42] Paul K. Jewett, *Infant Baptism and the Covenant of Grace* (Grand Rapids: Eerdmans, 1988), 7, 39–45.

[43] *On Original Sin*, chapters 3–4: *Nicene and Post-Nicene Fathers* Volume 5 (New York: Christian Literature Company, 1887), 238–39.

[44] See, for example, John Calvin, *The First Epistle of Paul to the Corinthians* (Edinburgh: Saint Andrew Press, 1960), 149–50.

[45] 1 Corinthians 7:14.

[46] Matthew 19:14.

[47] A further example of this approach is Pierre Marcel, *The Biblical Doctrine of Infant Baptism* (London: James Clarke, 1953).

[48] Acts 2:39.

[49] Mark 3:31–35.

[50] Jewett, *Infant Baptism and the Covenant of Grace*, 75–137.

[51] 1 Corinthians 4:7.

[52] 1 Peter 3:21.

[53] Matthew 7:13–14.

[54] Luke 23:39–43.

[55] Hebrews 6:2.

[56] Walter J. Hollenweger, *The Pentecostals* (London: SCM Press, 1972), 71.

[57] Matthew 28:19.

[58] Interestingly, the Baptist Union of Great Britain Declaration of Principle specifies immersion: 'Christian baptism is the immersion in water into the Name of the Father, the Son and Holy Ghost, of those who have professed repentance towards God and faith in our Lord Jesus Christ', *Baptist Union Directory, 2003–2004*, 7.

[59] Luke 3:21–22; Acts 10:38.

[60] A useful discussion of this is Paul S. Fiddes, 'Baptism and the Process of Christian Initiation', *The Ecumenical Review* 54 (2002), 48–64.

[61] Acts 18:24–28. It should be noted that it does not record that Apollos was baptised again even though he knew only the baptism of John. Perhaps it was judged that all the necessary signs of the Spirit were in him.

[62] The 1977 Baptist Union report, 'Visible Unity in Life and Mission' asserted: 'We could not commend to our churches any covenant which involved a bar to the administration of believers' baptism in the case of a paedobaptist whose conscience might lead him or her to the conclusion that fidelity to Scripture and the Gospel required such Baptism': Hayden (ed.), *Baptist Union Documents 1948–1977*, 195.

[63] Anthony R. Cross, 'Faith-Baptism: The Key to an Evangelical Baptismal Sacramentalism', *Journal of European Baptist Studies* 4.3 (May, 2004), 5–21.

5. The Feast of Life

Communion and Body Politics

Introduction

Baptism is the initiatory rite of the church but communion is its continuing rite. Baptism is meant to be administered once as a sign that Christ died for sinners once and for all time.[1] Communion is to be enjoyed often as a sign that we go on living in the benefits of Christ's sacrifice until Christ comes.[2] Baptism proclaims that through the death and resurrection of Christ our old life can be buried and we can become new creations in him.[3] Communion proclaims that through that same death and resurrection the way we began the Christian life is the way we continue it, through persistent trust in Christ's work and his presence among us. Communion goes under different names. It is called the Lord's Supper (or the supper of the Lord) in recognition of the fact that it was instituted as an evening meal between Christ and his disciples, at which he was the host.[4] It is called Holy Communion because, on the model of the sacrifice meals in the Hebrew Scriptures, it was and continues to be an intimate fellowship in which disciples share in the body and blood of Christ.[5] It is known as the breaking of bread because both in the Jewish meals from which it developed and in the meal itself this is the archetypal action of the sharing of food.[6] It passes under the name of the Eucharist (or Eucharistic celebration) because the word captures the essence: thanks-giving. Those who reject the idea that communion is in any sense a sacrifice of *propitiation* may still quite properly see it as a sacrifice of *thanksgiving*. In catholic traditions its name is the Mass because when the feast is ended the service begins: Mass comes from the Latin word for 'to send' and is related to 'mission'. Participants in the Mass are sent out to serve. Different traditions choose different names and increasingly they have become intermingled. All of these names are good. Even some baptists can now be heard speaking unselfconsciously of the 'Eucharist' as if they invented the term.

The aim of this chapter is to set out an approach to communion that is both biblical and spiritual. Baptism and communion are effective signs of God's kingdom and are placed as the two primary sacraments within the web of a wider pattern of practices which identify, shape and sustain the church and serve the transmission of the faith to new generations of believers.

A Baptist Concept of Sacramental Action

In celebrating communion the variety in the church reaches its farthest span. It stretches from the elaborate and splendid ceremonial of High Mass to the barest and most simple service of bread and wine. Theologies are erected to accompany the degree of ceremonial elaboration or lack of it. Usually those with the most ceremonies adopt the 'highest' theology of the Eucharist, ascribing to it all manner of potencies. Those who opt for simplicity settle for theologies to match. Baptists, being 'primitivists' and therefore always keen to return to the New Testament, tend to agree that the greater the ceremony the further we have travelled from the simplicity of Christ. This need not mean that they take a 'low' view of the presence of God in the celebration of communion, only that they want to put the emphasis where it belongs, on the inward rather than the outward.

In this book I have unashamedly used the word 'sacrament' and have done so in full awareness that it will jar with some. Although many baptists, particularly those more inclined towards the Reformed tradition which is an important part of their roots, refer happily to 'Word and sacraments', there is a widely felt aversion to the term sacrament and a preference among many for the alternatives: ordinance and institution. The ordinances of baptism and the Lord's Supper may be so called because they were instituted or ordained by the Lord himself as part of the church's basic order. 'Sacraments' are associated with more catholic traditions and with the idea that they are effective *ex opere operato*, or by virtue of their being performed, irrespective of whether or not they are received in faith. So, baptism brings regeneration of itself (so-called 'baptismal regeneration') and the Eucharist feeds with the actual body and blood of Christ whatever the condition of the one who eats. To the baptist this sounds like magic and places within the control of human beings powers which belong only to God. When associated also with ideas of an exclusive priesthood and a church possessing absolute authority this notion of sacrament gives the church power over this life and the next, power it has frequently misused.

Suffice to say, none of the above is intended by the positive use of the word in this book. The Reformation principle is that faith must be present to give efficacy to any administration of the sacraments (although the Reformers did not necessarily follow through fully with this logic in relation to baptism). Furthermore, the active power of the sacraments comes from the Word which is expressed through them and which the sacraments embody and give form to.[7] I use the word sacrament deliberately to counteract the common baptist reaction against the catholic traditions. If the idea of *ex opere operato* is mistaken so is the common reaction which strips the sacraments of any spiritual power at all and leaves them as 'mere symbols' to be observed as a matter of sheer obedience rather than as means of grace. Theology often proceeds by reaction, rejecting a position by swinging to an opposite extreme and choosing to take from the biblical witness only that which supports the reaction. There is clear biblical evidence to suggest that baptism and communion are far more than 'mere symbols' which we perform 'as a witness'. They are indeed both symbol and witness and even more: dynamic means of grace which, when they are received in faith and used as instruments of the free and gracious Spirit of God, become moments of spiritual encounter working in us the very things they dramatise and symbolise. Although the word sacrament (like 'Trinity') is not itself found in Scripture, and although the word itself comes from the Latin meaning a 'pledge', it came to be used to signify this kind of divine action of the Spirit through consecrated earthly means. This is the sense in which it is used here.

A broad understanding of God's sacramental action lies behind these statements. Everything we know about God within Christian revelation proceeds on the understanding that God mediates God's own self to us. This is primarily through the Son and the Spirit who are the agents through whom the Father has first of all brought creation into being and then brought about redemption. God's Spirit is the Spirit of life which breathes through all creation.[8] Redemption is brought to pass as God the Son gathers to himself the complete identity of a human person and becomes incarnate as Jesus of Nazareth in order through that one human and earthly being, now risen and glorified, to mediate God to humankind.[9]

A fundamental aspect of the way God works in the world is to do so mediately, incarnationally, using the earthly as the vehicle for the heavenly. This is true of Jesus' humanity and of the events with which his ministry is completed, the cross and the glorification of Christ's humanity in the resurrection. These earthly events are the means used by God to embrace as God's own the lost human condition and to exchange sin for righteousness.[10] These are the primary sacramental actions from which all else derives. But the church itself can be seen as a sacrament,[11] a community in which Christ by the Spirit continues to take form and which we call the 'body of Christ'. This church finds the authority of God in Christ mediated to it through a book, the product of a process of printing and manufacture and comprised of human words which have the potential to become living and active and to cut through to the heart by the Spirit.[12] This word is interpreted and applied by means of preaching, an act of human communication which spreads abroad the message of good news.[13] And the church is served by people called as ministers and set aside for the task while never ceasing to be flesh and blood, yet who make present the grace of God as the Spirit moves upon them. All of these fundamental aspects of the life of the Christian community operate with the principle of *sacramentality*, the freedom of God to take earthly means and make them means of grace for the salvation of human beings. Water, bread and wine fit into this pattern.

Baptism, about which much has already been said, is an example. Paradoxically Baptists, who take their name from the rite, can have a low view of what happens in baptism. In the desire to avoid any sense of a magical rite which we control and to preserve the priority of faith, there is an instinct to reduce baptism to an act of bare witness with little expectation that anything would happen in the baptismal act which has not already happened in the regeneration of the heart. It becomes therefore an outward sign of an inward grace and nothing more. But the New Testament does suggest more. It shows that baptism is eventful. When Jesus himself was baptised, suddenly the Holy Spirit came upon him.[14] On the day of Pentecost Peter instructed inquirers that when they repented and were baptised they would receive the gift of the Holy Spirit.[15] Throughout the Acts spiritual events happened before, after and through the baptisms recorded there. When in Acts 19 the disciples of John were baptised in Ephesus by Paul and he laid his hands on them the Holy Spirit came upon them and they spoke in tongues and prophesied.[16] In outlining the meaning of baptism in Romans 6, Paul could say 'we have been buried with him by baptism into death,'[17] as though this took place through the act of baptism itself. Peter can even claim that baptism 'now saves you,' and then goes on to clarify that this is not in the same way that it might remove dirt from the body but through its role as an appeal to God for a clear conscience.[18] Even so, this is language that no baptist would invent: most would be worried that it might be taken to imply baptismal regeneration. Yet, strikingly, virtually every saving gift that the New Testament attributes to faith it also ascribes to baptism.[19]

The point to be drawn from these accumulated references is not that of itself baptism can save but that Christian initiation involves faith and baptism in intimate connection. James Dunn summarised it epigrammatically in this way:

> Faith demands baptism as its expression;
> Baptism demands faith for its validity.
> The gift of the Spirit presupposes faith as its condition;
> Faith is shown to be genuine only by the gift of the Spirit.[20]

In the New Testament baptism was not an optional bolt-on to conversion but an intrinsic part of it. It was conversion-baptism. When baptism is the means by which people offer their lives to God in repentance and confess their faith then the Spirit of God is pleased to use the moment and the action to work in people's hearts those things of which baptism speaks. Baptism is a symbol, but not a *mere* symbol since symbols enable participation in the realities of which they speak. This does not mean that baptism is the only point at which it becomes possible to participate in the reality. Seen as part of a process baptism should express and deepen that which is already under way and that which goes on happening even beyond baptism. But baptism serves as a focal point, a moment of deepening participation in the benefits of Christ, an objective moment when the work of God within us can be marked with the seal of God's Spirit and verified as God's own.[21] Another way to imagine this is that baptism is a place of rendezvous or a 'trysting-place'.[22] God is able to meet us at any place and any time; but has appointed certain times as places of rendezvous and given the assurance that Christ will meet us there. Baptism is such a time.

If the word sacrament is used only hesitantly among baptists, there seems to be greater confidence about the term 'means of grace'. God has appointed means of grace, ways in which we might draw upon the grace of God and be strengthened in faith. Baptism is one such in that it provides an objective point to which we may look back, not least in order to reassure ourselves about our own standing before God. However we may feel about ourselves, we have been marked out by baptism as disciples of Christ, as those whom he will own as his own because we have owned him as ours.

Communion as a Sacrament

The picture I have painted about God's sacramental action is a broad canvas. Yet within this two rites have a unique status and acquire a clearer focus: baptism and communion. They enjoy this unique status since both are set before us in the New Testament as 'dominical' sacraments, which is to say they were instituted by Christ himself. They are for that reason not to be neglected. But they share a further quality in that both these dramatic rites make direct reference to the central events of the story of salvation, the death and resurrection of the Lord. This distinguishes them from other practices we shall consider in due course. In the act of burial and resurrection dramatised in baptism and in the bread and wine which make reference to the body and blood of Christ given for us, we are drawn to the primary sacramental action of God in making the cross and resurrection the means of human salvation. This is why these two sacraments may be called 'norming norms'. They keep the focus of the church in the right place. They enable the crucial story to be told time and again, and dramatically so. They apply that story to our own lives and require us to live in the light of it. In this way, they become means of grace not only to those who already confess faith but to those who are being incorporated into the church. As new people come to participate believingly in these signs so they are incorporated into the body. So the practices of the church are also important means of transmission, of the imparting of faith to new generations.

The first three Gospels record for us the origin of the communion service in the last supper Jesus shared with his disciples.[23] John's Gospel does not repeat this but adds further narrative and teaching to what is clearly the same event.[24] The supper is portrayed within the context and the meaning of the Jewish Passover festival, itself one of the means by which the Jewish faith was transmitted down the generations, and is to be seen as an adaptation of the annual Passover meal.[25] Passover was the time when the Jewish people recalled that God had delivered Israel from captivity in Egypt. It was celebrated in family groups and involved the sacrifice of lambs and the sprinkling of blood upon the doorposts of the house as a sign of protection from God's judgment.[26] The Passover was a perpetual remembrance of God's saving acts and a means of making them contemporary so that each generation could regard the deliverance from Egypt not as a past act for a former generation but as 'for us'.[27] Jesus took the Passover meal and transformed it into a way of interpreting the meaning of his impending death. He adapted the traditional breaking of bread at the beginning of the meal and the sharing of the cup after it as symbols of his own sacrifice. His body was to be 'given for you' and his blood 'poured out for you' as a new covenant in his blood[28] for the forgiveness of sins.[29] Jesus understood himself to be doing something on behalf of Israel that would result in a new quality of relationship with God, but this would be at the cost of offering up his own life as a sacrifice. Beyond the cross Jesus looked forward to a day of fulfilment in the kingdom of God when once more he would eat and drink with his disciples.[30]

The clearest and earliest indication that Jesus was understood here to be instituting a perpetual practice for his disciples is found in Paul's description of the meal in 1 Corinthians 11:23–34.[31] He explains this is a tradition 'from the Lord', by which he means that it is traced back to Jesus himself through the apostles,[32] which Paul himself received and then delivered in his turn to the Corinthians. This passage is sometimes referred to as 'the words of institution' and is regarded by some as an essential reading for any communion service, setting the meal within its proper context of meaning. The emphasis falls here both on remembrance and the expectation of Christ's future coming.[33] When Acts is read in the light of these verses it is tempting to find in any reference to 'the breaking of bread' the practice of communion. The first disciples 'devoted themselves to the apostles' teaching and fellowship, to the breaking of bread and the prayers'.[34] They worshipped day by day in the temple and 'broke bread at home and ate their food with glad and generous hearts'.[35] On the first day of the week the believers met to break bread.[36] Perhaps in this we see the emerging Christian practices of worship on the first day of the week and communion, but we cannot be entirely sure that the reference is not simply to eating together in the spirit of fellowship: this is sometimes called an 'agape' meal or a love-feast. The first Christians clearly combined sharing their food with communion as is clear from Paul's instructions to those who would abuse this practice. They should rather eat at home before they came to worship.[37] In this instruction we may also see the beginnings of a transition from the full agape meal to a specifically religious rite.

It is tempting to see Eucharistic references in the account of the disciples on the road to Emmaus. Jesus, risen from the dead but incognito, came alongside them and accompanied them on their journey. They prevailed upon him to eat with them. He assumed the role of the host, taking the bread, blessing it, breaking it and giving it to them: at that moment their eyes were opened in recognition. Later they recounted 'how he had been made known to them in the breaking of bread'.[38] This account of encounter with the risen Christ strengthens the sacramental perspective on communion. Christ is present among the disciples who gather in his name and this presence may be known with particular intensity and in life-giving ways in the breaking of bread.

The Meaning of Communion

Communion, like baptism, is multi-layered. The custom of early Christianity was to refer to both baptism and the Eucharist as *mysteries*, by which was meant not that they are impenetrable or incomprehensible but that they are densely packed with meaning: it is not possible to exhaust what they have to say. When we participate in them in faith we indwell the realities to which they refer. But we know more than we can tell; we commune at levels deeper than we can analyse. Nonetheless, there is much that can be said. Communion witnesses to the fact that we live within the tension created by a great memory and a great hope. It has past, present and future dimensions.

The past dimension: Communion is retrospective and is concerned with remembrance. It looks back to events that have happened which are believed to be decisive for the salvation of the world. Those events include the incarnation of God in Jesus Christ and Christ's self-giving upon the cross for us. In these particular events God participates in human and created existence and does so in order to heal what is assumed. In seeking and saving the lost, the first action is to come to where the lost are and in this way to restore and renew the image of God in humanity.[39] The actions described in Luke 24:30 were enacted by the Son of God in his condescension: in Jesus God took human flesh, and when he had blessed it he then broke it in sacrifice in order that he might give it. In a parallel way, God in Christ takes us, blesses us with the Spirit and then breaks us in sacrifice that we too might be given for the world. This is the story of salvation by means of divine participation, of the mysterious exchange of our polluted life for his glorious life.[40] It finds its response in thanksgiving and devotion, in careful self-examination and repentance,[41] in an appropriate mood of reflection and sobriety. Essentially the recollection is of a *finished* work, something completed on behalf of the world that endures forever. But there is more:

The future dimension: Communion is also to do with a great hope, one Jesus referred to when he spoke about a fulfilment in the kingdom of God when he would eat and drink once more with his disciples.[42] In part this expectation was fulfilled in the resurrection which was in its own way both a coming of the Lord and of the kingdom of God. So we read the testimony that Jesus ate and drank with them after he rose from the dead.[43] But beyond this the promise is capable of even greater fulfilment. Isaiah had spoken of a time when God would prepare a feast for all nations, a feast of life when God would swallow up death forever and wipe away the tears from people's eyes.[44] Jesus had referred to this visionary hope when he said, 'I tell you, many will come from east and west and will eat with Abraham and Isaac and Jacob in the kingdom of heaven.'[45] The communion feast is also therefore an anticipation of what is to come, of the 'marriage supper of the Lamb', the vision of which gloriously completes Revelation and the New Testament canon.[46] In the light of this, sober reflection cannot be the only note appropriate to communion. There must be joyful celebration of what is to be and of the full presence of Christ among his people once more. The ancient liturgical bidding *Maran atha*, 'Come, Lord Jesus', so ancient that it is still preserved in the Aramaic spoken by Jesus and his immediate followers, is a suitable prayer with which to conclude such a service.[47] This leads us to:

The present dimension: It would be a mistake to imagine that the past and present dimensions leave the present empty. In the tension between the two there is the living presence of Christ among his own people which is given an added quality in communion. *Maran atha* might equally be the prayer that begins a service of communion. Christ is, of course, always present by the Spirit in the world of which he is the creative and the re-creative agent. But this does not mean he is always present in the same way. There is an added quality to that presence when 'two or three are gathered in my name'.[48] The fact that God is the God who comes does not mean he is ever absent, only that God is able to move from one degree of presence to another. As the risen Lord was present to the two disciples in Emmaus, and ate and drank with other disciples after he rose from the dead, so he makes himself present in the feast of life of which he continues to be the host. This is where the word 'communion', or fellowship is particularly apposite. The bread and wine which we share become for us communion with God: 'The cup of blessing that we bless, is it not a sharing in the blood of Christ? The bread that we break, is it not a sharing in the body of Christ? Because there is one bread, we who are many are one body, for we all partake of the one bread.'[49]

The 'Real' Presence

Historically, the church has spoken about the 'real presence of Christ in the Eucharist', a term which has usually referred to the exact way Christ is found in the elements of bread and wine. This is a well-worn debate which is shaped as follows:

Transubstantiation

The Roman Catholic position affirms that at a certain point of the Mass, when the priest consecrates the elements and proclaims 'this is my body', bread and wine undergo a transformation. Whereas the outer appearance (the 'accidents') of both remains the same, the 'substance' (that which lies beneath) is transformed into Christ's body and blood.[50] The elements are therefore due the utmost reverence and to ingest them is quite literally to receive Christ. This is a very physical doctrine based upon a literal reading of the words of Jesus, 'I am the living bread that came down from heaven. Whoever eats of this bread will live forever; and the bread that I will give for the life of the world is my flesh.'[51] It is in continuity with those strands of early Christian thought which see salvation in very physical terms: Christ comes to us in our flesh to infuse into it his own immortality; our participation in this is through receiving the 'medicine of immortality' by means of which his physical presence is sustained and extended. Of course, restricting the authority to consecrate the elements to the authorised priesthood once more puts great power in the control of the church, outside which there can be no salvation on this account. A more recent, and more rational, version of this is 'transignification' according to which the substance of bread and wine remain the same;[52] but at a certain point of the Eucharist what those elements signify undergoes a change so that they are no longer to be seen merely as the fruit of the grain and the vine but as representing the body and blood of Christ. Here the change is not to the elements but to perceptions of what they signify among the people who celebrate.

Consubstantiation

Luther developed a slightly different version of the above but still one which attached to the presence of Christ a realism locating it in the elements. This time the bread and wine are not to be understood as being transformed but rather as *accompanied* by the actual body and blood of Christ as they are received by the believer. The molecules of the flesh and blood are administered 'in, with and under' the bread and wine. Behind this lies a peculiarly Lutheran doctrine of Christ known as the *communicatio idiomatum*, the communication of properties between the divine and the human natures of Christ. On this basis it is possible to talk about the human nature of Christ in directly divine terms; to assert for instance that God was born and walked on the earth, that God was crucified, that God's blood was shed for us upon the cross. Christ's humanity has divinity ascribed to it. By derivation his physical humanity has the property of infinity or omnipresence attributed to it so that the body and blood of Christ are capable of being infinitely extended as they are made available in the Eucharist alongside the bread and wine. In the Eucharist this is what is taking place and Christ really is present through bread and wine.

Memorialism

By contrast with the metaphysical nature of the above options, this approach, usually identified with the Swiss Reformer, Ulrich Zwingli (1484–1531), seems like a model of common sense. The meal is to be understood as an act of remembrance and recollection in which nothing happens to the bread and wine other than what is taking place in the minds of those who receive them. The words of Jesus about the bread of life are metaphors which are not to be taken literally any more than Jesus' words, 'I am the gate.'[53] Bread and wine are memorials of Christ and nothing more. This is a position with which many baptists are quite comfortable. In some baptist circles there are even pointed rituals which have grown up in a defiant way to establish the point. One is that any bread left from communion is thrown out for the birds rather than treated with any special reverence. Paradoxically some catholics are also happy with this position on the grounds that free churches lack the priesthood with the power to consecrate the elements anyway, so a claim for any 'real presence' would constitute more of a problem than the doctrine of 'real absence'.

Communion and the Spirit

Common-sense memorialism lacks a lively doctrine of the Spirit. Not for the first time we should be able to see that a healthy Christian theology is one which thinks in trinitarian terms and makes room for the Holy Spirit as the one through whom God is present and active. The real presence of Christ in the Eucharist is not to be located in the bread and wine as such but in the way in which the Holy Spirit is present among the people of God in the act of sharing bread and wine together as themselves the body of Christ. It is the sacramental action of taking bread and wine and sharing them as believers with each other in the name and power of Christ that constitutes living participation in the one God. Debates about the bread and wine are arid if the whole point is that *the people* are one loaf and one body and that it is the spiritual presence of Christ among them which is at issue. Paul spoke about the importance of 'discerning the body' and saw that a consequence of failing to do this was that many in Corinth were 'weak and ill, and some have died'.[54] Some interpret this to mean that if we take communion without having examined ourselves first, or when we are not truly of the faith, we may receive the elements 'in an unworthy manner' and find this damaging to us.[55] Sobering though this is, Paul might rather mean that when we act selfishly without 'discerning the body' or having due regard for the body of Christians of which we are part, people will be harmed by this. This is exactly what was happening in Corinth with their love-feasts being more like exercises in greed and riotous assembly. This is not the Lord's Supper, says Paul.[56] They have failed to 'discern the body'.

Communion is a celebration by the church using bread and wine to 'speak' of the salvation won for us in Christ. It is characterised by thanksgiving and a sense of communion with God inspired by the Holy Spirit. It takes place in such a way that the visible word of the drama is interpreted by the spoken word of Scripture. It is not a priestly re-offering of Christ as sacrifice but a renewal of the benefits of Christ accomplished by his once for all offering of himself for the sins of the world and his ensuing resurrection. It is an act of communion among the people of God in which we remember that we are bound together and allow those bonds to be renewed by the Spirit. It is a sacrificial offering of ourselves. As with so many other aspects of the church's life, there is great freedom as to how and when this feast of life is to be celebrated. For some it is so central as a means of grace that weekly or even daily participation is called for. For others this comes monthly, or quarterly or in a few cases annually, on the pattern of the Passover. Regular celebration does seem to be implied by the references we find in the New Testament.

The meal can encompass a wide range of moods from sobriety to joy and it can be carried through practically by means of several arrangements. Earlier baptists were happy to use one loaf, one cup and fermented wine. The pendulum swung for reasons of hygiene, health and taste towards many small cups and cubes of bread. The simplicity of the meal ought not to mean that aesthetic considerations and a sense of beauty and order are discounted. There is much to be said for returning to the practice of one loaf and one, or perhaps several, cups and to the use of real wine, which was good enough for Jesus. There are ways of accommodating people's personal needs at all of these points. The baptist preference has been for a congregation to remain seated and for lay people to serve them with bread and wine. This is another of those defiant touches which make it clear there is no sense of sacerdotal priesthood at play. This has been underlined in some traditions by the small detail, lost on later generations, that when the president at communion has shared the bread she or he is then immediately served by a layperson, since we believe in the priesthood of all believers. As baptists have become less reactionary against other traditions so they have begun to experiment with their forms, one of which is to receive communion one by one at the hands of some appointed for the task, and perhaps to receive prayer for God's blessing at the same time. This is a good innovation since in the kingdom of God, all 'things are yours';[57] we are free to make use of what is ours and to resist attempts to narrow us down according to sect, personality or liturgical legalism. Communion is indeed a feast of life and a foretaste of the feast that has no end.

The Politics of Practice

We should not underestimate the extent to which we are shaped by the practices and disciplines in which we engage. They have the effect, often unconscious, of embedding within us certain values and mindsets. This is why in Judaism great emphasis is laid upon the sabbath and the festivals of the faith in transmitting to the rising generations the stories and traditions that have made the people of Israel unique. It is why care is taken to ask and to answer questions about the meaning of those festivals. 'Why do we do this?' 'It is because…'

The Christian faith also has its practices. Two of these are dominical ordinances which are traced back to the Lord himself. Others are practices to which the New Testament bears witness, and these we examine shortly. Others are later Christian elaborations which have no direct biblical mandate but which have seemed like a good idea, such as Christmas or Easter. These were originally pagan festivals which were given a new meaning when Christian missions took hold in the West. The time gaps between them were filled with other festivals which ensured that certain fundamental emphases were constantly revisited, such as Lent, Ascension, Pentecost and Trinity. At this point, we are concerned to show how the central Christian sacraments and practices have *political* significance, that is to say, they shape the ways in which the

Christian community orders its life and expresses its convictions.[58]

Baptism is an example of this since the basic Christian confession, which every baptismal liturgy does well to include, is 'Jesus is Lord!' This is a political as well as theological statement. Because Christ alone is Lord, no other loyalty can take his place. The primary political analysis of the Hebrew Scriptures is that which identifies idolatry as a betrayal of the living God. To make anything other than the Lord our highest loyalty is to be in profound error. The baptised Christian therefore rejects as an idol any nation, kinship, celebrity, or combination of blood and soil which sets itself above the Lord of the universe. All these may have their validity in their place, but their place must be kept. If baptism settles the Christian's fundamental loyalties then communion expresses the terms on which the Christian community is to live out its life. There is here a fundamental equality between all believers in that whatever rank, status, social class or gender we start with, we are all equally dependent upon the grace of God and equally indebted to the work of Christ. We eat and drink bread and wine and do so together. In the early church slave and free, Jews and Gentiles, male and female found themselves sharing in the Lord's Supper in a new social reality which contradicted the assumptions of the prevailing culture and at the same time held open the possibility of social transformation. They were all one in Christ Jesus.[59] The Lord's Supper at that time was part of the love-feast and so equality was expressed in economic sharing at the table, which is why Paul condemned the Corinthians for their greed and selfishness.[60] This is a new creation, a new community of reconciliation and peace which fulfils the eternal purpose of God revealed in Christ.[61] The church is an international community whose members are citizens of God's kingdom first and only then of any earthly nation. The challenge is to live this out.

In expressing its life, the early church assumed or developed practices which did not have the central place or symbolism of baptism and communion but which nonetheless served to bind the body of Christ together and to build it up.

Common among these was the *laying on of hands* in symbolic action and with various meanings. Jesus placed his hands upon the children and blessed them.[62] This was clearly seen as an effective and beneficial act and not as mere words. Good and gracious words spoken very personally and in the name of God have the ability to impart blessing to people. The laying on of hands is therefore associated with healing, as when Jesus cleansed the lepers.[63] After Saul's conversion on the way to Damascus, Ananias laid hands on him and his sight was restored.[64] When baptisms took place in the Book of Acts they were sometimes accompanied by the laying on of hands which was itself followed by the gift of the Holy Spirit.[65] There is a clear implication here that the Spirit was given on these occasions through the laying on of the apostles' hands,[66] and so the act carries the meaning of impartation of the Spirit. In other places it is associated with commissioning or ordination as individuals are set aside for particular ministries and receive grace for the task.[67] The laying on of hands then is part of the church's ministry in relation to the blessing of children, prayer for the sick, the liturgy of baptism and commissioning or ordinations. The physical nature of the act captures a sense of solidarity and mutual dependence appropriate to the body of Christ.

Anointing with oil in the name of the Lord is prescribed in James 13:14 as part of the ministry to the sick and was also practiced by the twelve with very positive results when they were sent out by Jesus on a mission to the villages of Israel.[68] Oil symbolises the presence and power of the Holy Spirit which restores and heals. It has been used consistently in the more catholic traditions for a variety of liturgical purposes and there is every reason why anointing should be a frequent part of ministry in free-church contexts. It is appropriate for there to be a jar of oil on the communion table and the intimacy of the communion service provides an excellent opportunity for the anointing of the sick. This practice identifies the church as a healing community within which the vulnerable and needy can find security, peace and grace.

The *right hand of fellowship*[69] and the *holy kiss*[70] or *kiss of love*[71] are practices which identify the Christian community as one of reconciliation and the laying down of hostility. They allow small glimpses into the nature of the church as an affectionate community whose strength is its sense of belonging and the mutual exchange of love. Practices such as these vary culturally from place to place but all cultures have their ways of demonstrating affection. Although the right hand of fellowship is mentioned only once, it occurs in such a way as to suggest it was a commonly understood and formal sign of friendship. In contemporary practice it has long been a way of welcoming new members into the committed membership of a church. Although these are relatively small symbols they accumulate in such a way as to build strong community and to shape people's lives for good. The practices of the church are important and require both consideration about what they mean and nurturing so that they are not lost. In recent years there has been a pleasing recovery of the laying on of hands, of anointing and of the sharing of the peace, which functions as an equivalent to the holy kiss. These enrich our worship and our practice. Along with baptism and communion they shape our communities and our lives. Because churches are communities of the Spirit they can all serve as means of divine grace.

The Active Presence of God

Following Augustine, a sacrament has been routinely defined as 'an outward and visible sign of an inward and spiritual grace'. John Calvin's definition was that it is

> an outward sign by which the Lord seals on our consciences the promises of his good will towards us in order to sustain the weakness of our faith; and we in turn attest our piety toward him in the presence of the Lord and of his angels and before men.[72]

Both definitions are promising but somewhat lacking in dynamism. John Howard Yoder however based his understanding on the promise of Jesus that, 'What you bind on earth is bound in heaven' (Matthew 18:18) and defined a sacrament as a human action in which, 'God would at the same time be acting "in, with and under" that activity'.[73] So, 'Where they are happening, the people of God is real in the world.'[74] If God has indeed given us these practices in order to make him real as they are activated by the Holy Spirit, maintaining these activities for the benefit of the people of God should be a conscious and thoughtful activity.

Notes

[1]   Hebrews 10:12.

[2]   1 Corinthians 11:26.

[3]   2 Corinthians 5:17.

[4]   1 Corinthians 11:20.

[5]   1 Corinthians 10:16–18.

[6]   Luke 22:19; 24: 30–35; Acts 2:42.

[7]   Neville Clark, 'The fulness of the church of God' in Alec Gilmore (ed.), *The Pattern of the Church: A Baptist View* (London: Lutterworth Press, 1963), 100.

[8]   Psalm 104:29–30.

[9]   1 Timothy 2:5.

[10] 2 Corinthians 5:21.

[11] Avery Dulles, *Models of the Church: A Critical Assessment of the Church in all its Aspects* (Dublin: Gill and Macmillan, 1976), 58–70.

[12] Hebrews 4:12.

[13] Romans 10:14–15.

[14] Matthew 3:16.

[15] Acts 2:38.

[16] Acts 19:1–7.

[17] Romans 6:1–3.

[18] 1 Peter 3:21.

[19] Cross, 'Faith-Baptism', 4.

[20] James D.G. Dunn, *Baptism in the Holy Spirit* (London: SCM Press, 1970), 228.

[21] Ephesians 1:13.

[22] George R. Beasley-Murray, *Baptism Today and Tomorrow* (London: Macmillan, 1966), 41: 'Baptism was given as a trysting place of the sinner with his Saviour. He who has met Him there will not

despise it, but will seek to conduct others to it for the same kind of meeting.' Elsewhere Beasley-Murray adds to this, 'But in the last resort it is only a *place*: the Lord himself is its glory, as He is its grace': *Baptism in the New Testament*, 305.

23 Matthew 26:26–30; Mark 14:22–25; Luke 22:14–23.
24 John 13–17.
25 Luke 22:7–8.
26 Exodus 12:1-28; Deuteronomy 16:1–8.
27 Deuteronomy 6:20–25.
28 Luke 22:19–20.
29 Matthew 26:28.
30 Matthew 26:29; Luke 22:14–18.
31 Paul's letters were written before the Gospels were compiled.
32 Compare this with 1 Corinthians 15:3–11.
33 1 Corinthians 11:25–26.
34 Acts 2:42.
35 Acts 2:46.
36 Acts 20:7.
37 1 Corinthians 11:17–22.
38 Luke 24:28–35.
39 Luke 19:10; 1 Corinthians 15:47–49.
40 2 Corinthians 5:21.
41 1 Corinthians 11:27–32.
42 Luke 22:16–18.
43 Acts 10:41; Luke 24:42–43.
44 Isaiah 25:6–10.
45 Matthew 8:11.
46 Revelation 19:9; 22:1–8.
47 1 Corinthians 16:21; Revelation 22:20.
48 Matthew 18:20.
49 1 Corinthians 10:16–17.
50 'In the most blessed sacrament of the Eucharist "the body and blood, together with the soul and divinity, of our Lord Jesus Christ and, therefore, *the whole Christ is truly, really, and substantially contained*"': *Catechism of the Catholic Church* (London: Geoffrey Chapman, 1964) paragraph 1374, 309.
51 John 6:51.
52 This and a related concept, 'transfinalisation', were condemned by Pope Paul VI in his encyclical *Mysterium Fidei* (1966).
53 John 10:7.
54 1 Corinthians 11:30.
55 1 Corinthians 11:27.

[56] 1 Corinthians 11:20–22.

[57] 1 Corinthians 3:21.

[58] John Howard Yoder, *Body Politics: Five Practices of the Christian Community before the Watching World* (Nashville, TN: Discipleship Resources, 1992).

[59] Galatians 3:28.

[60] 1 Corinthians 11:17–22.

[61] Ephesians 2:11–22; 3:11–13.

[62] Mark 10:16.

[63] Mark 1:41.

[64] Acts 9:17.

[65] Acts 8:17; Acts 19:6.

[66] Acts 8:18.

[67] Acts 13:3; 2 Timothy 1:6.

[68] Mark 6:13.

[69] Galatians 2:9.

[70] Romans 16:16; 1 Corinthians 16:20; 2 Corinthians 13:12; 1 Thessalonians 5:26.

[71] 1 Peter 5:14.

[72] John Calvin, *Institutes of the Christian Religion* Book IV, chapter 14 1 (ed. John T. McNeil; Philadelphia: Westminster, 1960).

[73] Yoder, *Body Politics*, 1, 6.

[74] Yoder, *Body Politics*, 72.

6. A Kingdom of Priests

The Government of the Congregation

Introduction

There is no doubt that baptist churches grew up as a reaction against the model of church around them. Baptists believed the model was both contrary to the Scriptures and oppressive in practice. The exercise of power lay at the heart of their concerns. Could the power of the institutional church really be identified with the power of God? But the question went beyond the church. We have seen that in the genesis of baptist movements social and religious questions were linked and to dispute one was to challenge the other. This is why baptists were persecuted as a dangerous threat: they called the prevailing order into question. This all throws into relief the matter of church government and order. If the order of things inherited from the mediaeval church was wrong, what was the alternative? How might power be managed differently? How should the church be governed? How should the social order be governed?

It should be recognised that nothing happens without power and that powerlessness is far from being a good thing, as some romantic souls seem to suggest. We all have power, even if it is only that of occupying certain space. It is impossible to do without power. Power is necessary for life, let alone a fulfilled and flourishing life. Yet power is not one undifferentiated phenomenon. It has many textures and forms, good and bad. Power can be the ability to dominate or 'lord it' over others and can take form as manipulation, force of both physical and psychic kinds, violence or the threat of violence. It can also take the form of influence, of legitimate authority, of competence and skill, of personal charisma or of sacrificial love.[1] In essence, the question of how the church of Christ should be governed is a question of how power is to be understood and managed and here we come very close to a key aspect of the baptist way.

There is no doubt that Jesus was a man 'anointed with the Holy Spirit and with power',[2] and that he impressed his contemporaries with the authority of his actions. But the power of Jesus was the moral influence and impact of a profoundly spiritual man sent from God, not that of a system exercising control over others. Jesus was in conflict with a mentality of sacred power within the Jewish religious establishment of his day, an establishment that had become corrupt and against which he engaged in prophetic protest when he overturned the money-changers' tables in the temple.[3] Despite this, the church that developed in his name consistently reproduced the same faults against which he had protested and the free church is an attempt to rescue it from these ways.

The Common Ownership of Power

Miroslav Volf is accurate in capturing the free-church concern when he writes:

> I argue that the presence of Christ, which constitutes the church, is mediated not simply through the ordained ministers but through the whole congregation, that the whole congregation functions as *mater ecclesia* (mother church) to the children engendered by the Holy Spirit, and that the whole congregation is called to engage in ministry and make decisions about leadership

roles ... Traditionally, believers' church ecclesiology has champ-ioned both voluntarism and egalitarianism – voluntarism in the sense that the incorporative act is 'deliberate on the part of the candidate and the community alike' and egalitarianism in the sense that responsibility for the corporate life of the church ultimately rests on the broad shoulders of the whole community.[4]

Baptists have argued that because believers participate in the life of the Father through the Son and by the Spirit, and because when they gather in the name of Christ he is in the midst of them, each local congregation is competent to govern its affairs by discerning the mind of Christ. In this sense, each congregation is empowered to do what is necessary for its own life.[5] This way of thinking suggests that far from being concentrated in a priestly hierarchy, authority and power are diffused throughout the whole body of Christ and are the common property of the church:

That being thus joined, every Church has power given them from Christ for their better well-being, to choose to themselves meet persons into the office of Pastors, Teachers, Elders, Deacons, being qualified according to the Word, as those which Christ has appointed in his Testament for the feeding, governing, serving and building up of his Church, and that none other have power to impose them, either these or any other.[6]

We have noted the importance of the doctrine of the 'priest-hood of all believers', which lies at the basis of these affirma-tions. Christ's ministry towards humankind is defined by means of a threefold office: he is prophet, priest and king. To participate in Christ is also to participate in his priesthood and through him to have access to the Father in the Spirit. This is not to be understood in an individualistic way but in terms of the participation of each within the unified priesthood of the whole church in Christ and through him. The priesthood is that of all believers together rather than of each believer separately. It is equally possible to speak of the *prophethood* and the *kingship* of all believers. All believers may find themselves speaking the word of the Lord since, 'I will pour out my Spirit upon all flesh and your sons and your daughters will prophesy.'[7] Likewise, all believers participate in Christ's freedom to rule and to govern and are actively responsible and engaged under Christ's lordship in the shaping of their own affairs and those of the congregations of which they are members. The call of Christ therefore is not to passive subjection but to active discernment of what is pleasing to God, to responsible engagement and decision-making in the service of the kingdom of God, to the common ownership of the power of the congregation so that it is no longer a matter of having power exercised over the congregation but of it being distributed among them as a stewardship in which they all share. We begin to see how this is not only a radical vision of church but potentially also of the social order.

The first article of the Baptist Union of Great Britain's Declaration of Principle[8] reads:

> That our Lord and Saviour Jesus Christ, God manifest in the flesh, is the sole and absolute authority in all matters pertaining to faith and practice, as revealed in the Holy Scriptures, and that each church has liberty, under the guidance of the Holy Spirit, to interpret and administer His laws.

This is an affirmation of both authority and freedom. Absolute authority belongs not to the church or its ministers but to Christ who is the revelation in his incarnation of God. This revelation is made known through the Scriptures which are the normative and canonical witness to him, the Hebrew Scriptures by way of preparation and the Greek Scriptures by way of recollection. There is no assumption of infallibility on the part of the church but of liberty and responsibility in interpreting the Scriptures with the help of the Holy Spirit. and exercising authority in their application. The church is both an *acoustic* and a *hermeneutical* community: it exists by listening to the Word of God through the Scriptures and it seeks to interpret the significance of the Word for the world in which it lives. Its power to do this is a consequence of the church's catholicity because in each church the whole church, from which each local church draws its life, expresses itself. It has long been held that the local church is more than a lonely outpost of the 'real' church: it is in itself a manifestation of the catholic church, the body of Christ and as such is qualified for this task.

Alternatives to Congregationalism

In terms of church order, then, Baptists are congregationalists. They believe in the freedom of the local church to govern itself. If it is the case that identity is constituted by a genetic structure, a certain combination of genes, then in the Baptist genetic code this is a dominant gene not necessarily shared with other baptists. We could say:

> believers baptism + congregational government + liberty = Baptist identity

Congregationalism takes its place among a variety of ways of conceiving the governmental order of the church and can be illuminated by contrast and comparison with them.

Episcopalianism, for instance, is the majority tradition. It could also be called 'episcopo-centrism' since it believes that the church should gather round the bishop who is the guarantee that Christ is also present. Episcopalianism sees the church in historic and universal terms. It originates in Jesus who appointed twelve apostles to be with him and to bear the teaching and authority he entrusted to them. With the one exception of Judas Iscariot, who was replaced to keep the band of twelve intact[9] and with the subsequent and some-what irregular addition of Paul to the ranks of the apostles,[10] the apostles continued as the normative witnesses to Christ and his resurrection in the early church. In their ministries, the apostles gathered helpers around them (assuming that they worked in the same way as Paul).[11] As they established congregations, the apostles appointed and authorised elders or presbyters to represent them locally and carry on the work.[12]

The picture emerging here therefore is that of the 'orderly transmission' of apostolic authority to a new generation of leaders. As the apostles passed from the scene, their authority was transmitted through this process to successors who were accorded the title of bishop, an adaptation of one of the two terms used synonymously in the New Testament for elders, *episkopos* and *presbyteros*. The process of development is clear: churches would be founded and pastors appointed; those churches would grow and found other congregations and the pastors would grow in authority to become bishops; further growth would take place and they would become archbishops. It is also clear that there was a particular necessity for this sense of mainstream and orderly continuity at a time when both the canon of Scripture was still in formation and the interpretation of essential doctrine was yet to be shaped by the creeds. Who but the bishops could speak authentically when there were several competing versions of Christianity? These processes have embedded within the church, quite understandably, a sense of the historic episcopate which can trace its lineage back to the apostles and act as the guarantor of authentic Christianity.

In this tradition episcopal validation is of great importance both for churches, which look to a bishop as a matter of fundamental belonging to the Catholic Church, and for clergy who are ordained and then permitted to preach and officiate at the Eucharist by continuing obedience to their bishop. The authority to consecrate the elements in the Eucharist is dependent upon episcopal validation. The historic guardian of the episcopal discipline is the Roman Catholic Church, and in the East the Orthodox churches, but Anglicans also claim to be in the apostolic succession by virtue of a line of unbroken episcopal descent from the early church. The validity of this is denied by the Roman Church since Anglican churches are not 'in communion' with the Bishop of Rome. This entire structure has been seen until recently through the paradigm of 'sacred power', as an authority structure requiring submission and obedience and carrying the penalty of excommunication for those who defied it. More recent tendencies have moved the paradigm towards connectedness, relationship and organism in the same way that the branches of a tree need to maintain connection with the roots in order to be nurtured and sustained.

At the time of the Reformation the structures of the church were severely ruptured for a second time. In 1054 the Roman Church and the Orthodox churches experienced the Great Schism, mainly, but not exclusively, because of papal assumptions of authority which went far beyond what was traditionally agreed. The Orthodox could, however, still claim to be maintaining their kind of episcopal continuity. The churches of the Reformation were less able to claim this. In England the monarch simply assumed the functions of the papacy as his own and ruled as the head of the English church and state. Lutherans also looked to the state authorities – however they were constituted – to govern the church and sometimes maintained or re-adopted the term 'bishop'. However, episcopacy was no longer seen in terms of *historic* apostolic continuity: rather, the bishops were senior pastors among the clergy, although they could claim to be apostolic in that they maintained the apostolic doctrine.[13]

The Reformed developed a more consistent theology of church government which has come to be called *presbyterianism*. For the Reformed and other Protestants the claim of the historic episcopate to be the guarantee of authentic Christianity was seen to be demonstrably false by the corruption of the church over which it presided and the oppressive and persecutory use of sacred power in which it engaged. Tested against the Scriptures the whole mediaeval church system was shown, in fact, to be a denial of true Christianity, more anti-Christian than Christian, and needed to be either swept away or radically reformed. Replacing it involved a turning from hierarchical leadership towards the local.

Presbyterians locate governmental authority in the eldership of the congregation which comprises both ordained ministers and appointed lay people. Each congregation belongs to a wider group of churches, called a presbytery, which has the power to ratify decisions made by the individual congregations. The members of each congregation are involved in this process through their power to call their own ministers and to elect their lay elders. In this way, a balance is maintained between the local church, the authority of the wider presbytery and that of the national or regional church which, acting through an assembly, determines the broader disciplines and policies of the church or denomination. The logic here is that even though local congregations are competent to order their life, there is also a wisdom that belongs to the wider church which needs to be brought to bear from time to time upon them. Local churches are therefore guarded by the wider communion of churches from decisions or actions which may be in error or destructive in other ways. Some churches in the baptist tradition, particularly in the restorationist or 'new church' streams and in older Brethren circles or those churches deriving from them, embrace a strong if more informal presbyterian pattern of government, at least in the appointment of local governing elders and sometimes in wider networking.

Connexionalism is that form of church government which looks to a central authority to lay down policies and decisions either through charismatic leaders or through a corporate body established to succeed such leaders. Some baptist bodies, being the product primarily of one person's labours or influence, may therefore operate like this, formally or informally. Connexionalism is associated in particular with Methodism which freely acknowledges it to be an improvised replacement for the authoritarian John Wesley rather than a scheme derived from theological first principles. The connexional conference lays down the doctrines and disciplines to be followed through by the churches and circuits of churches governed by it. A more personalised version of this can be seen in the Salvation Army, a variant of Methodism and also a renewal movement. When they had to replace William Booth, their charismatic founder, they chose to do so by appointing further generals in succession to him. Although in the United Kingdom Methodists and Salvationists reckon themselves denominationally to be among the free churches, their preference for centralised government means that they are not free churches in the sense defined in this book.

The Congregational Order

The alternatives to *congregationalism* enable us to see what is at stake. Having broken with a system of sacred power, Anabaptists and Baptists were among those who turned towards the local in their search for a better way. In their journey they went further than the Presbyterians and located governmental authority in the congregations themselves, always, of course, qualifying this as authority under Christ as witnessed to by the Scriptures and interpreted by the Spirit. The congregation's authority is never infallible, but it is competent and responsible. This autonomy, or self-government, is not authority to change the essential content of the faith which has been entrusted to us once for all for our reception,[14] but to apply it and the mission it entails in each church's own situation. Autonomy does not mean anarchy or defiant independency, nor should it even properly be seen as democracy since the intention behind it is to live as free and responsible communities under the rule of Christ and in fellowship and co-operation with all those who confess his name. Karl Barth helpfully described this order of the church, rather, as a 'brotherly [and sisterly] christocracy',[15] a community which makes the rule of Christ its intentional goal. The institutional forms through which this can be expressed may vary, but it is common for it to be focused in a church meeting:

> The church meeting, though outwardly a democratic way of ordering the affairs of the church, has a deeper significance. It is the occasion when, as individuals and as a community, we submit ourselves to the guidance of the Holy Spirit and stand under the judgments of God that we may know what is the mind of Christ.[16]

Negatively, through their experiences, Anabaptists and Baptists had learnt that there is a proper limit to human authority, and that dissent and disobedience were both necessary when the civil power requires something that is in conflict with the demands of God: 'We must obey God rather than any human authority.'[17] They asserted that the Christian conscience and the church should be free from external, civil domination. Positively, they saw themselves returning to the birthright of the early church and as discovering their freedom in Christ. This need not mean that the constructive insights of the other traditions are without value. Baptists have willingly accepted the ministry of elders in the church, sometimes seeing their pastors in this role and at other times combining it with the assistance of lay elders. Anabaptists owed a great deal to the pastoral and apostolic labours of Menno Simons (ca. 1496–1561), who travelled constantly to gather and rebuild the scattered flock after the turbulence of Münster. Baptists have made room for the wider, itinerant and translocal ministries of 'messengers' (their translation of the word 'apostle').[18] Contemporary Baptists in Latvia, Georgia and Moldova have no compunctions about using the word 'bishop' of their most senior overseers and Mennonites have done so long since. The issue is not whether such ministries are rightly recognised and received in the church – they are – but where the accent falls in the distribution of governmental authority. Baptists locate this finally not in bishops or elders but in the churches which commission those ministries for their task. Authority is the common property of the 'royal priesthood' of the people of God.[19]

Congregationalism does not go without its critics. It is considered to be *unbiblical* by those who read the Scriptures in episcopal and presbyterian ways, taking inadequate account of the reference to elders 'who rule well'[20] and to the injunction to 'respect those who labour among you, and have charge of you in the Lord and admonish you',[21] and to 'obey your leaders and submit to them, for they are keeping watch over your souls and will give an account'.[22] It is thought to be *unspiritual* because it treats all members of the church as if what they have to say is equally important and fails to distinguish properly between those who are spiritual and wise, and those who are immature or poorly instructed. It also proves to be *impractical* in that it makes decisions both slow to arrive at and unadventurous when they finally come.

However, in its favour the congregational order reckons explicitly with a basic fact that all systems of church government must confront and with a large matter of spiritual principle. People vote with their feet. If they do not agree with a course of action they will not support it however much they are told from above that this is what they must do. Congregationalism confronts this at the beginning and prizes the need for church members to shape and agree their own futures. The large spiritual principle is that the church is not a command structure or a system of sacred power. This is not the way God chose to work in Christ. God works our salvation by drawing out from us the response of obedient love, not by coercing us into conformity. This is the true nature of spiritual authority patterned on that of Christ. If the congregational polity leaves room for human failure it is because this reflects the ways of the Lord. It is high risk, but so are the ways of God.

There are other ways of framing the various possibilities for church government. Grenz, for instance, puts forward three general options which he describes as the hierarchical, the representative and the congregational – these correspond to the categories above.[23] In ecumenical discussions a very helpful distinction is made between personal, collegial and communal forms of oversight in the church that also correspond with the episcopal, presbyteral and congregational patterns already mentioned (the connexional can be included within the collegial dimension). Respect for these three forms is deemed a necessary guiding principle for the church.[24] However, the forms of church government vary between the traditions because of the relative degree of emphasis they place on each dimension.

Grounding the Positive Vision

The alternatives to congregationalism have great strengths and the criticisms against it are powerful. Providing a credible biblical grounding is therefore all the more important. It is not being argued here that there is only one way of reading the New Testament evidence: there are different ways of being the church with full integrity and eventually we shall return in this book to the matter of how they may interpenetrate. But it is claimed that the congregational way both captures important dimensions which the alternatives are apt to minimise, has a claim to be most true to the New Testament and that 'what was legitimate during the New Testament period cannot be illegitimate today'.[25]

The argument from Jesus

The first line of argument, and the strongest, comes from the teaching of the one who is now exalted as head of the church and who therefore should be allowed to determine what that church is. We have already noted several times the importance for the believers church tradition of the passage in Matthew 18:15–20 in which Jesus tells his disciples that, 'whatever you bind on earth will be bound in heaven, and whatever you loose on earth will be loosed in heaven' and that, 'if two of you agree on earth about anything you ask, it will be done for you by my Father in heaven'. All this is because 'where two or three are gathered in my name, I am there among them'. This marks the conferring of governmental authority on the church, the ability to make and apply ruling decisions with spiritual confidence. It is important to note that all requests and decisions have potency only because they are made in the name of Jesus, which means in conformity with what is known of his will, character and purpose. We should also ponder the use of the word 'agree' which refers to far more than an outward, formal conformity and instead to an agreement of the heart, to a deep and spiritual unity of purpose and desire. These are glimpses into the workings of a spiritual community, which knows how to discover depths of communion with God and with each other in the process of discerning the mind of Christ. It is the unity of the Spirit in the bond of peace.[26] Where such spiritual agreement exists, the church has authority before God and is effective in prayer. The church functions at its optimum when not only its leaders but also the whole body is in spiritual agreement in this way. Meeting in the name and Spirit of Christ, the church possesses an authority towards its members. The church is able to bind and loose, which means to allow or disallow in accordance with the Scriptures. It is competent to make decisions which will be owned by God and to exercise authority on God's behalf in its own sphere of competence. Here is the foundation of the belief that authority in the church belongs to the whole of the gathered community and not exclusively to some within it.

Jesus rejected elitist and authoritarian approaches to leadership and urged his disciples to do the same. This is clearest in Matthew 23:8–12 where he tells his followers that they are not to be called 'rabbi', 'father' or 'instructor' because they have one teacher and Father in God and one instructor in the Messiah. Moreover, 'you are all students' (or 'brothers') and, 'the greatest among you will be your servant' (vv. 8, 11). With these words Jesus was subverting patriarchal and hierarchical structures and replacing them among his disciples with something more egalitarian and communal. All forms of self-exaltation are inappropriate in the community he founded (v. 12).

For most of its history, much of the church has chosen to ignore these words completely. We now have a situation where the intentions of Jesus have almost become irrecoverable, given the weight of the superstructure we have built over them. Jesus intended to form a community in which the supremacy of God within it was not to be eclipsed by the perennial human tendency to seek for status and position. It is the concept of the gathering church which has most potential for coming close to this, diffusing as it does the authority of Christ throughout its members. Such a community is both most able to check the pretensions of its members and to give place to Christ in the midst. It is the simplicity of the gathering church that most seems to be in harmony with the teaching of Jesus.

The argument from the New Testament theology of the church

What is taught by Jesus is confirmed by the theology of the church and of the Christian life contained in the New Testament. We refer to four areas to make this point:

(a) The New Testament teaches that *Jesus Christ alone is head of the church*.[27] All churches accept this in principle but not all agree on its implications. For Christ to be the head means that the church in all its parts is organically related by the Spirit to Jesus Christ, from whom it draws its spiritual life. No other person or group of persons fulfils this function and the living headship of Christ should not be obscured by the belief that he uses intermediaries to infuse his life into the body. His government is exercised over each part and not mediately through a system of delegates. Christ does not delegate his lordship but retains it as his own. This argues for a form of church life which recognises the immediate participation of the people in the life of the head as priests, prophets and kings.

(b) The New Testament lays stress also on *the ministry and priesthood of all believers*. Priesthood has two dimensions. It brings access to God and the ability to minister to the people of God. This forms the foundation of Paul's teaching on spiritual gifts in 1 Corinthians 12: 'To each one is given the manifestation of the Spirit for the common good' (v. 7). Among the gifts listed are those of wisdom, knowledge (v. 8), prophecy and the distinguishing of spirits (v. 10). As these gifts may be manifested through any believer as the Spirit chooses, it points towards the access of all to the discernment and decision-making processes of the local church and to the fact that all may serve the body in these respects.

(c) Similar to this is the teaching of *the anointing of all believers*, to be found in 1 John 2:20, 27. John teaches that those who believe have an anointing from the Holy One and that 'all of you have knowledge'. John is here counteracting the influence of false teachers who were claiming to have true knowledge and calling into question the competence of the believers to know the will of God without them. His response is to affirm what they have already known of the preaching of the gospel and to confirm that the anointing they have received from the Spirit remains in them. There is no need for them to be swayed therefore by strong personalities: they may trust their own judgment in spiritual things over against those who make exclusive claims to have the truth.

(d) The final area, which is concerned with the nature of the Christian life, is much neglected. It concerns *the ability to make godly decisions*, which is the goal and mark of spiritual maturity. This particularly relates to Hebrews 5:11–14, where the author admonishes the Hebrew Christians for the immaturity that causes them still to need milk as though they were spiritual children. He then says, 'But solid food is for the mature, for those whose faculties have been trained by practice to distinguish good from evil' (v. 14). The ability to make ethical judgments and decisions is the mark of the mature Christian. This conflicts with the attitude of those who say the mark of maturity is the willingness to submit to decisions which others make on their behalf. The result of this is immature Christians who know how to do what they are told but not how to think.

The New Testament theology of the church implies it to be a community of disciples who are growing in confidence, understanding and ability to contribute effectively to the government of the congregation. It may well be that young churches which have yet to grasp firmly the contours of Christian truth may need higher levels of guidance and leadership. The goal for each congregation, however, is to enable it to mature and enter into its full range of competencies. This is what we see happening in Acts.

The argument from the example of the early church

New Testament theology does not stay in the realm of theory but is expressed in the actual life we find the early church living. It is not part of our case that all the decisions of the church were only ever made by the whole congregation, but we do find that at certain times and for strategic reasons it was necessary for all the people to share in crucial decisions. Three particular occasions stand out:

Acts 6:1–7
Here the church in Jerusalem was facing difficulties which threatened to divide those who were Hebrew-speaking from those who spoke Greek. Jealousy and suspicion were erupting and that the apostles were Hebrew speakers did not help. Their solution was to call together 'the whole community of the disciples' (v. 2) and to hand over to them the responsibility of choosing seven of their number who would help to maintain the unity of the church through impartial service. The criteria for making the choice were determined by the apostles but the actual selection was made by the church. How exactly this was done is not recorded. We do know that the apostles left the decision to the church, confirmed and worked with it once it was made and that as a consequence the church increased all the more (v. 7). This is an example of con-gregational decision-making in relation to the crucial matter of appointing leaders. The situation was delicate because of the potential divisions, but the decision was wise. Those chosen were all Greek-speaking (v. 5) and would command con-fidence from the part of the church which felt neglected. The whole process is an example of practical wisdom on the part of the apostles and the church, as Luke no doubt intended it to be, and a possible model for action today. There is also here a healthy balance of authorities: the apostles were appointed by Christ and both defined the area within which the church would decide and validated it once it had been made. The authority of the congregation today is also circumscribed by the authority of Scripture and the content of the faith that has been handed down to it. Yet within and because of these boundaries it has freedom of decision.

Acts 11:29–30
Here we find the church in action responding to a specific need. The prophet Agabus had predicted a famine and the disciples in Antioch made the decision, apparently spontaneously, to contribute money, according to the ability of each, to help the church in Judea. This is an example of creative initiative emerging from the body of believers in response to a need. They also made the decision to send their gifts to Jerusalem by the hands of Saul and Barnabas (v. 30), for whom this was part of their development in ministry. Once more there is a balance of authorities here, this time between the charismatic authority of the prophet and that of the church which responds by deliberation to the word given and reaches a common mind about a course of action.

Acts 15:1–35
Here we find one of the truly great decisions of the church, which has shaped Christianity. The existence of the Christian faith as an ethnically inclusive and international community is the result of the Council of Jerusalem, the first ecumenical council of the church. At stake was the reversal of the Jewish ethnic prejudices with which the church began and the inclusion in the church of Gentile believers on equal terms. In Jerusalem the apostles and elders engaged in debate and arrived at certain conclusions designed to admit Gentiles and make table fellowship between Jews and Gentiles possible.

It is not surprising that the apostles and elders of the church took the lead in the debate by virtue of their calling, experience and position. The debate itself was an attempt to reconcile the received interpretations of the tradition with the living testimony of seeing God at work within Gentiles. In the process a new way of reading Scripture was reached in the light of experiences which were undeniably of God, a reading which firmly grasped God's desire to include the Gentiles within the story of salvation. In verse 22 we read, 'Then the apostles and elders, with the consent of the whole church, decided to choose men from among their members and to send them to Antioch with Paul and Barnabas.' The church in question was the church in Jerusalem which, after the expert deliberations, had been brought into the discussion and affirmed the conclusions reached. Once more there was care in appointing responsible people to represent them.

These examples show a church which is creatively involved in responding to the Spirit of God, even to the extent of making decisions which affected its leadership, its programme, its very nature and future. The passages affirm a flexible model of congregational decision-making but not one which required every decision, however small, to be approved by the body of the church. Within the context of the apostolic faith handed on to them, we find the church involved in strategic decisions of policy at certain times and then leaving their executive outworking to the responsible individuals duly appointed.

The argument from Christian freedom

Because the gospel is about the freedom given us in Christ, freedom in all its aspects must be a value to which the church is tenaciously committed. Paul's exhortation in Galatians 5:1 not to 'submit again to a yoke of slavery' should always ring in our ears. For freedom Christ has set us free. There are many yokes of slavery which present themselves as servants of freedom. Paul had in mind the kind of legalistic religion which taught they could belong to the people of God only if all the demands of the law were kept. Freedom in Christ has many ramifications but they all amount to this: we are never to allow anything other than Christ to have dominion in our lives, whether this be a religious law, a political power, a charismatic personality or an ecclesiastical organisation, a 'sacred power'. Only in Christ do we find the end for which we were created. Lest this freedom be misunderstood as rebelliousness, Paul goes on to clarify, 'only do not use your freedom as an opportunity for self-indulgence, but through love become slaves to one another'.[28] Submission to Christ includes proper respect for those whom he sends as his ministers but their task is not to come between the believer and Christ.

Church order should be so constructed as to enhance the freedom of the Christian. Freedom is to be celebrated, not begrudged as though it were a regrettable necessity. People do not join a church voluntarily only then to lose their freedom. A church's life is built upon the ongoing consent and agreement of its members. This is what the congregational order sets out to embody and maintain. But freedom is not licence or anarchy. When it was said, 'In those days there was no king in Israel; all the people did what was right in their own eyes',[29] this was not a record of a desirable state of affairs but of an ungodly one. The congregational order is an *order*, a way of pursuing the things of God in acknowledgement of God's sovereign rule.[30]

In summary, there is much to suggest that although various forms of church order can appeal to the New Testament, there are good reasons for believing that the congregational form overshadowed the others. Paul expected the Corinthian church to take care of its own affairs, to address, for instance, the problem of internal schism,[31] to take responsibility for the administration of communion,[32] and to discipline erring church members.[33] This speaks of responsible congregational autonomy, but not of congregational individualism or isolation.[34] The New Testament churches were local, self-governing communities connected relationally and spiritually with other such churches across the Mediterranean world and aware of the wider movement of which they were a part. They were held together by a network of relationships of which the apostles and their companions were a significant part and whose spiritual authority was recognised and valued.

Beyond Distortion

It must be acknowledged that despite the honourable and lofty ideals represented here, actual practice has often been a distortion of what is possible. There is no doubt that the church meeting for many congregationally governed churches can be an opportunity for the highest and the best or for the very worst. Partly this is because its very nature can be misunderstood. Above all, there is the subtle but important distinction between a 'brotherly and sisterly christocracy' and democracy. Although the outward form of a congregational church meeting may look like democracy, the intention is different. It would not be inaccurate to describe its form as a 'guided democracy'[35] where leaders have an important role in giving guidance but this is accomplished most of all by the Spirit of God. The church exists to discern the mind of Christ, not the will of the majority. What the majority perceive to be the mind of Christ is very important: but the spirit of it all is not the will-to-power ('how can we get our way and who is on our side?') but the will-to-truth ('how can we discover together what is right and good and submit to it together?'). The intention is that God may be all in all to us. To this end, *voting* as a method of decision-making is secondary to *sensing*. Voting may be an appropriate and sometimes necessary way of making some decisions and of underlining others, but the search for spiritual agreement and a shared mind expressed through consensus should be the essence of the process. This is as much to do with prayer and worship as with analysis and discussion. As with the Council of Jerusalem, reflection upon Scripture, the sharing of wisdom and experience can lead to our being able to say, 'it has seemed good to the Holy Spirit and to us'[36] and this should always be the goal we have in mind. After all, '"For who has known the mind of the Lord so as to instruct him?" But we have the mind of Christ.'[37] This cannot mean that a church functioning even at its best will always be right in what it decides: we only ever make decisions within the light that we have and such light will always be limited. But, by and large, it is more important to be responsible than to be right. Infallibility is beyond us, responsibility is within our grasp.

The church which meets to worship God through Christ and in the Spirit is also the church which meets to discern the ways of God. There is no yawning cavern between meeting to offer praise and meeting to make responsible choices. They are both of a piece with knowing and loving God with heart, soul and mind.[38] If the church is not a democracy where the will of the majority is the decisive factor neither is it an autocracy, where one person rules, a patriarchy or matriarchy where the men or the women rule, an aristocracy where an elite determined by birth rule, or an oligarchy where a clique rules. The point about the church is that it differs from all these systems and transcends them. This is where Christ rules among his people. It is an experiment in a new way of being, one which anticipates the rule of God in the final kingdom.[39] This means that all have the right to speak but not all contributions will have equal value. By listening to what each may say it becomes possible to discern and discriminate together, as a common priesthood, where the word of the Lord may be found. All of us together are wiser than any of us on our own. But there can be no pretending that learning to listen to each other is an infinitely demanding task.

To expect such wisdom of the ordinary people of the church may seem to some to be asking more than is reasonable. But this seems to be God's chosen way in making frail flesh and blood the people of God, the body of Christ and the temple of the Holy Spirit. It is for us to respond with our best.[40]

Notes

[1] For a useful discussion on the taxonomy of power see David Michael Hughes, 'The Ethical use of Power: A Discussion with the Christian Perspectives of Reinhold Niebuhr, John Howard Yoder and Richard J. Barnet' (PhD Dissertation, Southern Baptist Theological Seminary, 1984).

[2] Acts 10:38.

[3] Matthew 21:12–17.

[4] Volf, *After Our Likeness*, 2–3, citing also James W. McClendon Jr, 'The Believer's Church in Theological Perspective' (Unpublished Paper, 1997).

[5] The first Baptist, John Smyth, wrote, 'We say that the Church or two or three faithful people separated from the world and joined together in a true covenant, have both Christ, the covenant, and promises and the ministerial power of Christ given to them': in W.T. Whitley (ed.), *The Works of John Smyth* (Cambridge: Cambridge University Press, 1915), 403 (spelling modernised).

[6] The London Confession, 1644, Article 36, Lumpkin, *Baptist Confessions of Faith*, 166 (spelling modernised).

[7] Acts 4:17

[8] The Declaration of Principle was adopted also by the Baptist Unions of Scotland and Wales, although in both cases with some additional material: G. Keith Parker (ed), *Baptist Confessions in Europe: History and Confessions of Faith* (Nashville, TN: Broadman Press, 1982) 39, 46–47.

[9] Acts 1:21–26.

[10] 1 Corinthians 15:8–11.

[11] Acts 19:22.

[12] Acts 14:23.

[13] In fact, there are major problems with the idea of an unbroken historic link with the apostles because of a gap in the sub-apostolic period that cannot be satisfactorily bridged. The evidence suggests that the idea of an unbroken line of bishops of Rome in continuity with Peter was an *ex post factu* reconstruction intended to bolster the developing claim of the bishop of Rome to precedence within the church: Duffy, *Saints and Sinners*, 11–23. Even despite this, the process of episcopal descent has a strong claim to continuity even if it is not unbroken.

[14] Jude 3.

[15] Karl Barth, *Church Dogmatics: The Doctrine of Reconciliation*, Volume IV/2 (Edinburgh: T&T Clark, 1958), 680–81.

[16] 'The Baptist Doctrine of the Church', in Hayden (ed.), *Baptist Union Documents 1948–1977*, 7.

[17] Acts 5:29.

[18] John F.V. Nicholson, 'The Office of Messenger amongst English Baptists in the seventeenth and eighteenth centuries', *Baptist Quarterly* 17 (1957–58), 206. See also the collection of essays on this theme, Stuart Murray (ed.), *Translocal Ministry: Equipping the Churches for Mission* (Didcot: Baptist Union, 2004).

[19] 1 Peter 2:9.

[20] 1 Timothy 5:17.

[21] 1 Thessalonians 5:12.

[22] Hebrews 13:17.

[23] Grenz, *Baptist Congregation*, 53.

[24] WCC, *Baptism, Eucharist and Ministry*, 25–26.

[25] Volf, *After Our Likeness*, 21.

[26] Ephesians 4:3–5.

[27] Ephesians 4:15; Colossians 1:18.

[28] Galatians 5:13.

[29] Judges 21:25.

30   Neville Clark: 'Rather we are bidden to take the nature of the Gospel itself with relentless theological seriousness and so to plot its implications for the form of the Church. Order is given that disorder may be overwhelmed. Structure is given that the Church may be the Church, that the divine community may body forth the fullness of Christ, and that the completeness and finality of the apostolic gospel may find expression': Gilmore (ed.), *Pattern of the Church*, 100–101.

31   1 Corinthians 1:10.

32   1 Corinthians 11:33–34.

33   1 Corinthians 5:3–5, 12–13.

34   Grenz, *Baptist Congregation*, 54.

35   Kevin Giles, *What on Earth is the Church? A Biblical and Theological Inquiry* (London: SPCK, 1995), 95–96.

36   Acts 15:28.

37   1 Corinthians 2:16.

38   Matthew 22:37.

39   1 Corinthians 15:28.

40   In the Preface to his book *Decision-Making in the Church: A Biblical Model* (Philadelphia: Fortress Press, 1983), the Catholic New Testament scholar Luke Timothy Johnson writes, 'Once or twice in this book, I call it an "essay for idealists," and that is probably as good a description as any for this slender volume. It tries to place the decision-making process of the church within a biblical and theological framework. You may regard it as a curio or a Molotov cocktail. I can't make up my mind how to regard it. It is a book which seemed to force itself upon me, and then develop a logic of its own. I certainly wrote it, but I am not altogether sure I like what I read in it. I don't know if this is because I did the job badly or well. If badly, I am embarrassed. If well, I am frightened', 9.

7. The Children of the Church

People of Promise

Introduction

Infant baptism, which believer baptists reject for theological reasons, nonetheless has certain strengths. It tries to occupy constructively the space left by the New Testament in relation to the children of believers. We are not atomised individuals; we live in families. The decisions we make affect not only our lives but also those of others whose lives are intimately related to our own. Children are widely regarded as being bound up in the bundle of life with their parents, so that they participate in the parental allegiances, not least in matters of faith and religious tradition. It would only be an extreme version of individual human rights thinking or a very oppressive state ideology that would deny to parents the right to educate their own children in their faith. Infant baptism is making a positive statement about the place of children in the church: they are included by extension within the covenant community of God's own people. As we saw, the most compelling theological argument for infant baptism builds on the parallel with circumcision as a sign of the covenant while extending it to include female as well as male children.

Believer baptists have a potential weakness here and it is one which, if external voices are to be listened to, has not yet been successfully overcome. Are the children of the church to be seen as a living part of the church? Are they within or without? Are they members of the body of Christ or not? If they are, how should this be marked with a sign? There is no disagreement between infant and believer baptists that there is a theological space here to be occupied with some responsible thinking and practice. They simply disagree how to fill it. For the paedobaptist, not baptising a child declares that it does not belong within the sphere of the church and this is unthinkable.[1] But it is not as though the only choices are between being little Christians or little pagans.[2] For the baptist, infant baptism says more than one is entitled to say for any other person since no one can respond in repentance and faith to the gospel on behalf of another, not even a parent. To obscure this is to obscure the gospel. But it is and should be the case that both Christian families and church communities have an immensely important formative role in shaping people and enabling the response of faith. There is something different then about being born into the community of faith, being a child of the church.

Baptists are apt to believe that individuals come to faith almost in isolation and then join the church as an expression of their newly discovered discipleship. Individuals therefore precede community. Something similar to this often happens, but, as a matter of fact, if there is any 'normal' pattern it works the other way round. The faith is transmitted through communities of faith who draw into their orbit those who are seeking faith and enable the conversion of their thinking to the point that they are able to make informed and lasting responses to the grace of God. The catholic insight is correct at this point. The church is not a humanly generated society of those who choose to associate together; it is a divine community which precedes us and admits us to its fellowship. Communities precede individuals just as the community of the Trinity precedes and creates that of the church. As the church is drawn by the Triune God into the divine communion, so it transmits its life by drawing others into its own communion through the publication and practice of the truth. Individuals learn through contact with the community to believe and to live Christianly. They are initiated into the practices of that community so that they become heirs of salvation. There is a sense then in which coming to faith should be seen as a gift of God through the church. The ancient dictum, 'outside the church there is no salvation' is problematic when it constitutes a claim to exercise sacred power over life and death; but seen organically and relationally, the church is indeed that community which acts as the instrument of salvation. The church is our mother, and none can have God as their Father who do not also have the church as their mother.

The Catechumenate

If it is wrong to think of the church as the humanly created product of our own choices, it is equally wrong to think of the church as an insular fellowship. In fact, the common designation of the church as the 'fellowship of believers',[3] while not untrue, is also not true enough. If that is all the church is then something is wrong. We have noted how the idea of the 'gathering church' seeks to escape any sense of insularity by pointing to the way in which churches, as missionary communities, are always drawing others in, or if not have forsaken their true nature. In understanding the church it is as important to focus on what is happening around the edges as on what takes place at the centre. True churches, engaged in mission, draw others into their own life. The evidence that this is happening is the presence around the committed core community of those others who are pressing in and wanting to join. We may call these 'seekers'.

In the early church, those who were seeking with intent were called the 'catechumenate'; they were 'under the sound of the gospel', undergoing instruction in the faith and moving towards confession of Christ in baptism. Most of them would have been part of the adult catechumenate, but children also belonged there. They were among those who were in the community of faith and were moving towards personal confession of it not as a merely cultural rite of passage, but as a sign that they too had embraced the way of discipleship. That faith could dawn upon them at any point in their progress.

Baptists then would not see children as members of the body of Christ on the basis of someone else's faith in a kind of 'half-way covenant' by which they are external members but not internally so in the heart.[4] But they would certainly believe that they are part of the community as catechumens or, to adapt an image, they are in the body in the sense that they are enfolded and embraced by that body.[5] They are mingled in among the people of God. Above all they are children of promise since, 'the promise is for you, for your children and for all who are far away, everyone whom the Lord our God calls to him'.[6] This promise means that how they are regarded is determined by what God has done on their behalf and the future in the purpose of God which awaits them on the basis of faith. Even infant baptism, while sharing the sense of promise, recognises that children are in a distinctive category in that they have yet to make that promise fully their own. This is why in some paedobaptist denominations the rites of confirmation or first communion are clearly delayed until children have attained some degree of definition apart from their parents. For the baptists, the appropriate way to mark inheritance of the promise is through the baptism of disciples.

The Status of Children

Believer baptists, being evangelicals, have a constant preoccupation with questions of salvation, and salvation is consistently interpreted in terms of eternal life. But properly understood salvation is more than the question of 'where we spend eternity' and baptism is more than a witness to a personal decision for God: it is rather part of that process of conversion by which our lives are made new and we begin to conform to the image of Christ. Regeneration and sanctification should not therefore be separated in the positive baptist vision: we are redeemed in order to live lives worthy of the Lord and to share in the mission of God. Inevitably however, for both theological and pastoral reasons, we must address the question of the status of children in terms of their spiritual condition. If humankind is lost,[7] dead in trespasses and sins,[8] and we are by nature children of wrath,[9] how does it stand with children? And how might this affect their place in the Christian community?

Those who believe that infant baptism conveys of itself the grace of regeneration might believe at this point they have given a satisfactory answer to these questions. To be baptised is to be saved. On this basis, the baptism of infants must be practiced on the widest possible scale – to leave a child unbaptised is to jeopardise its possibilities of eternal life. This whole position begs the question as to what kind of God saves or condemns infants and children on the basis of a ritual performed over them without their own knowledge, choice or will. It also comes into severe conflict with the God who is revealed in the Christ who welcomed and blessed children and proclaimed, 'it is to such as these that the kingdom of heaven belongs'.[10] As we have noted, this position is rarely advanced today, but the questions that it evokes are still pertinent. We have already pointed to the distinction between original sin and inherited guilt and while finding a place for the former have discounted the latter. There is a corporate condition which defines the whole of humanity and each person within it: human beings are collectively and without exception fallen. But this is only half the story: 'For as all die in Adam, so all will be made alive in Christ.'[11] Human beings are defined by 'Adam' but are redefined in Christ. They are linked to Adam by a process of human descent and imitation; they are renewed in Christ by means of faith and the regeneration of the Spirit.

We cannot say definitively how it is that the corporately fallen condition of the human race is transmitted from one generation to another. It could be that ontologically, within the very constitution of human nature, a disordered condition is genetically and biologically passed on. Scientists have recently, although controversially, been drawing attention to the phenomenon of 'genetic memory' by which living beings download their experiences in life into their genetic code to be transmitted to further generations.[12] It could equally be that each human being is socialised from birth into perverse patterns of behaviour. Human beings are not, after all, born as static creatures. They experience a process of formation and development and so are as much human 'becomings' as human 'beings'. Human social patterns, already fallen, will reproduce themselves in emergent members of the community. There is therefore an element of necessity in the constraint of each new person towards sin by their inner tendencies and their outer context. We are bound to sin.[13] We are sinners 'by nature'.[14] As such, we bring ourselves into condemnation by imitating the sin of those who have gone before us and throwing in our lot with them.[15] This accords with Scripture and with experience. It is just this bondage to sin, our inability to help ourselves, which excites God's compassion towards us.[16]

The crucial distinction in all of this concerns our degree of personal responsibility for what we cannot help doing. A determinist approach asserts that we cannot help anything we do and that any contrary sense we have of being responsible is an illusion. The alternative is that although we are certainly conditioned by the natures we have acquired, we are always *more than* our genes and our nature and that we can do otherwise if we so will. We are therefore generally to be held accountable for our wrongdoing, although not in the 'extenuating circumstances' of mental illness, for instance, when we were 'not ourselves', or of genuine ignorance or of external compulsion. The apostle Paul seems to recognise this category, namely, that it is possible for sin to be at work within us without it being 'reckoned': 'Sin was indeed in the world before the law, but sin is not reckoned where there is no law. Yet death exercised dominion from Adam to Moses, even over those whose sins were not like the transgression of Adam [i.e. knowing and culpable].'[17] The true tragedy of the human condition concerns the will that lies behind the will: by exerting the will we can do what is right, but we lack the will to use our wills aright. It is possible therefore both to talk about the freedom of the will and its bondage. We are responsible for what we do, but we are morally incapable of willing to do otherwise. Naturally our wills are free in that we can choose, but morally they are bound in that we consistently fail to choose the right. Regeneration in Christ by the Spirit is that work of God by which our inner will is made alive and willing towards God. It is being set free to want to love God.[18]

In relation to children, this brings us to the concept of an 'age of accountability'. Children are included in the disordered condition of humanity but sin is not 'reckoned' until they come to an age of accountability and assume responsibility for their actions. This is suggested by a variety of Old Testament texts, principally by those which refuse entry to the Promised Land to the whole generation of those who rebelled against God, but exempt from this the children 'who today do not yet know right from wrong'.[19] The age of twenty years is specifically (and generously) mentioned in another place as the threshold.[20] In those passages in which Jesus teaches about the children as exemplars of the kingdom and commends those who welcome them as welcoming also himself, it is also possible to discern a 'protected status' for the child in the eyes of God.[21] The Jewish ceremonies of bar- or bat-mitzvah[22] when a child assumes the responsibility to obey the laws and after which parents are no longer responsible for the sins of their child, are in accord with the idea of an age of accountability which in these cases is settled at thirteen and twelve, respectively. It may be, however, that the age differs from child to child and that the reality of true responsibility is known only to God.

In the light of this reasoning, it becomes possible to say something from a baptist perspective about what happens when a child dies before the age of accountability, as has been the case frequently in times past and still happens. There are differences of opinion here about how children might participate in the work of Christ: do they benefit from that saving work done objectively on behalf of all humanity only if they 'opt in' or 'automatically' unless they choose to 'opt out'?[23] Whereas there are many sentimental and compassionate reasons for wanting to believe the best, on their own these are not good enough. Strict Calvinists may want to say that the number of the elect is already decided so that the age at which a person dies does not finally matter one way or the other. Not surprisingly, Calvin himself seems to have been content to believe that the children of the elect are also elect.[24] There is a valid agnosticism that is content not to know but to trust that all is for the best and simply to ask, 'Shall not the Judge of all the earth do what is just?'[25] However, in the light of the way in which Jesus welcomed children, which cannot be separated or distinguished in any way from the way God the Father welcomes them since Christ is the revelation of the Father,[26] there are surely strong grounds for believing in the special status of children. This is not because of their supposed innocence or because they have the qualities of humility and natural trust; rather, it is because they are vulnerable and without status and the God who protects the widows and the orphans is on their side in eternity just as much as in time.[27]

Infants and children who die are in the safe hands of God.[28] It does not quite do, however, to say simply that they are saved since the believer baptist insists that the grace of God does not override or ignore our own responses to that grace. Whereas there are no specific biblical grounds for saying it, and lacking a biblical mandate any point of view must be identified as a theological opinion and not as a doctrine or an article of faith, there is a theological case for arguing that infants and children go on becoming in the life which is beyond death and hidden from our knowledge. In this continued becoming, response towards the grace of God is still asked of them, as it is of those who live, and the grace of God has such a response as its goal. Nevertheless, believer baptists would also generally insist that however God's grace is revealed, it is not only shown to the children of the church but to all infants and children who die.

Infant baptism, as we have noted, probably arose first of all as a pastoral response to the experience of infant mortality. It is not the only way of responding ritually to such a tragedy. A baptist way would be to hold the child and place it in prayer into the hands of God, possibly reciting verses of Scripture which speak of the compassion and mercy of God, God's care for the orphans and widows, and words of promise concerning the life which is stronger than death. Christians work with the presumption that God wills to save and is not wanting any to perish.[29] The reason Christ came into the world was not to condemn it but in order that the world might be saved through him.[30] These positive convictions provide the ground on which children can be commended with confidence to the Christ-like God.

The Church as Hospitable Space

Because the children of the church belong as catechumens and children of promise, the community of disciples constitutes a welcoming and hospitable space for them. When Jesus made reference to 'their angels which continually see the face of my Father in heaven',[31] he was not offering a doctrine of personal guardian angels so much as affirming the place of children among the people of God, who are protected by the angels of God.[32] The church is a community within which children may become, being formed and shaped by the relationships that surround them. This is an immense blessing and one which marks out the children of the church from others. There is something different about being born into the church which does indeed place children in some kind of relationship with the covenant of God.

One of the verses frequently used to justify infant baptism is 1 Corinthians 7:14 where Paul is addressing those wives who are married to unbelievers: 'For the unbelieving husband is made holy through his wife, and the unbelieving wife is made holy through her husband. Otherwise your children would be unclean, but as it is, they are holy.'[33] This could be taken to mean that the faith of the wife is attributed to the husband and her children and that the eternal destiny of both is determined, thereby justifying baptism. However, this would conflict with the call to discipleship which requires people to deny themselves and take up their cross, as is clear from the fact that the logic which would justify the baptism of the children would also justify that of the husband. It seems rather that Paul is addressing the fear of Christian wives that by being married to unbelieving, possibly pagan husbands, they are in some way rendered ritually or morally unclean, along with their children. Paul is saying that there is no need to fear (or to seek a divorce) because the process works the other way round: children and husbands are rendered holy by being married to a Christian wife or having a Christian mother. 'Holiness' is being used here in a way distinctive of Old Testament teaching which sees it as a condition transmitted by contact, a kind of spiritual 'radioactivity' related to being in the near presence of God.[34] To be in the church is to be in the sphere of the holy, in a community which is benignly radioactive with the grace and power of God. To be put outside this community is to be returned to the 'power of darkness' from which we have been rescued.[35]

These are primal and basic images which it is easy for modern people to overlook, but to be in the sphere of the Christian community is (or should be) to breathe an atmosphere of spiritual freedom which is distinct from the godless or idolatrous spirit of the age and which enables all who benefit from it to flourish. God embraces all children, but being born into the church counts for something. The children of the church have no distinct advantage over other children as far as eternal salvation is concerned but they are at the least among the people of God and surrounded by the blessings of the covenant.[36] They are in the realm where God is loved and worshipped in the Spirit and this is something to celebrate. It is a place where the blessing of God can rest in particular ways upon those who share in it. The theological space which the New Testament leaves in relation to children can be filled by means of this understanding and it can also have its own sign.

The Blessing of Children

When Jesus welcomed the children he took them in his arms and blessed them. The New Testament mandates no particular sign for the purpose of welcoming children and blessing them; but what Jesus did on this occasion leads quite consistently to the development of a rite which has come to be called 'the blessing of children and the dedication of parents'. In a previous chapter pointed out that in addition to the two dominical sacraments, the New Testament gives evidence of practices such as the laying on of hands, anointing with oil and the kiss of peace. Beyond these, the Christian church has for good reasons developed other festivals and rites. In the past, baptists have looked askance at these on account of their sometimes pagan origin or their lack of specific biblical mention. These rites are not all in the same category. There are few baptists, for instance, who would think twice about celebrating marriage in a Christian context or holding a funeral service, even though neither of these rites is mandated in Scripture. They are later elaborations by the church to fill a gap in the actual experience of Christian people who for psychological and personal reasons need rites of passage in their pilgrimage. It is not as if the Bible fails to address these matters. Marriage is prized in almost sacramental terms as a picture of the commitment of Christ to his church and vice versa.[37] The death of a believer is a natural point at which to affirm the hope of resurrection.[38] And the birth of a child is a very fitting moment at which to give thanks for the goodness of God's creation and the promise of salvation through calling on the name of the Lord which is extended to all people. This has been recognised from the time of Balthasar Hübmaier, one of the first Anabaptists, who, on 16 January 1525, wrote:

> Instead of baptism, I have the church come together, bring the infant in, explain in German the gospel, 'They brought little children' [Matt. 19:13]. When a name is given it, the whole church prays for the child on bended knees, and commends it to Christ, that he will be gracious and intercede for it. But if the parents are still weak, and positively wish that the child be baptized, then I baptize it; and I am weak with the weak for the time being until they can be better instructed.[39]

In its present form, the rite of the blessing of children developed at the end of the nineteenth century as a way of responding to the religious, psychological and personal need for a rite of passage marking the birth of children.[40] At first it was observed in the home as a family rite but as it gained in acceptability so it came to be a common practice of baptist churches embracing the welcome of children into the Christian community.

A solid scriptural and theological basis can be provided for it. Hannah and Elkanah brought their child Samuel 'to appear in the presence of the Lord', to give thanks for him and to devote him to the service of the Lord.[41] Similarly, and the parallels are not accidental, the infant Jesus was presented to the Lord by his parents after thirty-three days, the required time of ritual purification on the birth of a son, in the temple in Jerusalem with a sacrifice of thanksgiving.[42] This was the customary practice in Israel and was the occasion when Simeon blessed him and his parents, and both he and Anna prophesied over Jesus.[43]

We have already noticed several times the significance of Jesus welcoming the children, taking them in his arms and blessing them. Jesus did this when his disciples would have kept them away; it is recorded that Jesus was indignant about this and rebuked them sternly saying, 'Let the children come to me; do not stop them.'[44] These are strong words. The children were taken as object lessons in what it means to be in the kingdom of God. To enter the kingdom means to become like a child in laying aside concerns for status and position: children had no status in Israel and they are symbols of the reversal of values that takes place in God's kingdom.[45]

In the Old Testament era it was customary for families and communities to impart blessings at significant moments – for example, Isaac blessed Jacob;[46] Jacob blessed his sons;[47] Solomon blessed the assembly of Israel;[48] the priests blessed the Israelites.[49] Baptists have been so keen to downplay any suggestion of magical impartation or human agency that they have tended to neglect this dimension, reducing the benediction (literally: speaking good words) at the end of a service to a sign that it is ended. In this they are quite unbiblical in that words are believed in Scripture to be potent. By the word of the Lord the earth and the heavens were created, and this creative potency still adheres to the words of Scripture and to words spoken in the name of the Lord. If it is true, as we know it to be, that malevolent words can cause damage to a person's inner being, the opposite is even more true, to speak good words is to bless. To bless is to impart life-giving vitality in the name of the Lord in order that people may flourish and grow healthily.

None of these biblical instances creates a mandate as such for the rite of the blessing of children, but taken together they form a strong biblical basis and encouragement for the practice. Infant blessing is appropriate in the light of them. Yet the rite is more than the blessing of children. It is a dedication of the parents to the vocation of Christian parenthood, to the task of nurturing children into the ways of God. It is a moment when they can give thanks publicly and accept both the responsibilities of the task and the prayers of the people of God for wisdom and grace in fulfilling it. More than this, it is an opportunity for the community of the church to welcome into its enfolding embrace children of promise and to recall its own responsibility to let the children come to Christ.

The Shape of the Rite

Much has been made here of the rite of blessing for the simple reason that if it is the case that there is a 'deficit' in affirming the place of children then the blessing of children is a practice that will help celebrate children and affirm their place among the people of God. As a continuing practice, the rite of blessing will shape the assumptions and instincts of the community. For this reason there is a lot to be said for the repeated use of the same order and for the careful design of a form of words that says what needs to be said clearly and with dignity.

It is clear that this should begin with Scripture, the selection of passages which speak about the blessing of children and acknowledge them as gifts from God.[50] Children also need to be seen as heirs to the promise of salvation. The blessing of the children by Jesus will be the centrepiece of any use of Scripture. The note of thanksgiving on behalf of parents and church is essential as is some form of commitment on the part of both. For the parents this will be a commitment to the vocation of parenthood, to bring their children up in a Christian way and on the part of the church at the very least to prayer and the provision of an atmosphere of loving acceptance. The community is both receiving and welcoming the newly born and then blessing children and parents in the name of the Lord, preferably with the use of the Aaronic blessing.[51] Prayers of intercession in the light of the promise should also be added and will include the prayer that in due time the child may come to accept Christ as Lord and confess him in the waters of baptism.

The Scope of the Rite

As described, the rite is most applicable to Christian parents. However we need to reckon with the fact that what Christians take to be the norm in family life is in fact increasingly abnormal. Parents may be on their own, may be married to non-Christian partners, may be cohabiting but in stable relationships, or may not even be Christians at all. Each church, and each pastor, will need to develop policies to cope with the diversity. On the one hand, they will wish to safeguard certain values and hold to them, and, on the other, to be accommodating and welcoming wherever possible. However, the blessing of children can be seen as much as a rite of creation as a promise of redemption.[52] In principle, and unlike baptism and communion, it may therefore be open to parents who have not yet confessed Christ but who recognise the need to give thanks and desire the blessing of God upon their children and themselves. In this case, it is possible to adapt the rite so that it has integrity for them and does not ask them to make promises they cannot fulfil. All the biblical promises would still apply to their children and to bless in the name of the Lord what God has created is still appropriate. At this point, there is some validity to the argument of infant baptists that it is the faith of the church which renders the rite meaningful and effective, the difference being that infant blessing does not make any presumption about the response of the child. When it comes to 'irregular' liaisons, such as cohabitation, care obviously needs to be taken not to legitimate what is deficient. But once more, children themselves are hardly responsible for the situation into which they are born and most would not want to exclude children from a blessing for reasons the children themselves cannot help. The options are always there for pastors to offer some kind of ministry, sometimes in the home or family circle, which is suitably adapted to the situation, as funerals and sometimes weddings often must be. The concern is to balance integrity and honesty with an openness to serve and bless others and minister to them.

Pastoral Issues and Questions

We can now address some more frequently asked questions, and without presuming to give the 'right' answers, attempt to give responsible ones.

Is there a minimum age for baptism? Answers to this will certainly vary and will be determined by where the emphasis is laid. We have already made the distinction between adult and believers baptism, the effect of which is that the relevant criterion is not age but faith: this is the baptism of *believers*. [53] However, how old does one have to be to have true faith? Some conclude that since children can truly and sincerely believe, they can also be baptised at a relatively young age. The danger here is that infant baptism is replaced by 'infantile' baptism, baptism which is neither fully grasped by the recipient nor truly persuasive to those who witness it. Others distinguish stages of faith and while fully affirming each stage in its own value, argue that baptism should be deferred if possible to a later stage. The 'affiliative faith' of childhood, which is formed through close identification with parents and family, needs to grow into the 'owned faith' of more mature years before baptism becomes appropriate. [54]

In an earlier chapter I introduced the term 'baptism of disciples', which seeks to say more about the meaning of baptism than the term 'believers baptism'. The baptism of disciples captures that element about baptism which understands it as a denial of self, a turning of the back on the alternatives to the living God and a taking up of the cross to follow Christ.[55] Those who are baptised need to reckon with the demands of the baptised life. This does imply some degree of 'adult' understanding about the demands of baptism and the life of discipleship and asks the question whether it is responsible to administer baptism without some evidence that this has been grasped, at least in outline. Baptism is not about cheap grace but about following after the Crucified. The age at which people may grasp this will vary, but the tendency of this emphasis is to encourage a delay in baptism into and beyond the age of accountability.[56]

Having said this, baptism at any age in which there is evidence of faith should never be counted as invalid. When there are demands for a new baptism 'because I now understand it properly' these should be resisted in favour of encouraging people to embrace at greater depth the commitment previously made and signified in baptism.

Should children participate in communion? Virtually every denomination is confronted with the question of the place of children at communion, and some find it easier to answer than others. In paedobaptist communities the logic of infant baptism suggests that infants and children should equally be admitted to communion. When they are not until they are confirmed this undermines the claim of infant baptism to be full baptism since it still has to be completed by the personal ownership of the act in confirmation. Some Anglicans, as an example, are moving towards the admission of children to communion on the basis of their infant baptism. Catholics introduced a new rite of 'first communion' early in the twentieth century which takes place at around the age of eight and precedes confirmation. The Orthodox churches have long since admitted baptised infants immediately to the eucharist. For baptists, if children are believers and have received baptism they should go on to receive communion. With other children the situation is complicated.

The process of Christian initiation is clear enough. Repentance and faith are accompanied by baptism which leads to church membership and participation in communion. This follows the pattern of Acts 2:37–42. Baptist practice used to be very strict at this point only permitting those baptised as believers, or who had a letter of introduction from a similar church, to be in membership of the church or to take communion. This was known as 'closed communion' and 'closed membership': both membership and communion were restricted to those baptised as believers. In the English experience, although there had always been some churches which recognised both believers and infant baptism, the norm began to change in the nineteenth century as churches began to reject 'sectarianism' and open up communion to all who professed faith. The invitation at communion was routinely given to 'all who love our Lord Jesus Christ and are in love and charity with their neighbour'. This is known as 'open communion' but was still often combined with closed membership. Once people who were not baptised as believers, and in some cases not baptised at all, were admitted to communicant the pressure mounted for this so-called 'communicant membership' to be reflected in the constitutional church membership. Churches began to introduce 'open membership' which could be entered by transfer from another church or sometimes on profession of faith without the necessity of believers baptism. All of these changes were resisted by those who considered the integrity of a Baptist church was being diluted in the process; some churches moved off into the Strict Baptist denominations. Over time, then, the norm moved from being closed communion and closed membership to open communion and open membership with variations in between. The English norm here is markedly different from Baptist churches in most other countries which adopt a less liberal polity.

Another change which influenced developments was liturgical. Communion services used to take place, and in many places still do, as an additional service after the regular service allowing opportunity for those who were not qualified, or chose not to participate, to leave. With belief growing in the centrality of the Eucharist, this came to seem unsatisfactory. Instead, communion was increasingly included as the climax of a service, sometimes being celebrated on a weekly basis. This meant people, including children when they were present, were not encouraged to leave and the choice to participate or not was posed more starkly: should children be served with the bread and wine, and who should make this decision? Should it be the children themselves, a parent or those serving communion (possibly putting them in an awkward position)? More importantly, if children were permitted to participate in one dominical sacrament, on what basis were they refused the other, baptism? Moreover since communion was open and neither believers baptism nor any other kind were stipulated as prerequisites but only faith, what was the basis for refusing children communion when they showed evidence of faith? Practically speaking, open communion reverses the likely order of the sacraments since worshippers are more likely to encounter a communion than a baptismal service: first communion, then baptism. Again, practically, because baptism is a once for all and very public act and communion a repeated and more or less private (although in company with others) rite, the decision to be baptised is made more slowly. All of these changes have happened without the longer-term consequences necessarily having been assessed.

The choice here is quite difficult: either return to the practice of closed communion and closed membership or bring some kind of order to the practice of open communion. The first option is almost unthinkable for those who wish to see the church fashioned as an open community.[57] The second may be more untidy but there can still be coherent disciplines of various kinds. This is one: communion is an open meal to be shared by all who love Christ and trust in him. It is a way in which people are drawn among the people of God into the deeper life of the body. As Jesus ate and drank with sinners, so in the communion issues of correctness, although still important, are secondary to matters of open and gracious acceptance. Children are included in this and appropriate disciplines are necessary for discerning in them, and indeed in everybody, the faith which enables them to eat and drink. For children, this is an educational and guidance process best carried through by parents, appropriately instructed and informed about the signs of true faith. Children of the age of accountability, which might credibly be agreed as thirteen or fourteen, may request and receive communion from those who serve. Other children of faith can be served by their parents. All other children and adults who desire may receive the blessing with the laying on of hands. Nobody is left out. But baptism, as a once for all event, still marks a threshold into the way of discipleship. Open communion need not imply an immediate access to baptism for children any more than it does for others who are welcome at the table. First the evidence must be there not only that there is faith to receive but the will to take up the cross and follow wholeheartedly after Christ.

Notes

1 Donald M. Baillie, *The Theology of the Sacraments* (London: Faber & Faber, 1957), 80–82.
2 G.R. Beasley-Murray, *Baptism Today and Tomorrow*, 103.
3 Ernest A. Payne, *The Fellowship of Believers: Baptist Thought and Practice Yesterday and Today* (London: Carey Kingsgate Press, 1944).
4 Jewett, *Infant Baptism and the Covenant of Grace*, 116–19.
5 Doctrine and Worship Committee, Baptist Union of Great Britain, *Believing and Being Baptized: Baptism, So-called Re-baptism and the Children of the Church* (Didcot: Baptist Union, 1996), 41–42. The Baptist Union Report on 'The Child and the Church' (1966) cites the words of an early Baptist writer, John Tombes (d. 1676): 'The children of believers are born into the bosom of the Church': Hayden (ed.), *Baptist Union Documents, 1948–1977*, 220.
6 Acts 2:39.
7 Luke 15:3, 9, 32; 19:10.
8 Ephesians 2:1, 4.
9 Ephesians 2:3.
10 Matthew 19:14.
11 1 Corinthians 15:22; see also Romans 5:15–21.
12 *www.questinstitute.co.uk/dynamic/resources/memory.pdf.*

13 Alistair McFadyen, *Bound to Sin: Abuse, Holocaust and the Christian Doctrine of Sin* (Cambridge: Cambridge University Press, 2000).

14 Ephesians 2:3.

15 Romans 5:12.

16 Romans 5:6–8.

17 Romans 5:13–14.

18 Romans 7:21–25.

19 Deuteronomy 1:39.

20 Numbers 14:29–31.

21 Matthew 18:1–14; 19:14.

22 'Son' or 'daughter of the commandment'.

23 'The Child and the Church', 212, 214.

24 John Calvin, *The First Epistle of Paul to the Corinthians* (Edinburgh: Saint Andrew Press, 1960), 149: 'But the fact that the apostle ascribes a special blessing to the children of believers here [7:14] has its source in the blessing of the covenant, by whose intervention the curse of nature is destroyed, and also those who were by nature unclean are consecrated to God by his grace.'

25 Genesis 18:25.

26 John 14:8.

27 Deuteronomy 10:18; 24:19; Psalm 10:14, 18; 146:9; Jeremiah 22:3.

28 Charles Haddon Spurgeon believed that finally the number of the saved would be greater than that of the lost: 'We know that infants enter the kingdom, for we are convinced that all of our race who die in infancy are included in the election of grace, and partake in the redemption wrought out by our Lord Jesus. Whatever some may think, we believe that the whole spirit and tone of the word of God, as well as the nature of God himself, lead us to believe that all who leave this world as babes are saved': *The Metropolitan Tabernacle Pulpit* Volume 24 (Passadena TX: Pilgrim Publications, 1972), 583. See also Spurgeon, *Infant Salvation: A Sympathetic Word to Bereaved Parents* (London: Passmore and Alabaster, no date), 13–17.

29 2 Peter 3:9.

30 John 3:17.

31 Matthew 18:10.

32 Psalm 34:7–8; 91:9–12.

33 1 Corinthians 7:14.

34 Exodus 19:16–25 and *passim*.

35 Colossians 1:13; 1 Corinthians 5:5.

36 Report on 'The Child and the Church', 210.

37 Ephesians 5:25–27; Revelation 21:2.

38 Romans 8:11.
39 Williams, *Radical Reformation*, 135.
40 A history of the rite is given in W.M.S. West, 'The Child and the Church: A Baptist Perspective', in William H. Brackney and Paul S. Fiddes (eds.), *Pilgrim Pathways: Essays in Baptist History in Honour of B.R. White* (Macon, GA: Mercer University Press, 1999), 75–110.
41 1 Samuel 1:21–28; 2:11.
42 Luke 2:22-24; Leviticus 12:2–6.
43 Luke 2:25–38.
44 Mark 10:14.
45 Matthew 19:13–15; Luke 18:15–17.
46 Genesis 27:1–29.
47 Genesis 49.
48 1 Kings 8:14
49 Numbers 6:22–27.
50 Suggestions can be found in Baptist Union of Great Britain, *Patterns and Prayers for Christian Worship* (Oxford: Oxford University Press, 1991), 109–17.
51 Numbers 6:22–27.
52 P. Beasley-Murray, *Radical Believers*, 45.
53 Acts 8:36 [and 37?].
54 John Westerhoff, *Bringing up Children in the Christian Faith* (Minneapolis: Winston Press, 1980), 26–28.
55 Matthew 16:24–28; Luke 14:27.
56 Marlin Jeschke, *Believers Baptism for the Children of the Church* (Scottdale, PA: Herald Press, 1983), 112–24. Jeschke speaks of 'accountable' and 'covenanted' faith.
57 Wright, *New Baptists, New Agenda*, chapter 5.

8. Ministers and Members

Ordination and Enabling

Introduction

Any organisation that intends to endure through time and be effective will quickly lay down certain principles and patterns. It needs to appoint leaders, to work out its beliefs and purpose, its values and culture, to establish ways of working and to develop rituals and practices. The Christian churches are no different in any of these respects, but they must be distinctive and true to their own sources in Christ and their identity in him. Above all, Jesus made it clear that in his community leadership was to be done differently. In Matthew 20:24–28 he says,

> You know that the rulers of the Gentiles lord it over them, and their great ones are tyrants over them. It will not be so among you; but whoever wishes to be great among you must be your servant, and whoever wishes to be first among you must be your slave; just as the Son of Man came not to be served but to serve, and to give his life a ransom for many.

In a parallel passage in Luke 22:24–30 there is a significant variation with the words 'and those in authority over them are called benefactors', being added (v. 25). Those who exercise power over others often clothe themselves with ideology and present themselves in a benevolent light: but the inner reality remains the exercise of domination. This has been the free-church criticism of the system of sacred power that for a long time masqueraded as the church of Christ: the legitimating ideology was that of shepherding the flock, the inner reality was that of domination and it stands contrary to the way of Jesus Christ who presents himself to us as the one whose self-sacrificing service we are to imitate.

A Christian understanding of the role of leaders is therefore twofold. On the one hand, there is the undoubted need for them to be proactive and to exercise authority; it is after all not good enough for leaders passively to wait for others to take all the initiatives. On the other hand, there is the expectation that all this will be done not for the sake of domineering over others or to pursue self-interests but to serve others and the purpose of the church self-sacrificially. Jesus, whom we imitate, succeeded in both these ways, being proactive and exercising authority and doing it all in the spirit of the servant.

The Leadership of Some and the Ministry of All

In a Christian understanding of ministry all Christians are called to serve (minister) within the church and the world. Ministry is a shared characteristic of the whole church.[1] The New Testament abolishes any idea of the rulers and the ruled, the latter existing for the sake of the former, and replaces it with a concept that applies to all: *diakonia* or service. In the church only Jesus Christ rules. In order to serve all are given gifts. From the exercise of gifts there develop 'ministries' and sometimes ministries need to be recognised in specific offices, such as those of the pastor or teacher, the elder or deacon.[2] If the personal, collegial and communal dimensions of oversight all belong to the church, here we concentrate on the personal dimension, and its exercise in a collegial form.

We have several times encountered the idea of the priesthood of all believers. Priesthood, which in the Old

Testament is defined by descent from the families of Aaron or Zadok and therefore is a limited status, is in the New Testament generalised to all and defined by gifting and call. The church is a royal priesthood. In the New Testament the term 'priest' (and related terms) is never used of a dedicated office within the church other than that which is occupied by Jesus Christ himself, who is our great high priest.[3] Otherwise, the church as a whole is a priesthood to God, offering sacrifices of thanksgiving and service. All believers together constitute the priesthood.

Within this general commitment to ministry on the part of all, *some* are called to particular spheres of ministry. The Roman Catholic Church distinguishes at this point between the 'royal priesthood' of all believers and the 'ministerial priesthood' of the ordained. Historically, this has sometimes been interpreted as 'clergy' and 'laity'. 'Clergy' has a dual meaning in that it can be derived from 'clerk' (so 'clerk-in-holy-orders'); this refers to the fact that at one time only the clergy were educated and could write. It may also derive from *kleros* meaning 'inheritance', and imply that the clergy are a special possession of God. 'Laity' derives from the Greek *laos*, meaning 'the people'. The use of clergy-laity language can be unfortunate if it implies a radical distinction between the two such as 'officers and soldiers', giving to the former a form of rank or a set of powers which it exercises over the latter including, in a system of sacred power, the right to command. However, there is also a distinction here between 'professional' and 'non-professional', between those who make their living by serving the church and those who make it elsewhere. In this sense, 'laity' can be a hard word to avoid using without having to substitute whole sentences for it.

Over recent years, it has been correctly argued that the relationship between the some who lead and the many who minister in other ways is not primarily that of rank or command but of enabling and equipping. The *locus classicus* for this is Ephesians 4:11–13:

> The gifts he gave were that some would be apostles, some prophets, some evangelists, some pastors and teachers, to equip

the saints for the work of ministry, for building up the body of Christ, until all of us come to the unity of the faith, and of the knowledge of the Son of God, to maturity, to the measure of the full stature of Christ.

Varied ministries are given to serve the body by enabling it to minister as a whole. The distinctions are distinctions of gift and contribution with the intention that all are engaged in the one task of building the body of Christ into a unity. The ministries are given perpetually, throughout the church's existence in time, since the completion of the work of growing into maturity and unity is eschatological.

Discussion of the church has often become in the more catholic traditions a debate about 'holy orders' on the grounds that if properly ordained ministers are essential for the *esse* of the church, for its very right to be called church, the search is on for those who are 'proper'. However, this understanding is problematic because ecclesiology risks becoming 'hierarchology'. The early episcopocentric idea that the true church can be identified because it is where the bishop is became a discussion about valid ordination in the episcopal tradition and therefore about the preconditions for the proper administration of the sacraments. In reaction to such 'clericalism' or 'sacerdotalism', a fixation on priesthood, some believers churches have gone to another extreme in rejecting any kind of hierarchy and insisting on radical equality, as with some branches of the Quakers. This extends to the rejection of any kind of presidency in meetings for worship and, of course, of any sacraments. Others have rejected the priestly and episcopal tradition and yet reinvented similar forms of hierarchical ministry, as was the case with some early Restorationists.[4] This has moderated in time.

There is a genuine tension here. Leaders or ministers are given to enable the ministry of all. But the ministry of all does not just happen – it is brought about in large measure through the ministries of those who are specifically gifted, called, 'ordained' and authorised to enable it to happen. Those whom Christ gives for specific offices of ministry might best be seen as catalysts for the life of the body as a whole, but, thankfully, they are not the only ones. A crucial distinction can be made here between a 'hierarchical' view, which always sees the transmission of authority as working from top to below, and an 'ordered' view, which recognises the value of offices of leadership and ministry but insists that they must be validated and appointed 'from below'. Baptists are in the second of these traditions. An alternative way to express this is to say that although believers churches reject a priestly hierarchy they do accept and respect a 'hierarchy of responsibility' (as the New Testament clearly does) within the church.

The Origins of the Ministries

Jesus is portrayed as taking great care in the appointment of the first apostles. He went up into a high mountain (presumably to pray) and 'called to him those whom he wanted, and they came to him'.[5] The twelve whom Jesus called were symbolic of the twelve tribes of Israel which Jesus in his ministry was renewing. From his larger band of disciples Jesus formally and identifiably appointed these twelve to be 'with him' as his close companions, named them 'apostles', which means 'those who are sent', and authorised them to preach and to have authority to cast out demons. Later on, Jesus commissioned them for a specific mission and added to what has been said the power to cure diseases and to heal.[6] On a further occasion, Jesus appointed seventy and commissioned them in a similar way to go before him. The seventy here are reminiscent of the seventy elders anointed by God to assist Moses in his task.[7]

In these actions of Jesus we are entitled to see a pattern for the continuing work of the ascended Lord in the church, for which he perpetually provides. Christ continues to call those whom he chooses; as they respond they also are identifiably appointed within his community as those commissioned to preach, to heal and to have authority in Christ's name over evil influences. They are sent by Christ to be received by others as Christ's own, indeed, as Christ himself.[8] In due course Jesus strengthened the authority of the first apostles by bestowing upon them the power to bind and loose,[9] and by giving to Peter particularly the command to 'feed my sheep'.[10] This is the apostolic ministry and in its fundamental task it cannot be said to be valid only for the first generation of believers. It is certainly the case that as the primary witnesses to the life of Christ and the resurrection, the twelve, with readjustment for the defection of Judas and then the anomalous but valid inclusion of Paul, performed a unique and historically unrepeatable function.[11] They therefore had a normative authority which belonged to them alone and which formed the basis for the formation of the New Testament canon which now constitutes that norm. But in all other aspects of their commission – preaching, healing and liberating in the name of Christ, the apostolic ministry is perpetuated by the continuing activity of the risen Lord in the church and the process of appointing and commissioning new generations of leaders. So it is that in the early church James, Barnabas, Stephen, Philip, Prisca and Acquila, Apollos, Silas, Timothy, Titus, Luke, Mark, Junia and a host of others, named or otherwise, emerged by a process of spontaneous generation and community recognition to serve as leaders. Paul and Barnabas on their missionary journeys selected and appointed elders in each church with prayer and fasting, handing over immediate pastoral care of each church to them.[12]

The later writings of the New Testament give evidence that the securing of the apostolic succession in ministry became a vital issue as the church progressed from the first to the second generation: '(W)hat you have heard from me through many witnesses entrust to faithful people who will be able to teach others also.'[13] In view here is a process of tradition, of 'handing on' the gospel and responsibility for teaching it. Four generations are involved: that of Paul representing the apostolic generation, of Timothy which was the immediate heir to it, then those who would be trained and taught by Timothy to succeed him, and a further generation, as yet out of sight, which those teachers would teach. It is entirely correct then to speak both of an apostolic tradition and of an orderly transition in ministry. But essentially the tradition is not safeguarded *externally* by the act of laying on of hands from one generation to another but *internally* by faithfulness to the apostolic testimony; and that testimony is the property and responsibility not of ministers alone but of the 'household of God, which is the church of the living God, the pillar and bulwark of the truth'.[14] The true apostolic tradition is the faithful transmission of the original testimony to Jesus Christ. That handing on is still happening and it works in the same way: by the free activity of the Spirit in generating gifts and awakening members of the church to a sense of call and the recognition and validation by the churches of those who have the capacity to fulfil the task.

The Pattern of the Ministries

In summary, the pattern of New Testament ministries should be seen as flexible rather than rigid, as admitting variety and as being adaptable to local custom and circumstance. There is principled accommodation to the needs of the situation and this should warn us against taking a single order from Scripture that acts as a 'one-size-fits-all' template. However, just as the same needs arise consistently, so patterns of ministry have a general consistency to them. For instance, we can distinguish roughly in the New Testament between translocal and local ministries, those which were intended as gifts to the wider church and those which fulfilled their mission in the local.

Translocal ministries

Ephesians 4 is, once more, a key passage and sets out a number of offices or assignments in the service of the church: apostles, prophets, evangelists, pastor and teachers. As with other such lists, Paul is probably identifying representative ministries rather than an exhaustive set.[15] Debates about whether this order is fivefold, fourfold (pastors and teachers being one ministry) or even sixfold (there being pastors, teachers and pastor-teachers) only serve to warn against being too rigid or prescriptive in interpretation. On the other hand, if the ministries are a perpetual provision of what is needed there will be a recurring pattern or what can be called a 'stable underlying pattern of office'[16] from generation to generation. We are wise to identify those patterns and to order our own thinking around them. It would be wrong to do this in a tight and restrictive way. Those who are pastors may, indeed should, also function as evangelists;[17] prophets can also be teachers and vice versa; apostles may be excellent pastors and are nothing if not evangelists. The boundaries between these ministries are porous and which is dominant may depend on particular assignments at specific times. But the whole range of ministry is required by the church if it is to mature.

To call these ministries 'translocal' is to acknowledge that they are not limited in service or jurisdiction[18] to one congregation but belong to the wider church of Christ. This is the context in which Paul places them. They are therefore transferable ministries and those who exercise them might well expect to be re-assigned from time to time. This precise point about jurisdiction is an area of disagreement among Baptists some of whom have insisted that to be a minister is to be at the head of a local Baptist church and to be confined as a minister to it,[19] while others have been equally insistent that ministers represent the whole church of Christ and are the representatives in the local of the catholic church, its teachings and its sacraments.[20] The ordained ministry on this view is universal and acts as a stewardship of the Word and sacrament entrusted to and standing over the universal church.[21] The disagreement here is reflected in other ways in baptist thinking.[22] The position taken here favours the more universal point of view. The proving of gifts on a local basis is of course essential; but since the church is not only local but a communion of churches, ministries are properly located in both spheres and both local and translocal manifestations can call and send ministries in their name.

It is appropriate to ask in what sense it remains possible to speak of apostles and prophets within the underlying patterns of ministry provided in perpetuity for the church. The term 'apostle' is used in the New Testament with a degree of latitude. There were clearly the original apostles who were the normative witnesses to the resurrection, who were intrinsically unrepeatable, and any claim to this status in the later church is both absurd and bogus. But there was a wider group of apostles in the early missions of the church, including James, Barnabas and others[23] who were involved in building the church and in the outward and cross-cultural thrust into the Mediterranean world. In this missionary sense, the ministry of apostles may be seen as both renewable and perpetual 'until'[24] the church finally attains its goal. This aspect of the apostolic ministry came to be separated out and continued in the ministry of the bishop which emerged in the second century. Although this is thought of by episcopalians as 'the apostolic ministry' the word 'bishop' is derived from one of the two New Testament words for 'elder', which were *presbyteros* and *episkopos*. This usage shows a degree of sense in that to be called bishop rather than apostle avoids confusion; it also designates a ministry by means of a word the New Testament itself uses and so maintains continuity. Prophets differed from teachers in not only passing on the tradition but having a degree of inspiration in the Spirit which was extraordinary, and in the case of Agabus, powers of accurate prediction.[25] Considerable dangers lurk at this point and putative prophets have worked their share of destruction in the history of the church by claims to predict the future. Perhaps the kind of prophetic ministry most to be desired is exemplified in the Old Testament by the people of Issachar, 'who had understanding of the times, to know what Israel ought to do'.[26] The ministry of the prophet is not about new revelation but about the application of the revelation of the ways of God in Christ to changing times and unforeseen circumstance. Those who are gifted for this are to be prized in every generation as the Word is made newly relevant.

Within the catholic tradition the underlying pattern of ministry is seen to be threefold: bishops, presbyters (priests) and deacons (or assistant ministers).[27] The order of bishops exercises translocal jurisdiction, presbyters are their local representatives and deacons act as assistants in the local church. Some Baptists have also acknowledged a threefold order which it has defined as messenger, elder and deacon: messengers are trusted pastors called to a wider sphere of service among several churches, elders are pastors who have oversight of local churches, and deacons are lay leaders in those congregations who assist both in overseeing the churches and stewarding their affairs. Other Baptists have seen a twofold order of elders and deacons: if there are messengers they are simply 'extruded' elders.[28]

Local ministries

Meshing in with the translocal are roles and offices which are concerned with serving the local congregation. These are identified as elders and deacons and precise directions are given in the Pastoral Epistles about the necessary qualifications for both.[29] The roles and the terms which designate them seem to be borrowed from the organisation of the synagogue which would function as a natural model for early Christian congregations with a core of Jewish believers. The precise differences between these roles is not set out, but the terms themselves and the qualities listed suggest that elders were concerned with general oversight, possibly the ministry of the Word and prayer, whereas deacons were devoted to ministries of assistance and help perhaps among the needy.[30] Both roles required spiritual maturity and the frequent distinction between elders who are engaged in the spiritual and deacons who do the practical reflects modern dualism rather than biblical spirituality. Translocal ministries mesh into the local offices when they are exercised locally and may be considered part of the eldership at this point, as Peter describes himself.[31] In more contemporary terms, elderships may be composed of both 'professional' and 'lay' people or of translocal and local ministries, although the dominant Baptist custom up until recently in the United Kingdom has been to see the 'professional' ministries as the eldership and deacons as lay ministries. Globally, the variety among baptists at this point is considerable.

Ordination

Baptists have from the beginning practiced ordination according to their own understanding and even from the nineteenth century accorded the title 'Reverend' to their ministers.[32] Local churches were responsible for testing a call to ministry, sometimes over a lengthy period, and for calling their own pastors. They believed themselves fully competent to discern a call from God and to perform the ordinations of those called. Gradually, other ministers became involved in the laying on of hands and with the further growth of theological education and forms of accreditation in the twentieth century, ministerial recognition and ordination became more of a denominational process and decision. Ordination implied recognition of a charismatic *ordering* or *ordinance* of ministry in the church by the Lord himself. However, some Baptists and others in the believers churches have had hesitations about ordination, some failing to find a biblical basis for it[33] and others believing that it separated ministers out too much from the churches into a clerical class. They have preferred to speak of pastors and others being 'recognised' and 'commissioned' but not ordained. Behind this reaction there is confusion about what is intended by the act or rite of ordination. Some struggle to disassociate the language from the theory of priestly and sacerdotal ministry which confers special sacramental powers on some and denies them to others. This is felt to conflict with the idea of a fundamental equality in the body of Christ. It needs to be tested therefore whether there is a biblical basis for ordination and what powers, if any, it is intended to confer.

There is no doubt that there was a clear concept of ordination to priesthood in the Old Testament and that this was restricted to certain elite families in Israel.[34] This is transformed in the New Testament into the royal priesthood of all believers. There is point therefore in arguing that baptism is a kind of ordination and that when believers are baptised it is into the messianic anointing that came upon Jesus in his baptism and which enables them to carry forward his mission.

With the loss of both Temple and priesthood, the Jewish people found a precedent for rabbinic ordination, conferring a teaching rather than a priestly role, in the way Moses laid hands on Joshua, bestowing upon him both the spirit of wisdom and authority.[35] It is possible that rabbinic ordination had some influence on emergent Christianity; however, even before this the New Testament witnesses to rudimentary practices of commissioning or ordination. Jesus called and appointed the twelve, as noted. The apostles appointed the seven chosen by the Jerusalem church with the laying on of hands and prayer as they stood before them.[36] The church leaders in Antioch were told by the Spirit to 'set apart Barnabas and Saul for the work to which I have called them' and sent them off with fasting, prayer and the laying on of hands.[37] In turn, Paul and Barnabas 'appointed' elders to succeed them (the word in Greek suggests with the laying on of hands).[38] Paul reminds Timothy to 'rekindle the gift of God that is within you through the laying on of my hands',[39] and says, 'Do not neglect the gift that is in you, which was given to you by the laying on of hands by the council of elders.'[40] Paul also advises Timothy, 'Do not ordain [or lay hands upon] anyone hastily.'[41] If these events constitute commissioning or 'leadership affirmation', but not ordination, it is difficult to know what the difference is. Commissioning may, indeed, denote prayer and appointment to a time-limited task or mission; and ordination may more strongly imply being set aside for an enduring and open-ended life commitment. But the two are so close it is hardly worth arguing about. At any rate, to say there is no biblical basis for ordination is short of the mark: the basis is as strong as for other practices of the church.

The key issue is the meaning of ordination. Clearly, individuals are being identified for particular ministries and given both formal recognition and authorisation by the church to fulfil them. The ministries to which they are appointed are offices within the church of a local or translocal nature. Although believers are equal in the body of Christ, there is also within this a distinction of service and function which requires that certain roles are accorded recognition by the church for their proper exercise. Ordination involves a re-ordering of relationships in that once ordained to office some members of the church are no longer just members: they serve for the good of the church in particular offices necessary to the church's well-being and should be accorded the respect due to those offices.[42] This also involves a representative role in that they are mandated by the church to represent it to the wider church and to the wider community. In the baptist traditions, neither commissioning nor ordination is understood to empower any sacerdotal function in the liturgy of the church. However, this does not exclude the fact that within the priesthood of all believers those in office will mediate God's grace and blessing to those whom they serve: this is a desirable 'priestly' ministry of which, of course, all believers are potentially capable and that accrues added meaning when mediated in a representative capacity. Furthermore, it might be expected both that those who are ordained in this way will feel it laid upon them as a charge and duty to live in accordance with their office and that God will answer the prayers that are made on their behalf at their ordination. Once more, ordination is more than a 'mere' symbol: it becomes a means of grace. This by no means implies that the ministries of those who are not ordained will be in any way inferior to those who are. The New Testament testifies that the divine if irregular spontaneity evident in the commissioning of a Saul,[43] or the unaccountable but exciting appearance of an Apollos,[44] can never be fully legislated for. There will always be a creative interaction between the spontaneous working of the Spirit in the church and responsible attempts to order the life of the community. The practice of ordination is both appropriate for those who believe in the freedom and order of the church and wise as a way of undergirding ministries and giving stability to them. Following the biblical precedent makes sense. Ordination provides an opportunity not only for the local church but for the wider communion of churches and churches of other traditions to affirm and receive the ministries of those whom Christ is calling.

Ministry and 'Necessity'

In what ways should the ministries under discussion be described as 'necessary'? Earlier on we discussed the 'ecclesial minimum'; ministers did not figure for baptists as absolutely necessary in order for church to be church. In the catholic tradition it is deemed otherwise. For this tradition, 'the church is where the bishop is', so valid ministry belongs to the *esse* of the true church in so far as the historic episcopate connects and validates it. From 180 onwards, the authority of the Roman Church was consistently legitimated by the claim to an unbroken chain of transmission from Peter and the apostles through the bishops of Rome. To be sure, this tradition struggles to find evidence that its version of the historic episcopate is any more than pious romance justifying the growing hegemony of the Roman Church, a fact sometimes recognised most clearly by Catholic historians.[45] As the Roman Catholic theologian Hans Küng identifies, 'According to this view the whole responsibility and authority of Peter lived on in the Roman bishop, an idea from which, with increasing rapidity, fundamental juridical conclusions were drawn.'[46] There is a world of difference between seeing Peter as the first confessor of Jesus and as one with monarchical and legal jurisdiction or ruling authority over the whole church.[47]

Baptists have been more likely to insist that a church can be a church without a duly ordained minister;[48] but ministers belong most certainly to the *bene esse* of the church, to that which promotes its well-being, upbuilding and growth. They are given to the church to do it good and to enable it to thrive. No sooner do we think about the church engaging in mission than we must also think about the means and the people through whom this will be done, and here we identify ministries and ministers. However, some Baptists have insisted that ministers do indeed belong even to the *esse* of the church and that this was the belief of the earliest Baptists.[49] For one thing, a church cannot come into being unless someone is *sent* to bear the Word which enables people to call upon the name of the Lord. [50] The presence of a commissioned ministry is therefore implied in the very coming of a church into being. Both early Anabaptists and Baptists believed that the life of a Christian community needed to be under some kind of pastoral oversight and that this clearly belonged to the fundamental order of the church. A church was only completely organised when it had appointed elders and deacons and was constituted by 'officers and members', suggesting the importance of office for them.[51] We might say that whereas it is possible for believers to be church together as they meet for fellowship, they only become *a* church (that is an ordered community) once they have appointed some kind of oversight. Ministries are vital for the *bene esse* of the church; for its *esse* they are *almost* necessary, but not quite absolutely. Ordered communities of disciples at the very least will need the local ministries of elders and deacons (however they are in fact designated) and it is in the very act of appointing such ministries that a group begins to become a church. In addition, they are wise to seek the oversight of the translocal ministries in order that they may have the benefit of those gifts and people Christ bestows on the church for its growth into maturity and unity with the whole body of Christ.

A related question here concerns whether it is possible to celebrate the sacraments of baptism and communion without ministers presiding at them. This has been argued by Catholics, at least in the case of communion, on the grounds that the priest alone has the sacred power to transform the bread and wine at communion into Christ's body and blood. For some Protestants, communion is one of the church's 'norming norms' and so only those who are duly appointed as guardians of the church's teaching should preside. The first of these restrictions is for sacerdotal and the second for disciplinary reasons. Both would agree that whereas ministers should baptise whenever possible,[52] there are 'emergency baptisms' which any lay person could perform. Baptists have been more ambivalent on the issue of communion. Some have argued that only ordained ministers should preside either for simple reasons of discipline and good order, or because for them not to do this would mean that the ministry is only *convenient* for the church and not *necessary*.[53] On this view, the practice of 'lay presidency' among Baptists came out of necessity because of the growing number of churches and as a defiant reaction in the nineteenth century against Anglo-Catholicism. Its potential danger is in undermining the 'need, nature and function' of the pastoral ministry, although this might be mitigated by asserting that whereas pastors preside by right of office others must be specifically invited by the church to do so.[54] For others, the sacraments belong properly to the universal church of which ministers are representatives, therefore the task of ministers is to mediate into the local sphere what belongs to the whole church and they are the appropriate persons to do so. Because the Word and sacraments order the life of the church in a definitive way their administration belongs in a peculiar way with those ordained as ministers of the whole church.[55] Generally, this is resisted as too great a concession to the catholic way. The counter insistence is made that the sacraments belong to the church not to the ministers of the church, and if the universal church is really manifested in the local congregation this empowers those congregations to administer the sacraments.

It is the church which preaches the Word and celebrates the sacraments, and it is the church which, through pastoral over-sight, feeds the flock and ministers to the world. It normally does these things through the person of its minister but not solely through him (sic). Any member of the church may be authorised by it, on occasion, to exercise the functions of the ministry, in accordance with the principle of the priesthood of all believers, to preach the word, to administer baptism, to preside at the Lord's table, to visit, and comfort and rebuke members of the fellow-ship.[56]

Notice here the cautionary note that the non-ordained still have to be 'authorised' by the church and cannot take the responsibility to preside at communion upon themselves. Baptists also believe in the sacramental importance of preaching and are happy that many should preach, ordained or otherwise. To claim that at communion only the ordained should preside is therefore to place communion on a higher plane than preaching. This does seem to be in conflict with fundamental baptist instincts. Generally, the preaching of the Word has been understood to provide the context in which the visible words of baptism and communion acquire significance.[57] More 'catholic' Baptists have appreciated the title 'ministers of Word and sacrament' with its suggestion that the sacraments belong especially to the ministerial task. Others have preferred the simpler term 'ministers of the gospel'. However, if the ministries are concerned with the oversight, upbuilding and ordering of the church, its teaching and practice then, even if ministers do not always preside themselves, it is still their responsibility as overseers to ensure that both baptism and communion are properly administered. In that sense, responsibility for the ministries of Word and sacrament cannot be evaded and the 'necessity' of ministers is located in their responsibility to be authoritative teachers and guardians of the faith.

Ministry and Authority

A consistent theme of this book has concerned the rejection of any practice of 'sacred power' in the sense that the church exercises power over people. The church is a community of disciples in which power is commonly owned, managed and distributed. Its members exercise power *with* but not *over* each other. This does not mean ministries within the church are *disempowered* but that they are appropriately *empowered* by the church according to what is believed to be the workings of the Spirit in gifting and enabling those ministries. Ministers should be seen therefore to possess genuine authority, and we have identified this as a hierarchy of *responsibility* rather than of *sacerdotal power*. Ultimately, this authority derives from the Word of which they are called by God to be bearers and interpreters, from the activity of the Spirit in gifting them for their task, from the understanding and insight that has been gained through experience and study, from the moral weight of their lives as disciples of Christ, from the call of a congregation to fulfil their vocation in or from its midst, and from the wider recognition of a communion of churches which has been involved in the process of testing and proving their ministry and the loving sacrifice they exhibit in imitation of Christ. This authority is not the power to command except in those rare instances when the object of the command is an evil influence which needs to be overcome in the name of Christ.[58] It will also be the authority to assert and guard those decisions and disciplines which have been agreed by congregations in fulfilling their calling and mission. However,

> In the Christian congregation...authority cannot be imposed but only won through humble service. This was the truth about authority embodied in Jesus himself (Mk 10:42–5). It is when pastors have won trust through their serving that people will allow them to lead them in initiating new things or putting an end to the old. No other authority is of any worth.[59]

Properly speaking spiritual authority comes from Christ to whom all authority is given in heaven and earth.[60] The church does not give authority except in the sense that it accords to ministries a spiritual authority which it has come to recognise and to which it adds its approbation. That authority is to be exercised with accountability towards God and the people of God.[61] Furthermore, despite the importance of the local church, that authority does not depend entirely upon local approbation since it also resides in that of the wider Christian community. Ministers therefore have – by virtue of their calling from and direct accountability to God and by reason also of their calling within the wider church which they represent and serve – an authority as teachers, prophets and guides, which may on occasion confront local congregations and be directed as a rebuke to them. This is especially the case when fundamental Christian teaching is at stake: ministers are entrusted with the stewardship of guarding the truth.[62] In part, this authority is *conferred* by the ordination of some to office but, more importantly, it is *acquired* through faithful exercise of that office over time. To balance things, the faithful church is itself 'the pillar and bulwark of the truth' and as such has a reciprocal authority and right to confront deviation from the truth in those it appoints as ministers.[63] The tasks of ministry include promoting and maintaining those ways of life which are in accordance with Christ. This is the authority of 'oversight', of watching, protecting and guiding the people of God. In this sense, and without any feeling of 'sacred power', ministers are said in Scripture to be 'over' the people of God,[64] to 'have charge'[65] of them and even to 'rule' in the church.[66] Believers are enjoined to submit to them and even obey them.[67] Modern people tend to find this language difficult but it should not for that reason be avoided. Within the church there are real expressions of spiritual authority which we are called to welcome and receive, but they are based on trust, mutual respect and willing acceptance and are not intended to deprive believers at any point of their freedom in Christ and their conscientious responsibility before God or for themselves.

Ordination and commissioning, then, may be seen as ways in which spiritual calling and authority is recognised and accorded. It clearly implies that those so ordained remain dependent upon and accountable to the churches which assign them to these roles. Experience suggests that assignments, gifts and ministries vary in nature: some are given for a moment, some for a season and others for a lifetime. We have indicated that baptism may be seen as a form of ordination in that all believers are anointed by the Spirit for service. However, God's provision of distinct local and translocal ministries, and New Testament precedent, suggest that particular moments of commissioning and ordination with the laying on of hands are appropriate for some or all of these offices. Accordingly, some baptist churches ordain deacons and elders as well as pastors, evangelists and others to their ministry. Clearly, what is distinctive here is not ordination as such but the office to which one is appointed. Others commission local but ordain translocal ministries as a way of indicating that whereas local ministries might be for a season, translocal ones are longer lasting and probably even lifelong. Once more, we do not necessarily seek the 'right' practices here, only responsible ones. Paul's injunction to Timothy, 'Do not ordain anyone hastily', perhaps suggests that this rite is to be used sparingly.[68]

Two rules of thumb might help us: *Commissioning* is appropriate when the local office in view involves some oversight of a congregation and when it is considered to be an enduring office in the church: this commission is relevant to the local congregation in which the assignment is fulfilled and is not necessarily transferable. *Ordination* is appropriate when the ministry in view falls within the spread of translocal ministries as a ministry of the wider church and is transferable within the communion of churches which have had a say in its testing and recognition. This is indeed a 'setting apart'[69] for ministry, but this should not be interpreted to suggest that those so ordained form a separate class. They remain first of all members of the church who have been called from within the church to 'stand before' it in a particular ministry.[70] They exist to enable and enhance the ministry of all in an intentional and proactive way, not to encourage a passive 'laity' by reserving to the 'ministry' all the work of service.

Those who are set aside for ministry have in principle the right to be supported financially in what they do and to make their living from the gospel, even if they choose not to make use of this.[71] 'Those who are taught the word must share in all good things with their teacher.'[72] It appears that Jesus also was supported financially by those who were in a position to do so.[73] It would be entirely wrong for ministers of Christ to enrich themselves by means of their work and position, but the principle that they have a right to share in the common wealth of God's people suggests they should be supported at a level commensurate with that of those they serve. To do this is both a sign of the value placed upon their work and of the proper honour shown to them.[74]

Ministry: A Positive Vision

The danger of any high vision of Christian ministries is that it might be thought to suggest a correspondingly low vision of the people of God as a whole. At this point, as at others, Christian theology requires to hold important truths together and see the connection between the two. The health of the Christian ministry and that of the church are organically and essentially related. Healthy churches give rise to healthy ministries which in turn inspire healthy churches. The effective ministry of the whole people of God is the goal in view and will not be brought to pass without those enabling and commissioned ministries bestowed by Christ for our lasting good.

Notes

1. Ephesians 4:11–13; WCC, *Baptism, Eucharist and Ministry*, 20–21.
2. 1 Corinthians 12:4–11, 27–31.
3. Hebrews 7:26; 9:11. It is sometimes argued that the word 'priest' is a shortened form of 'presbyter' and therefore refers to a teaching elder rather than a sacerdotal ministry: Gordon Kuhrt, *An Introduction to Christian Ministry* (London: Church House Publishing, 2000), 9.
4. Wright, *Radical Kingdom,* chapter 5.
5. Mark 3:13–19.
6. Luke 9:1–6.
7. Luke 10:1–12; Numbers 11:16–25.
8. Matthew 10:40–42.
9. Matthew 16:19; 18:18; John 20:21–23.
10. John 21:17.
11. Acts 1:21–22; 1 Corinthians 9:1.
12. Acts 14:23.
13. 2 Timothy 2:2.
14. 1 Timothy 3:15.
15. Compare Ephesians 4:11–13 with 1 Corinthians 12:27–31.
16. Doctrine and Worship Committee, Baptist Union of Great Britain, *Forms of Ministry among Baptists: Towards an Understanding of Spiritual Leadership* (Didcot, Baptist Union, 1994), 19.
17. 2 Timothy 4:5.
18. I am using this word in the sense of interpreting the law of God rather than imposing it.

19 Arthur Dakin, *The Baptist View of the Church and Ministry* (London: Baptist Union, 1944), 45

20 Payne, *Fellowship of Believers*, 38–40; Clark, 'The Fulness of the Church of God', 8: 'Theologically the minister is not essentially a congregational figure. He is the representative of the one body set within the congregation to promote its Christological ordering and its edification in love, and as such he (sic) is the living embodiment of catholicity.'

21 Neville Clark, *Preaching in Context: Word, Worship and the People of God* (Bury St Edmunds: Kevin Mayhew, 1991), 17–19.

22 Wright, *New Baptists New Agenda*, chapter 8.

23 Acts 14:14; Romans 16:7; Galatians 1:19; 1 Corinthians 15:7.

24 Ephesians 4:13.

25 Acts 11:27–30.

26 1 Chronicles 12:32.

27 J.B. Lightfoot classically traces this development in *St. Paul's Epistle to the Philippians*, 181–269.

28 These views are similar to evangelical Anglican understandings of bishops as 'senior presbyters': Timothy Bradshaw, *The Olive Branch: An Evangelical Anglican Doctrine of the Church* (Carlisle: Paternoster, 1992), 175.

29 1 Timothy 3:1–7 on elders or 'bishops' and 8–13 for deacons.

30 Compare 1 Timothy 3:2, 8 and Acts 6:2–4.

31 1 Peter 5:1–2.

32 The apparently unproblematic word 'minister' raises several issues on closer inspection. It is avoided by some because it is deemed that to call *some* by this name is to undermine the *many* who are called to minister. For preference, either more precise terms such as 'pastor' or alternative generic words such as 'leader' are employed. The New Testament is by no means as coy as this and happily uses the term (*leitourgos* or *diakonos*) of some ministries while also affirming the service of all: Romans 15:6; Ephesians 6:21; Colossians 1:7; 4:7. 'Minister' is simply a generic word for 'servant' and as such spans a variety of ministries including all those identified here as translocal and local. It has come to be used particularly of those who are 'professional' but in my view is misused when it becomes a synonym for pastor. On this basis evangelists are not ministers and pastors who are assigned to other roles, such as theological teaching, can be said to 'leave the ministry'. In fact these are just different forms of ministry. Generally, the Christian churches use a bewildering array of terms for describing its ministers and they are far from

being equivalent to each other.

33 John E. Toews, 'Rethinking the Meaning of Ordination: Towards a Biblical Theology of Leadership Affirmation', *The Conrad Grebel Review* 22.1 (Winter, 2004), 2–25.

34 Numbers 8.

35 Deuteronomy 34:9.

36 Acts 6:6.

37 Acts 13:1–3.

38 Acts 14:23.

39 2 Timothy 1:6.

40 1 Timothy 4:14.

41 1 Timothy 5:22.

42 1 Thessalonians 5:12–13.

43 1 Corinthians 15:8.

44 Acts 18:24–28.

45 'Neither Peter nor Paul founded the Church in Rome, for there were Christians in the city before either of the Apostles set foot there. Nor can we assume, as Irenaeus did, that the Apostles established there a succession of bishops to carry on their work in the city, for all the indications are that there was no single bishop at Rome for almost a century after the deaths of the Apostles. In fact, wherever we turn, the solid outlines of the Petrine succession at Rome seem to blur and dissolve.' Duffy, *Saints and Sinners*, 2.

46 Küng, *Church*, 446.

47 Küng, *Church*, 458.

48 In 1930 the Baptist Assembly agreed in response to the World Conference on Faith and Order at Lausanne in 1927 that, 'We cannot agree that the ministry, as commonly understood, is essential to the existence of a true Christian Church, though we believe a ministry is necessary for its highest effectiveness': Payne, *Fellowship of Believers*, 38.

49 Payne, *Fellowship of Believers*, 39.

50 Romans 10:14–16.

51 'A particular Church, gathered, and completely Organised according to the mind of Christ, consists of Officers, and Members; And the Officers appointed by Christ to be chosen and set apart by the Church (so called and gathered) for the peculiar Administration of Ordinances, and Execution of Power, or Duty, which he entrusts them with, or calls them to, to be continued to the end of the World are Bishops or Elders and Deacons': Second London Confession, 1677 and 1688, Chapter 26 Article 8,

Lumpkin, *Baptist Confessions of Faith*, 287 (spelling modernised). See also B.R. White, *Authority: A Baptist View* (London: Baptist Publications, 1976), 17.

[52] Although Paul did not seem keen to insist on his own rights in this regard: 1 Corinthians 1:17.

[53] Payne, *Fellowship of Believers*, 50.

[54] Payne, *Fellowship of Believers*, 58

[55] Neville Clark, *Pastoral Care in Context: Vision of God and Service of God* (Bury St Edmunds: Kevin Mayhew, 1992), 32–33.

[56] 'The Baptist Doctrine of the Church', in Hayden (ed.), *Baptist Union Documents 1948-1977*, 8.

[57] John Smyth, 'Propositions and Conclusions Concerning True Christian Religion 1612–1614', Article 74: 'That the sacraments have the same use as the word hath; that they are a visible word, and that they teach to the eye of them that understand as the word teacheth the ears of them that have ears to hear…' Lumpkin, *Baptist Confessions of Faith*, 138.

[58] Luke 10:17–20.

[59] Fiddes, *Participating in God*, 100.

[60] Matthew 28:18.

[61] Hebrews 13:17.

[62] 2 Timothy 1:13–14.

[63] 1 Timothy 3:15.

[64] Hebrews 13:17.

[65] 1 Thessalonians 5:12–13.

[66] 1 Timothy 5:17.

[67] Hebrews 13:17.

[68] 1 Timothy 5:22.

[69] Acts 13:2. The older term 'separated ministry', sounds somewhat severe to modern ears.

[70] One of the New Testament words translated as 'leading' literally means 'standing before': Romans 12:8.

[71] Romans 9:8–14.

[72] Galatians 6:6.

[73] Luke 8:1–3.

[74] 1 Timothy 5:17–18.

9. Relating and Resourcing

The Communion of Churches

Introduction

Baptists believe that the universal church of Jesus Christ is manifested in each local congregation of believers. For this reason, they have been strong in their commitment to the local church. But the church stretches beyond the local and some account needs to be given of how individual churches share in communion with other churches. In discussing the ecclesial minimum there was a missing element at this point. It is debatable whether any church can be truly church if it does not give recognition and demonstrate 'universal openness' to other churches.[1] Not to do this is to fail to 'discern the body'.[2] The same theological logic that undergirds the local church works for the wider church. If it is the presence of Christ in the gathering congregation that renders it competent, then that same Christ is present in the wider communion of churches and lends to it also an authority and wisdom that need to be heeded. It cannot be right therefore for churches defiantly to insist that they do not need other congregations or can exist without reference to them. The *competence* of the congregation was never meant to be an *omnicompetence* which removes the need for interdependence. If openness to others is a fundamental condition of the *esse* of the church, then supportive and co-operative fellowship certainly belong to the *bene esse* of the churches and the *plene esse* of the church will only be accomplished when all Christian congregations are working together in the bonds of the Spirit for the glory of God.

In rejecting the system of sacred power which the institutional church had become, baptists had also rejected the means by which some degree of uniformity was maintained in the churches of Christendom. It was inevitable that fragmentation should follow from this. The Catholic and Orthodox churches are by no means exempt from schism and division within themselves, but Protestants had opened a door which it proved difficult to shut. Separation from others can become a hard habit to break. The Protestant wing of the church has gone on fragmenting ever since for doctrinal, sociological, organisational and personality-based reasons. The spirit of separation often has a self-righteous and judgmental edge to it which renders it particularly unpleasant. Nonetheless, baptists insist that separation has sometimes been justified when issues by which the faith stands or falls have been at stake. There is also an argument, although a dubious one, to say that separation has led to a multiplicity of denominations which has assisted rather than hindered the church's expansion. But if the system of sacred power has been the fundamental flaw of the catholic tradition, the lack of concern for the unity of the church has been that of the baptists. It is not enough to insist that in the invisible church there is a spiritual unity that transcends the divisions. Such spiritual unity demands to be embodied in the real world, not appealed to as a Platonic form in some eternal realm beyond it. The prayer of Jesus, 'that they may become completely one, so that the world may know that you have sent me',[3] must be the decisive insight into what God wills for the whole church. At this point, baptists need to give responsible answers.

The Church: Local, Universal and Eschatological

Baptists have often insisted that there are only two dimensions to the church, the local and the universal.[4] The church is the sum total in heaven and earth of those who belong to Christ; it is manifested in the world in local congregations of those who believe. The baptist view has characteristically been that, properly speaking, there are no intermediate bodies or institutions which are entitled to the name 'church' in the usages we find such as the Methodist 'Church' or the Episcopalian 'Church'. Baptists have normally avoided this custom to describe the networks in which they come together, preferring more provisional terms such as association, union, convention, conference or fellowship. Although people frequently refer to the Baptist Church, this is not a self-designation because as a term it awakens within Baptist minds the fear of a centrally organised body which claims governmental authority over local congregations. The term might possibly be used of a gathering of Baptist believers in an assembly or synod, but the focus here would be upon the act of gathering not upon the permanent institutional form.

There is a further way in which it is possible to think about the two dimensions of the church. There is the church of the present and the church of the last day, and arguably this is the pattern the New Testament offers us.[5] Revelation 7 portrays a vision in which,

> there was a great multitude that no one could count, from every nation, from all tribes and peoples and languages, standing before the throne and before the Lamb, robed in white with palm branches in their hands. They cried out in a loud voice, saying 'Salvation belongs to our God who is seated on the throne, and to the Lamb!'[6]

This is a vision of the one, holy, catholic and apostolic church. It is the church that will be gathered in the presence of God in the fullness of time and in the fullness of its being. It does not currently fully exist but is coming into being. It is one because God is one and participation in God's life binds all its members together. It is holy because God is holy and has communicated holiness to all. It is catholic because it is a whole, incorporating within itself the diversity of humanity and excluding none who wish to enter. It is apostolic because it confesses the salvation that comes from God through Christ and lives to bear witness to it. What passes for church in the present is a provisional and incomplete but at the same time real anticipation of what is to come. When particular denominations take these four marks of the church and apply them exclusively to themselves (as for instance in the claim that the Roman Catholic Church is the one, holy, catholic and apostolic church) then they actually add to the failure of the church. The churches of the present are laid under an obligation to become what is revealed to be the will of God and to move towards it with intent. The four 'marks of the church' are not yet fully true of any one part of the church. They cannot be said to be our present possession, except by way of anticipation and promise; but they do set the agenda for the church of the present time.[7] They represent 'work in progress'. When Christians confess their faith in the one, holy, catholic and apostolic church they are proclaiming what will be the case and the cause which God in Christ is committed to bring to pass by the Spirit. The unity, cohesion and connectedness of the whole body of Christ is crucial for the fulfilment of God's purpose and any vision which does not lift up its eyes to see this will be faulty.

Associating and Association

British Baptists have traditionally chosen the word 'association' to describe their way for local churches to relate to each other in networks or communions of churches. It captures something of the gospel because in the body of Christ we need each other. The active participle 'associating' expresses this even more because it suggests a continuing activity in which we invest, not something we take for granted. The term also protects the freedom of local congregations from external compulsion and points to the essential insight: churches freely choose to relate to other congregations in order to express life together as the body of Christ more fully and for common purposes in the service of mission. No church has power over another, and no group of churches has power over individual churches. The only true power is the moral power created by love and mutual service.

This concept of association has been present among English Baptists since their beginnings in the sixteenth century. One of the earliest Baptist doctrinal statements was the Particular Baptist Confession agreed by seven local churches in London in 1644. It affirmed both the autonomy of the churches and their interdependence. We have previously noted Article thirty-six which states:

> Being thus joined, every Church has power given them from Christ for their better well-being, to choose to themselves meet persons into the office of Pastors, Teachers, Elders, Deacons, being qualified according to the Word, as those which Christ has appointed in his Testament, for the feeding, governing, serving and building up of his Church and that none other have any power to impose them, either these or any other.[8]

But Article forty-seven adds:

> And although the particular Congregations be distinct and several Bodies, every one a compact and knit City in itself; yet are they all to walk by one and the same Rule and, by all means convenient, to have the counsel and help of one another in all needful affairs of the Church, as members of one body in the common faith under Christ their only head.[9]

The later Confession of 1689 underlines this point:

> All members of each local church are engaged to pray continually for the good and the prosperity of all churches of Christ, wherever located, and upon all occasions to assist all other believers, within the limits of their own areas and callings, in the exercise of their gifts and graces. It follows therefore that churches should seek fellowship with one another, so far as the providence of God provides opportunity for the enjoyment of such benefits.[10]

A further statement indicates what this might mean:

> When difficulties or differences occur in respect of doctrine or church government and peace, unity and education are at risk, one church may be involved, or the churches in general may be concerned. Again, a member or members of a church may be injured by disciplinary proceedings not agreeable to the truth and church order. In such cases as these, it is according to the mind of Christ that many churches in fellowship together should meet and confer together through their chosen representatives, who are able to give their advice on the matters in dispute to all the churches concerned. It must be understood, however, that the representatives assembled are not entrusted with any church power properly so called, nor have they any jurisdiction over the churches themselves to exercise discipline upon any churches or persons, or to impose their conclusions on the churches or their officers.[11]

Churches, then, are to hold fellowship with each other for the purpose of mutual support and correction, but this must not be allowed to become the usurping of the freedoms or powers of any member church or the exercise of power by one church or groups of churches over another. What is envisaged is a free association of churches held together by mutual trust and moral authority.

Documents prepared for the inaugural meetings of the Abingdon Association in 1652 indicated the emerging theology of association. After affirming that churches ought to hold 'a firm communion with each other', the statement is supported by the argument that there is the same relationship between one church and another as there is between the members of one church. As each believer should be a part of a church for the purposes of mutual support and correction, so churches should manifest the same care over each other. Love between the churches is part of our love for all the saints and enables the work of God in which each church is engaged to be carried on. Churches may exhort, counsel and assist each other and the love expressed between them is a sign to the world of that love which enables churches to be recognised as true churches.[12]

It can be seen in these documents that belief in the competence of the local church does not preclude the need to be associating with other congregations. There is a struggle in evidence to manage power appropriately, to avoid the pattern of 'sacred power' while replacing it with high levels of moral authority and influence within the communion of churches. The *associating* of churches together became formalised into actual *associations* by agreeing confessions of faith and holding assemblies. Between 1640 and 1660 various associations formed in a way parallel to the regional associations called into being by the parliamentary forces in the English Civil War. Since then Baptist churches have commonly established associations or their equivalent wherever they have taken root.

The title to this chapter distinguishes between relating and resourcing and implicitly suggests that these are the two primary functions of associations. Relating amplifies the associating aspect of inter-church communion and indicates that the life of the people of God together consists primarily in the relationships they enjoy. In this they reflect the life of the Triune God and the essence of church, which is not first of all an institution but a communion of those who are related in Christ. Where depth of relationship between fellow Christian believers and their communities is lost, what is left becomes merely formal. But this is not to despise institutional form, especially if institution is understood most broadly as a 'stable pattern of relationship'. Miroslav Volf, as we have seen, enters this territory and suggests that even within God there can be said to be such a pattern of relations and that therefore sociality and institutionality are inseparable.[13] The way God has being can become the model for our own institutional ordering and places the emphasis on mutuality, participation and the distribution of power.[14]

There is likely to be institutional ordering in any project that aims to extend its life beyond the immediate generation; just as nothing *happens* without people so nothing *lasts* without institutions. This is what is intended by the word 'association': it is the institutional dimension to associating, the organisational pattern of resourcing, legal, financial and otherwise, which is constructed to serve in the preservation and extension of the Christian community. If this can err by being sheer form without relationship, then without association relationships on their own can also fall short in what they are practically capable of delivering. They need resourcing in varied ways to assist in the carrying forward of their project. How exactly these resources might take form will vary from culture to culture, but all cultures will require them in some way.

A Biblical Basis for Associating

How does all of this reflect the patterns of the early church? If New Testament theology is a guide to the ordering of the church, we might expect that both in principle and practice it will throw light on this dimension of the church's life.

The early Christian churches appear to have been loosely connected by means of networks of relationships stemming from the apostolic activity which had given rise to them. It is not inaccurate to describe this as a communion of essentially autonomous congregations. We see this emerging between the church in Samaria and that in Jerusalem as described in Acts 8. After the preaching of the gospel by Philip, many Samaritans responded and were baptised, but there was a delay in the manifest outpouring of the Holy Spirit until Peter and John came down from Jerusalem and laid hands on them.[15] Given the suspicion and hostility between Jews and Samaritans, the delay served the purpose of connecting the new church with the mother church in Jerusalem and sealing the relationship with the apostolic witnesses. In a similar fashion, when Gentiles in Antioch came to faith, the church in Jerusalem sent Barnabas to investigate the situation. He recognised the genuine nature of what was happening and was able to validate it and then, along with Saul, to teach and train the new believers.[16] Soon after, we find the church in Antioch sending financial help to Jerusalem. But then this church under the influence of the

Spirit became a strategic centre for further missionary work and a crucial community in forging the multi-ethnic identity of the new movement.[17] Romans 15:26 also speaks of contributions being made by the churches of Macedonia and Achaia for the poor of Jerusalem, and 16:1–2 of Phoebe, a minister of the church at Cenchreae, who is being commended to the Church in Rome.

Such verses offer a picture of widely scattered churches reaching out to each other in support and mutual affirmation, with travelling ministries, those of the apostles and others such as Prisca and Aquila,[18] making connections between them. The word 'associating' describes this process well. It was not the establishing of a graded hierarchical organisation with the church in Jerusalem or Rome acting as headquarters. The relationship of the apostles to the churches was certainly authoritative by virtue of their position in the movement, but even here the keynote is struck by Paul's words: 'I do not mean to imply that we lord it over your faith; rather, we are workers with you for your joy, because you stand firm in your faith.'[19] Paul's relation to the churches he helped to found was of a father to beloved children, reliant upon exhortation and appeal.[20]

Synods and Councils

I have argued that the local church is competent to govern its own affairs, but that it is not omnicompetent. Nowhere is this more so than in deciding the large issues of the faith which demand the collected experience and wisdom of the whole church. The doctrine of the autonomy of the local church allows each congregation considerable scope for exercising conscientious judgment in the application of the gospel to its situation. Yet the gospel has a given-ness to it and so there is a limit: it is not up to individual churches or Christians to reinvent the faith that has been given. Even so, there are times when strategic and far-reaching judgments do need to be made and on which a great deal hangs. Although it has been given as a stewardship to be guarded, the gospel needs to be interpreted, especially as it encounters new cultural contexts and new questions. There are times when to stay with the old interpretations is actually a form of unfaithfulness and a leap needs to be made into a new paradigm which is truer to the gospel than what it replaces. Here we are not in the sphere of individual choice but of the mind of the church, the *sensus fidelium*, the consensus of the faithful. Decisions of this order of magnitude cannot be made in the local congregation. They require the wisdom of the wider church as its representatives come together in synods and councils. The word 'synod' means 'a common way' and refers to those councils of the wider church where the intention is to discuss and pray together to find a common way through the often-complex issues with which the church has to deal. The definitive decisions over the essence of Christian belief about God were made at a series of 'ecumenical councils' in the first centuries of the church's life when the church remained relatively undivided. With growing division, the possibility of further such councils has gone, but in more partial ways the denominations and sub-traditions of the church all have their ways of consulting together and seeking God's wisdom in their imperfect state. In principle, the practice of synods has a firm biblical basis which should lead all the churches to respect these processes highly and give careful attention to them.

It sounds risky to talk about leaps into new interpretative paradigms but essentially this is what happened within the faith of Israel because of the coming of Christ. The traditional interpretations of Hebrew Scripture were radically reworked by those who saw Christ as the coming of God, giving rise to a way of reading the Scriptures which was both decisively new and entirely faithful to their essence. The first Christians interpreted the tradition afresh in the light of the risen Christ.[21] Such was Christ's impact that the full meaning of his coming took time, and is still taking time, to run its course. The most significant example of this in the early church concerned the nature of the Christian community: was it to be defined ethnically and by means of religious culture as

Judaism had been, or was it to be defined irrespective of these on the basis of faith and the reception of the Spirit alone? The first of these possibilities was entirely in line with traditional Jewish interpretation and had its advocates in the early church which could make strong appeal to the authority of tradition. But Paul characterised them as the 'circumcision faction'.[22] The truth did not lie with them but with the modernisers who were reinterpreting the tradition in the light of what they saw God doing among the Gentiles. If it was true that God had opened the door to the Gentiles to receive the Holy Spirit and enter the community of disciples, the received tradition needed to be reinterpreted. In very personal terms, we see Peter shifting paradigms and moving from his restrictivist Jewish background into a new inclusivism.[23] This meant both a departure from the inherited way of reading Scripture and a radical discovery that it could still be read faithfully but in a new way. The cumulative effect of the experience of Gentile conversion and the opposition to it of the circumcision faction was to precipitate the need for the synod or council at Jerusalem through which a common way forward was found.[24]

The Council of Jerusalem is clearly presented in Acts as a model for discerning the mind of Christ through collective discussion. Certain things stand out clearly.

- It would have been impossible to resolve the issues at stake without such a gathering, at which various points of view were represented. Not every issue can be resolved at the level of the local church since the perspectives required to see things clearly will rarely be contained within one church. Neither would a more limited consultation carry conviction and confidence across a broad spectrum of diverse churches.
- Although Luke does his best to present the run-up to the Council and its aftermath in a constructive light, it is clear that the matter under discussion was a tense one and that feelings about it ran high. There was also no shortage of misunderstanding and misrepresentation even among believers.[25] Confusion often accompanies clarity in the decisions of the church.

- Debate which moves towards clarity and common understanding is a necessary process. The truth does not necessarily come easily but through the struggle to interpret and to sift. The Council of Jerusalem involved 'much debate'[26] and this can become tiresome for those who do not have much patience for it.

- The Council was concerned to interpret both Scripture and the tradition in the light of new experiences which were narrated at considerable length.[27] These experiences of Gentile conversion were understood by reference to the primary Christian experience of the reception of the Spirit which was the criterion for their authenticity.[28]

- The debate and the experiences gave new insight into the meaning of key Scriptures which were brought forward to speak to the new situation they were facing.[29]

- Although the Council of Jerusalem included the full participation of various interested parties, there was still the need for it to be managed by those competent to do so. In this case, that role was taken by James, the brother of the Lord and the leading figure at this time in the Jerusalem church. It is significant that Peter did not take this role and that the summing up of the debate and the mediating of a way forward lay with James.[30] Even so, what James summarised had to carry the consent of the apostles, elders and the whole church.[31]

- The product of the Council was a compromise formula, admitting Gentiles without the demand of circumcision but asking for certain moral and ritual observances in agreement with the law of Moses.[32] The practical intention behind this was to enable Jews and Gentiles to enjoy table fellowship together, so this was not a sacrifice of principle but of preferred practices. On this level, compromise is not only necessary to enable people of differing cultures to co-exist; it is also an act of grace in deferring to the needs and sensibilities of others.

- Although the Council of Jerusalem came to a clear recommendation, the matter remained open as to how churches would receive the proposals. The conclusion of the Council was an exhortation, not a command, and in principle the churches were free to receive it or not, although the consequences of its not being received would have been truly problematic. In the event, the church in Antioch received it gladly in the spirit in which it was sent.[33]

The Council of Jerusalem both sets out in model form the ideal way in which difficult decisions might be arrived at in synods and councils and demonstrates the importance of such representative gatherings in the later history of the church. Their true authority is that of the wisdom they mediate (although in truth later councils also became entangled with imperial power, so confusing the nature of their authority). Their wisdom should be listened to carefully and received gladly when it is recognised.

Associations and Competence

I have laid stress several times on the competence of the local church. Because Christ is there by his Spirit the congregation is empowered to govern its own affairs. It is competent, but not omnicompetent. Some matters take wider circles of the church to resolve, as at the Council of Jerusalem. It might be expected then that an association of churches has competence in relation to those decisions that need to be taken in the mission of God within the area in which it serves. Local churches might see their own or a somewhat larger context in a strategic light, but regional perspectives go beyond one congregation. Issues to do with strategic church planting or evangelisation, or in relation to government fall naturally here. Since an association in principle has such competence it should use it and neither see itself merely facilitating the vision of local churches or implementing the yet larger strategy of a national union or convention. An association is a sphere of competence in its own right and should not abdicate its authority in this regard.

The tendency to do this, to be squeezed between the local and the national, is well illustrated in regard to ministerial recognition. If the local church can call and ordain ministries within its own sphere of competence, as baptists have consistently argued it can and as the first Baptists certainly did, associations have an analogous competence within their own sphere. They can affirm and recognise as competent to minister among the churches of the association those who are already serving within individual congregations. In this way, they can, if asked to do so and if the relevant criteria they establish have been met, extend the recognition accorded by local churches into the wider sphere. In many countries in Europe, the national Baptist unions are smaller in size than English associations and yet confidently exercise their competence. The point is to believe fully in the appropriate degree of competence that the presence of Christ makes possible and not to underestimate it.

Being Church Beyond the Local Church

The further we move away from the grassroots of the Christian churches the more difficult it becomes to have a strong sense of ownership. Christian disciples are most likely to feel a sense of participation in those local communities which play a large part in their own lives. In moving out from this base such ownership is less likely to be the case and here lies one reason why baptist Christians often have a strong local ecclesiology and a weaker sense of anything beyond. Episcopocentric churches almost by definition give the wider church a priority, at least theologically, in this regard and are clear among themselves that the life of the local is drawn from the church catholic. Baptist believers are more likely to believe that it springs up from below and flows out into the broader stream. The truth is somewhere between the two. Practically speaking, however, the life of local churches will be connected into associations by means of representatives who have the responsibility to act as two-way communicators: from the local church to the wider fellowship and back again. Christians are connected not only in regional and national communions but also internationally and at this point the number of people who have direct experience of international synods is likely to be relatively small. As a consequence the sense of the universal church will remain for most people an abstract one. Episcopal traditions define bishops both as guardians of the church's teaching and as focal points of unity within and between the different parts of the body of Christ. The expectation is that the church universal will be held together by a network of personal contact and communication which draws the church together in a matrix of fellowship. An Anglican bishop is enjoined both to guard the faith and to guard the unity of the church;[34] this personal dimension is much more likely to prove effective than any form of bureaucracy and expresses the priority of relationship over institution which both reflects the trinitarian life of God and is in accordance in its own way with the values of the baptist tradition. For non-episcopal baptists this points to the need for representative individuals to act as life-joints within the body of Christ for the sake of its unity, a point to which we shall return.

There are deeper points at stake in all of this. In the local community it is possible in realistic ways to give expression to covenant, the mutual commitment of believers to each other for the sake of Christ. Beyond the local church it becomes progressively more difficult to do this except in the ways I have indicated, through representative individuals among whose responsibilities and goals is that of maintaining the unity of the whole communion they serve, and beyond that of the whole church. A baptist theology of the wider church will almost certainly be drawn from the theology of the local church. We noticed this in the formation of the Abingdon Association: just as each church member belongs to a community of disciples, so each community should belong to an association. This logic could be extended to the national level and then the international. All parts of the church belong together and should seek connection and relationship in order to reflect the ordered yet dynamic life of the triune God. The role of individuals will be significant in this. As the body of Christ is 'joined and knit together by every ligament with which it is equipped',[35] so the body of Christ is held together as people called and gifted to do so take care for the growth into unity of the whole: this is of deep importance both to God and to the mission of the church. This brings us to the question of oversight.

A Theology of Oversight

As a local church forms so it stands in need of ministries which will sustain its well-being and extend its mission. These are the translocal and local ministries to which I have referred and which I have described as 'almost necessary' for the being of the church and most certainly necessary for its well-being and full functioning. If the wider dimensions of the church represented by associations and unions, are modelled theologically on the local church, this suggests that each dimension of fellowship in regional, national and international spheres also needs ministries to sustain and nurture it, taking care of the particular concerns and needs which arise in their sphere. This is not to suggest that baptists should develop hierarchical structures. In a hierarchy the power flows from the top down whereas baptists operate ecclesiologically from the bottom up. A hierarchy suggests a pyramid in which each level of authority is responsible to the next one up. Instead we suggest an *extensive* ordering where the churches are continually reaching out to new dimensions of fellowship and where the model is one of interlocking circles, each with its own forms of oversight accountable to those who appoint them from below and without any suggestion that there is a command structure from above. What is important here is what flows *between* the interlocking circles, and that should be spiritual life communicated through the joints which hold the whole body together. Without formal authority there should nonetheless be moral and spiritual authority at work within this dynamic. There is both relating and resourcing as relationships forged nationally and internationally become the vehicle for the effective sharing of resources in ways which enable those who have to share with those who have not. The New Testament bears witness for the need of a 'fair balance' within the churches of Christ. At the moment, the disparities of wealth between the nations are enormous and for the church to take seriously the challenge of a fair balance between those who have a present abundance and others with overwhelming need would be truly to be a paradigm for the nations and to fulfil its mission.[36]

All of this is to do with being church at a level which is wider than the local. If associations and unions are not churches, then they certainly are expressions of church; they belong to the whole task and calling of being church; they are in the service of church. For Baptists this is an unresolved point of tension. For some, only local churches are truly church and the rest is a matter of convenience or indifference; for others, local churches are indeed church, but not the totality of the church: the interconnections which draw the whole body of Christ together are also part of the richness of God's temple as the church of the present imperfectly anticipates the true and complete church which will be gathered at the last. Although it is entirely accurate to say that denominations are not 'biblical' it is also not right to dismiss them of no value. Kevin Giles suggests a more positive reading of them:

> The church is to be defined as the Christian community. As the denomination is a true expression of Christian communal life, it is rightly called 'church'. Nevertheless, as it is but one historical form of the supra-congregational church, and a form that expresses the divisions among Christians that will not be known in heaven, it can only be given provisional theological endorsement; yet this is all that is needed. Every aspect of the life of the church in history is provisional, a pale reflection of the communal life to be revealed on the last day.[37]

It will not quite do to see translocal manifestations of church merely as human constructs without theological significance: they also are ways of being church.

The present discussion alerts us to the question of oversight, or *episkope*, within the church. If oversight is necessary for the local church, what form ought it to take for the association, a national body or an international agency? As we have noticed, ecumenical discussions have clarified that oversight within the church takes several forms which can be described as *personal, collegial* and *communal,* and each dimension of oversight is found in each form of church order, although in a different balance. Personal oversight is vested in individuals who have been set aside for the task either as translocal or local ministries. Collegial oversight is that of a college of elders within a congregation who share responsibility for pastoral care and teaching. Communal oversight is that of the whole congregation for all its members shared as part of the commitment to watch over one another in love. Baptist congregations will be used to the concept of mutual care and responsibility but will also agree that for this to be done best usually requires the appointment of a group of leaders who will have particular regard to the needs of the congregation, and that within such a group one or some will have particular gifts of teaching and a pastoral vocation recognised through ordination. The personal and collegial therefore serve as ways in which the communal responsibility can be carried through effectively. How might this be translated to the association sphere?

The same oversight functions are required but will be differently expressed. Churches will help and serve each other. A group of representatives will be appointed by the churches to have particular stewardship of those concerns and resources which the churches share corporately. Individual ministries will be called and assigned to watch over the needs of the association and to help carry through its ministry and mission. These ministries come close to the role which is otherwise called that of the bishop, but not the historic episcopate of the catholic tradition; it is based rather upon the gifts and abilities which are recognised in individuals, and appointment comes from below, through the churches, rather than above from a hierarchical structure. In English Baptist life the title General Superintendent, first introduced in 1916, was borrowed from German Lutherans (others of whom use the title 'bishop') and was more recently replaced by 'regional minister'. In America the generic term 'judicatory' is used to refer to all structures of ministry which work at the association level or equivalent.[38] The emergence of this kind of ministry even among baptist groups strongly suggests that the ancient insistence on the threefold ministry of bishops, presbyters and deacons has something to it, not as an insistence that this is the form ministries must invariably take but as a recognition of a recurring pattern based around the real needs of the church in all its dimensions. God gives the grace of ministries to address the needs of the church, and the 'bishoping' function belongs as an expression of personal oversight alongside the other forms we have identified. This is true in each sphere of ministry, including the national and the international: individuals given to the church by God are part of that good work of connecting the church in all its parts to each other. They function not as independent and unaccountable agents but in and from the other patterns of oversight which are also required. Yet they bring qualities and contributions which add to these other dimensions and sharpen their effectiveness, sometimes bringing a degree of precision which the others because of their collegial or communal nature are not able to provide.

Baptists are so attuned to the misuse of sacred power that they constantly run the danger, at least in their declarations, of devaluing the personal dimension of oversight at the translocal level. Consequently, they risk depriving themselves of the gracious gifts of God which they need to come to maturity. The better way is to celebrate those whom God has given, to respect and honour them and to pray that their work will be effective in the service of the kingdom of God.

Notes

1. Volf, *After Our Likeness*, 106, 278.
2. 1 Corinthians 11:29.
3. John 17:23.
4. For universal see Ephesians 1:22–23 and Matthew 16:18; for local see, for instance, Galatians 1:2 and Revelation 1:4.
5. Volf, *After Our Likeness*, 266–69.
6. Revelation 7:9–10.
7. Stanley J. Grenz, *Renewing the Center: Evangelical Theology in a Post-Theological Era* (Grand Rapids: Baker Academic, 2000), 308–24.
8. Lumpkin, *Baptist Confessions of Faith*, 166 (language modernised).
9. Lumpkin, *Baptist Confessions of Faith*, 168–69 (language modernised).
10. Chapter 26, Article 14: *The Baptist Confession of Faith of 1689: A Faith to Confess* (Haywards Heath: Carey Publications, 1975), 59. The 1689 Confession is the most famous of all Baptist Confessions and was later adopted also as the Philadelphia Confession of Faith. In Lumpkin's work it appears as the Second London Confession of 1677 and 1688, which was then reissued in 1689 after the Toleration Act of that year.
11. Chapter 26, Article 15.
12. B.R. White (ed.), *Association Records of the Particular Baptists of England, Wales and Ireland to 1660: Part 3. The Abingdon Association* (London: Baptist Historical Society, 1974), 126.
13. Volf, *After Our Likeness*, 234.
14. Volf, *After Our Likeness*, 236.
15. Acts 8:14–17.
16. Acts 11:22–26.
17. Acts 11:19–30; 13:1–3.
18. Romans 16:3–4.
19. 2 Corinthians 1:24.
20. 1 Corinthians 4:14.
21. Luke 24:27.
22. Galatians 2:12.
23. Acts 10.
24. Acts 15.
25. Acts 15:1–5.
26. Acts 15:7.
27. Acts 15:6–13.

28 Acts 11:17.

29 Acts 15:15–17.

30 Acts 15:19–21.

31 Acts 15:22.

32 Acts 15:20.

33 Acts 15:31.

34 The Church of England, *The Alternative Service Book* (London: Hodder & Stoughton, 1980), 388.

35 Ephesians 4:16.

36 2 Corinthians 8:13–15.

37 Giles, *What on Earth Is the Church?*, 211.

38 In other places I have argued for the use by Baptists of the term 'bishop' on the grounds that rather than create a new term to describe a biblical function, it is the better alternative to 'apostle' (which can sound pretentious), or 'messenger', an equivalent term formerly used by Baptists. It also has the advantage of being recognisable by the general population and by other traditions and of enhancing the role of the regional minister. See, Wright, *Challenge to Change*, chapter 7.

10. The Separation of Church and State

Dissent, Religious Freedom and Tolerance

Introduction

In the introduction to this book I identified a distinctive
feature: what is believed about the community of the church
has implications for what is to be believed about the wider
civil and political community. If it is believed that the church is
central to the saving purposes of God, that a messianic
community is being gathered through the preaching of the
gospel, and that the community has in some way entered into
the fuller purposes of God for God's world, then it follows that
we should be able to deduce from the church at least some
aspects of what the will of God for all communities might be.
This is a mighty claim. Indeed, it borders upon being too
mighty since the church as a community of continuing, if
redeemed, sinners always falls well short of its vocation: the
squalid reality of its achievements often calls into question the
high theory of its doctrine. Yet by the grace of God it is a claim
with which to persist. The church *at its best* has set before the
world an exemplary community which acts as salt and light
and has the power to transform. In this capacity the church has
often played the role of the social pioneer, incubating within
itself a love for humankind and ways of living together
inspired by its discipleship of Christ which have in due course
made their impact upon the wider community. It has done this

initially by venturing ways of behaving communally which have gone beyond what was commonly accepted and have therefore been at variance with the *status quo*. It is this aspect of the baptist traditions that have earned them in the past the description 'dissenters'. By following the pull of their own consciences and daring to be different, these radical believers have found themselves blazing trails for others to follow.

As an example, historians have not been slow to point to the influence of the participative forms of church government pioneered by baptist congregations upon wider societal structures. The rejection of sacred power hierarchically administered in favour of consent-based patterns of government espoused by these dissenters led to the development of 'a pluralist society in which men would learn to live in peace with others with whom they disagreed without resort to the scaffold or firing squad'.[1] After all, if the enforcement of religion was taken out of the hands of the secular power, the role of that power shifted towards the more modest one of providing the conditions within which people could negotiate their own religious convictions. In particular, A.D. Lindsay famously argued that democracy represented the social application of the priesthood of all believers and was the political analogy of the 'democratic' religious congregation.[2] As congregations determined the form of their own obedience to the Christian message, the claim followed that societies should have the parallel freedom to govern themselves. On this understanding, the nexus between a free church and a free society is the method used for making decisions.[3]

Dissent, Nonconformity and the Free Church

The terms 'Dissenter' and 'Nonconformist' have a peculiarly English character to them.[4] They also now sound dated and perhaps irrelevant. Indeed, Dissenters and Nonconformists have felt this themselves since at least the nineteenth century when they began for preference to define their convictions as 'free church'. 'Dissent' and 'nonconformity' were negative terms, concepts which allowed that against which they were a protest to define what they were. 'Free church', by contrast, was an attempt at positive self-definition: the church of Jesus Christ was to be free, most especially in that it was founded upon free profession of faith in the Christ who had set them free; churches were consequently free to govern themselves under Christ who alone is supreme governor and head of the church. This conviction is grounded in what are sometimes called 'the crown rights of the Redeemer' and the freedom to which it points is not that of mere human self-determination but of free obedience: Christ alone has the right to rule the church and no human being can usurp this right. As the church is called to be free so also it seeks its own image in civil society by derivation: society is to be free, free from religious compulsion, discrimination and penalty; free for the exercise of the informed conscience; free also from tyranny and domination. A 'free church in a free state' encapsulates the essence of the free-church vision.

Since this slogan provides the title for this book, its origins should be briefly investigated. It is sometimes attributed to Camillo Cavour (1810–1861), the Piedmontese statesman and then first prime minister of a united Italy. Alternatively, Jürgen Moltmann attributes the term to Guiseppe Mazzini (1805–1872), Cavour's fellow-countryman.[5] Cavour's mother was a Genevan by birth and a Calvinist in religion, both of which facts are of more than incidental importance for his eventual political philosophy. Cavour believed that as the Roman Catholic Church separated itself from the Italian state by renouncing temporal power and exercising an entirely spiritual power this would result in the world's renewal and the revival of humankind.[6] He seems to have derived this understanding at least in part from Alexandre Vinet (1797–1847), the French-speaking theologian who taught in Lausanne and Basel. He was the founder of the Swiss Free Church and, in his writings, a powerful advocate for religious freedom.[7] Although the term was clearly shared by both French and Italian movements for political liberation, its origin may also be attributed in part to Félicité de Lammenais (1782–1854), the French priest. Lammenais accepted the authority of the church in matters of faith but not of politics and so campaigned for the separation of throne and altar through his newspaper *L'Avenir*, the masthead of which proclaimed 'God and Freedom'. He was closely followed in this by Henri Lacordaire (1802–1861), the French Dominican, and Count Charles Montalembert (1810–1870), the Roman Catholic historian. These three represented the movement within the Roman Catholic Church towards the acceptance of democracy and freedom which found itself decisively rejected by successive popes of the time who uniformly saw 'a free church in a free state' as code for anti-Christian attacks on religion.[8] Although they were wrong in this, and the use of the term by Catholic thinkers ought to make this clear, the term certainly undermined papal assumptions about the very nature of the church and veered in the direction of the free churches.

If the term 'free church' brings us close to the essence or genius of the tradition we are expounding, the words dissent and nonconformity help to trace an important historical route that led to it. These words refer to the particular formative experiences of some Christians within the English context. Their experience is no doubt paralleled in other places and its memory has certainly been exported from its English home to those parts of the world, especially English-speaking, which have been, often through migration, a continuation of the story. Particular historical events, specifically the journey from persecution to toleration within newly Protestant England, have been of normative significance. The historian John Coffey has traced this transition in some detail.[9] In the Elizabethan age religious *uniformity* was considered an essential good for the preservation of English religious, national and political identity. This involved a close inter-weaving of the religious and the political. Since Henry VIII took over the role of the papacy towards the English Church, church and state were seen in England as one entwined entity rather than two distinct realms. Those who would threaten uniformity either by attempting to return to Roman Catholicism or by moving towards radical Puritanism were severely dealt with therefore as both political and religious dissidents. The Church became a primary means by which the authority of the monarchy was imposed and maintained. Failure to conform to the practices of the Church of England and non-attendance at or departure from its liturgies, were penalised.

The use of coercive measures to preserve Christendom had long been practiced with the approval of the church and had been given powerful theological justification by Augustine.[10] It came to be taken as the norm. The peace of the world, that is to say its power to coerce in order to preserve peace, was rightly if reluctantly to be used by the authorities to preserve the peace of the church. Admittedly, this was emphatically seen by Augustine as a disciplinary rather than a punitive measure, but it came with time to be used as an instrument for rooting out those who were perceived as threats to religious uniformity and so to political well-being. Dissenters and recusants (those Catholics who refused to attend the Church of England services) were alike harshly dealt with during the Reformation era and beyond. The high point of the attempt to achieve uniformity came after the restoration of the monarchy and the publication in 1662 of the *Book of Common Prayer*. After years of struggle and debate over the nature and direction of the English Church, years which included the political and religious conflicts of the English Civil War, a defining moment had arrived. Those who could not or would not submit to the Prayer Book's regulation were ejected from the Church and were known thereafter as Dissenters and Nonconformists. Even if the worst persecutions were brought to a close by the Toleration Act of 1689, other penalties and exclusions were to remain in force well into the nineteenth century.

The cost of such coercion to social cohesion meant that uniformity was to prove impossible to sustain over time, alienating as it did so many otherwise upright members of society. It gave way to the search first for *comprehension* in which the Church of England might embrace a wider range of theological convictions and then to *toleration*[11] of those who excluded themselves from the Church's ministrations or for whom the Church could find no place within the bounds of Christian orthodoxy. From the belief that uniformity was necessary to preserve the well-being of society experience had led, with many fits and starts, to the contrary belief that toleration alone could achieve this. Initially, this was, of course, the espousal of pluralism within a shared Christian faith and culture. With time it would become an inter-religious pluralism, with the acknowledgement of a diversity of religions and this would raise a range of questions which the early Dissenters could only guess at, and continues to do so.

English religious Dissent is the product of this historical experience and contributed significantly by its resilience to the emergence of toleration. However, nothing actually happens in a straight line. There is a reading of English history, sometimes described as the 'Whig' interpretation, which has argued that left-wing Puritanism, closely identified with Dissent, 'laid down the key principles of modern democracy, including individualism, egalitarianism, and the separation of church and state'.[12] Whatever the truth here, and I would argue there is much, it is not *simply* true. Dissent, if it eventually became identified with religious freedom, did not uniformly begin as such. Rather, it was a struggle over which *version* of the Christian religion should *constitute* the Establishment. Specifically, there was the contest between Episcopalianism and Presbyterianism. For a brief time during the English Civil War, Presbyterianism *was* the established church and, to quote Milton, 'new Presbyter was but old Priest writ large'.[13] In Scotland, Presbyterianism triumphed and relegated the *Episcopalians* to the status of dissenters and nonconformists. So-called Dissenters have sometimes wanted freedom for their own version of religion in order that, in the name of truth and God, they might deny that freedom to others who were, by their lights, in error.[14] It was only slowly that primarily on the left wing of the Dissenting movement the position that Coffey calls 'radical tolerationism' began to emerge in the writings of such advocates as John Milton and Roger Williams. It was to do so by means of sharp debate with more conservative Separatists and Independents who were by no means averse to the magistrates punishing ungodly behaviour or deviation in religion. Radical tolerationists, by contrast, advocated full liberty of conscience to all religions.

They broke with the Augustinian tradition by insisting that 'coercion could never be used to advance true religion'.[15] It is not that they disagreed with the Reformed aspiration after a free church in a godly society, more that they saw toleration as an aspect of godliness, and doubted that true reform of behaviour could be achieved other than through inward transformation: 'not by might, not by power, but by my Spirit says the Lord of Hosts'.[16] Achieving a 'godly' nation by force was simply another version of sacred power, as Milton so clearly saw. These calls for full religious freedom had all been foreshadowed in the English language by the Baptist pioneer, Thomas Helwys, the founder in 1612 of the first Baptist church in England:

> For mens religion to God is betwixt God and themselves; the King shall not answer for it, neither may the King be judg betwene God and man. Let them be heretikes, Turks, Jewes, or whatsoever, it apperteynes not to the earthy power to punish them in the least measure.[17]

We owe much to the pioneers of radical toleration. What once was a dangerously radical position has become, of course, the standard orthodoxy both in the Western churches and in Western democracies. Much has grown out of what D.H. Lawrence, himself a product of Midlands Congregationalism, once called the 'deep dung of Nonconformity'.[18] In many parts of the world, not least in the post-Soviet states of Eastern Europe, persecutory religious nationalism continues to make life difficult for what it regards as alien sectarian groups, such as baptists.

The Free Church Mind

By contrast with those Christians who support established or 'state churches',[19] Dissenters are inclined to see church and state as in principle incommensurate and therefore resist the idea of a church-state alliance or establishment. Church and state represent different kinds of power, the state that of coercion and the church that of moral persuasion. Any binding partnership between them is therefore a conjunction of forces that are at best awkward bedfellows and at worst mutually subversive. It is not that the church is an unblemished institution. It too participates in the fallen-ness of all human structures. But it is at least a community called into being by the redemptive activity of God in the power of the Holy Spirit which is orientated towards a kingdom that is not of this world. The more the Christian way is viewed as a costly and demanding if freely chosen following-after a crucified Messiah, the more incongruous and implausible a partnership of church and state comes to seem. This does not mean that the state is not necessary: it is given to maintain order and to preserve society. But it functions according to different principles from the church and a critical distance between the two needs to be maintained not to compromise the church's way of working. Even at times when the state is well-disposed to the churches, even to the point of giving financial support to socially useful projects, it is wise to be cautious and to avoid any arrangements that will bind the church to becoming something it does not wish to be.

Dissenters are used at this point to employing a *disjunctive* rather than a *conjunctive* logic,[20] and it is implied in the very term 'the crown rights of the Redeemer'. Conjunctive logic has at times in the history of church-state thinking been used to justify monarchy: there is one God, and so there should correspondingly be one pope, and one emperor. Divine monarchy validates political monarchy and the ecclesiastical monarchical episcopate. James I's political and ecclesiastical logic to undergird the episcopal system in the Church he governed was simple: 'no bishop, no king'. I have referred to the fact that theological ideas concerning the church seek their mirror image in the civil and political communities. Here we see examples of that: monotheism, monarchy and episcopacy are mutually supportive. Dissenting logic however has tended in the opposite direction. Because the Lord is King, there can be no other king. Divine kingship does not validate human kingship but calls it radically into question since God has no rivals. It is this disjunctive logic that we find Jesus employing in Matthew 23:8–12:

> But you are not to be called rabbi, for you have one teacher, and you are all students. And call no one your father on earth, for you have one Father – the one in heaven. Nor are you to be called instructors, for you have one instructor, the Messiah. The greatest among you will be your servant. All who exalt themselves will be humbled, and all who humble themselves will be exalted.

In these words, the supreme claim of God and God's Messiah overwhelms, relativises and subverts all other claims, whatever initial validity they may seem to have. Although Dissenters would certainly agree that the state is ordained by God as part of the order of preservation, the means whereby human life is kept from chaos and anarchy, it would not from this deduce it to be anything like an equivalent partner with the church in God's purposes for creation. The state, whatever form it happens to take, is a limited, this-worldly reality with a constant tendency to self-exaltation. It is closely associated in the biblical tradition with idolatry. Its role is to be acknowledged, respected and constructively enhanced but also watched, criticised and sometimes resisted since as a fallen power in possession of immense coercive potential it has the greatest difficulty in minding the things of God and seeking God's kingdom in any shape or form. To the Dissenter who seeks above all to be free for God, the desire for established status, when it is not incomprehensible, is apt to seem like a beguiling search for worldly significance, a falling-in with the power game that is contrary to the way of Christ, a lust to be acknowledged by those in positions of worldly power. This seems like 'being shackled to a corpse'.[21]

This approach certainly gives a more negative, or penetrating, analysis of human power systems than those which favour establishment or church-state partnership might at first sight do. It stresses the *disjunction* between church and state, the *incommensurate* nature of these two spheres, the fact that ultimately the state deals in coercion while the church acts by persuasion. To conflate these realms is fatal since on the one hand the church becomes a partner in coercion, as it so often has done, and on the other the state's worldly power is confused with the power of God. In Dissenting history this (rightly) negative appraisal has been balanced positively by a doctrine of creation and of the 'cultural mandate', the duty to build culture as part of what it means to be created in the divine image. The negative analysis is not an attempt to demonise the state or to deny responsibility for it, since it too belongs to the realm of creation and is providentially over-ruled by God for the preservation of humanity. But it is certainly ambivalent about the state and for that reason espouses a doctrine of *the separation of church and state*. The distinctiveness of the church requires it to maintain a critical distance in order that it might remain faithful to its own calling and identity and not become inappropriately entangled. To avoid confusion here, separation of church and state does not mean separation of church and society. The church is fully involved in society, doing its best to serve and shape it. But the state exists as the hard edge of society, being entrusted with the monopoly of coercive power as a hedge against disorder and anarchy. It is inappropriate for the church *as church* to be in partnership at this point since the church must maintain the clarity of its vocation. Individual Christians are certainly at liberty in their capacity as citizens to serve within the legislature, the executive or the enforcement services. They bring their Christian perspectives to bear upon their task; but they do not formally represent the church as church in these capacities. Like everyone else, they struggle conscientiously to do what is right.

What is crucial is to maintain the freedom of the church to be itself. Separation of church and state implies that whereas Christians will live as responsible citizens within the social order giving due acknowledgement in their proper sphere to legitimate rulers, they will not surrender the government of the church to any power other than Christ. The church governs itself so that it is wholly available to do God's will and not to dance to the tune either of the latest fashions in contemporary culture or to the currently powerful managers of the state apparatus.[22] In this, Dissenters can be seen once more to represent the sect-type of social existence, as discussed in chapter 2. We can see here its aspiration to *intensity*, to remaining true to the distinctive values and beliefs and forms of discipleship which are rooted in the particularities of Jesus of Nazareth rather than the generalities of human religion. Inevitably, such intensity leads to a degree of alienation from the prevailing value or power systems, but it is this critical distance that allows the church to maintain a distinctive and prophetic edge. It resists being co-opted by the state or giving it uncritical allegiance. A characteristic of the contemporary self is of course to be distrustful of intense religion of the sect-type. Is it not religious intensity that is at the root of some of our immediate fears and problems? In response, the Dissenter argues that when 'intensity' means close and faithful adherence to the way of Jesus Christ, this is not something to fear. What the world needs is not more religion but more Christ-like living. More greatly to be feared is the power of religious nationalism, when religious identities are so closely identified with ethnic or national interests or temporal power that they become both fused and confused. The Christian faith in its origin was one which expressly rejected the identification of the people of God with one single racial, ethnic or cultural identity in favour of a radical openness to all peoples, being a house of prayer for many nations. God's church is an international project which while scattered among the nations breaks free from exclusive or idolatrous association with any one ethnicity or nationhood in order to find its highest priority in the kingdom of God and the love of God for all peoples.

Dissent and nonconformity as I have described them can be seen to have taken their character from particular experiences in the English context. But at the same time they bear witness to something that belongs to original and normative Christianity. In its origins the Christian faith was a movement of both religious and political dissent. It dissented religiously within the established religion of its point of origin, Judaism, because of its belief that the Messiah had come in Jesus. It dissented politically within the Roman Empire because of its belief that Caesar was not Lord, since only Christ could be Lord. This was the ground of its earliest persecution. Dissent is more than a mere historical accident since it captures something that belongs to the essence of the Christian faith to lose which would be to leave Christianity hugely the poorer. This dissenting community went on to change the course of human history.

Tolerance in Society

It can be seen that baptist believers have been on the side of toleration and have consistently argued that the only way in which modern societies can survive is through its deliberate practice. Yet toleration is a more slippery subject than might at first appear and it is as well that we are clear what is meant by it.

It is undeniably true that the history of the Christian church has been characterised frequently by intolerance. Often this has taken the form of active persecution of perceived deviants, dissenters and heretics. Whereas in the contemporary world intolerance is regularly associated with fundamentalist Islam, a case could well be made that historically Christianity has been consistently more intolerant than the religion of Mohammed. Both Islam, in the Crusades, and Judaism, in the pogroms, have had cause to fear the sign of the cross which Christians themselves revere as a symbol of the overflowing love of God. It is not only *between* the religions that such intolerance has found expression. Intra-religious conflict tore Europe apart in the wars of religion which followed the Reformation. To be sure, religion was rarely ever simply religion; but once combined with national aspirations and personal power play it has in its intolerant state been as much part of the human problem as of the solution.

Western society has benefited enormously from the shift towards tolerance which is associated with the eighteenth-century Enlightenment. The conventional account of this pursues the line that in reaction to the wars of religion political philosophy began to look for an alternative to the religious state. It found it in the secular state, a state unhooked at least overtly from religious and ecclesiastical authorities and free to pursue its given task of maintaining order in its own right and without recourse to religious persecution. We should see in this on the one hand an *irreligious* and *secularist* reaction against the powers exercised by traditional religion, a reaction made necessary exactly because of the church's complicity in state coercion and oppression. But on the other it contains the modest triumph of a particular minority *religious* emphasis that had begun to emerge in calls for religious liberty first expressed in the writings of such baptist pioneers as Balthasar Hübmaier[23] and Thomas Helwys. In this respect, there really was light in the Enlightenment. The light consisted in the recognition that it was not the role of the state to enforce a religious line but to sustain the kinds of societies in which people are free to make their own conscientious religious decisions. Yet in detaching the state apparatus from traditional religious commitments, the Enlightenment opened the door to takeovers by ideologies which were resolutely hostile to the Christian religion. This is seen most obviously in the French Revolution, the immediate effect of which was an anti-religious crusade on a large scale. Arnold Toynbee summarises this:

> In the Revolution a sinister ancient religion which had been dormant suddenly re-erupted with elemental violence. This *revenant* was the fanatical worship of collective human power. The Terror was only the first of the mass-crimes that have been committed [since the Revolution] in this evil religion's name.[24]

If communism and fascism are also to be reckoned among the descendants of Enlightenment secularism, the anti-Christian and anti-religious impulses of this movement are by no means a deliverance from intolerance but an intensification of its worst aspects. The secularist claim that freedom from religion is freedom from intolerance is just not true. In being properly self-critical about Christianity's past intolerances, Christians also do well to believe that any other ideology, unconstrained by the drama of sacrificial love which is at the core of their faith, could have been infinitely worse. David Fergusson is surely right to point out that modern conceptions of tolerance owe more to the liberalism of John Stuart Mill than the free church tradition and that its 'account of the unencumbered self, detached from commitments and traditions is illusory'. To this he adds that the idea of an unencumbered state is equally illusory. With David Tracy he can point out that in modern society religion is viewed as 'a private consumer product that some people seem to need. Its former social role was poisonous. Its present privatization is harmless enough to wish it well from a civilized distance.'[25] This is far from being a satisfactory base for a truly tolerant society.

In the final chapter to this book I intend to say more about secularism and the challenges it poses to Christian faith. I shall distinguish there between secularism as an atheistic worldview and secularism as a political strategy for pluralist societies. Ideological secularism offers no real way forward since its incipient claims to an absolute position render it potentially as intolerant as any other claim to possess the truth. However, there are points at which the concerns of the free church tradition and those of secularism as a political strategy might be seen to coincide in part. Insistence on religious liberty and tolerance is a case in point. But we should be sure what kind of tolerance we are talking about. Some things should be the objects of intolerance: abuse or oppression, for instance. By tolerance we mean the willingness both to accept and respect differences between people; the recognition that diversity rather than uniformity makes for richness and life. Jürgen Moltmann helpfully distinguishes between *sceptical* tolerance and *productive* tolerance.[26] *Sceptical tolerance* is premised on the belief that no religious claims are true so all should be treated with equal disbelief. Behind this lies a concealed absolutism, a claim to know that all religious claims are untrue. Any claim to certainty is unacceptable. Contrasted with this is *productive tolerance* which acknowledges that people will truly believe what they believe and are entitled to do so. What is at stake is not their right to believe but how they behave towards others who believe differently. Drawing upon Lessing's play, *Nathan der Weise*, with its parable of the three rings representing Judaism, Islam and Christianity, Moltmann cites the words:

So let each man hold his ring
To be the true one - even so
Let each man press on uncorrupted
After his love, free from prejudice.

This is genuine and productive tolerance since it acknowledges the sincerity of real differences of belief and opinion
while insisting that the way those beliefs are held must match
the highest aspirations of those very beliefs themselves.
Tolerance of this quality reflects the heart of the Christian faith
revealed in Christ and his cross. Just here is the point of
divergence from liberal arguments for tolerance. For free
church Christians tolerance has a theological basis rooted both
in the illogicality of intolerance and the nature of Christian
belief. Religious intolerance proceeds from the belief that
those who are in error are dangerous to the common good and
so should be rooted out. But the measures taken against them
prove to be more dangerous to the common good than their
errors themselves. Moreover, their effect is more often to call
forth resistance and so entrench the error rather than remove
it. If true faith is God-given and sincere then it cannot by its
nature be instilled by coercive or persecutory methods. By
contrast there is a logic to tolerance in the acknowledgment
that people are responsible for their own faith and cannot
transfer this responsibility to either church or state. Recognition of the place of personal conscience therefore becomes
sacrosanct. Neither is it possible to pursue the common good
by coming into constant conflict over subsidiary issues about
which there remain legitimate questions. Rather an atmosphere of debate and dissent can actually be the means
whereby beliefs are challenged and tested in argument, with
all the possibilities this brings of growth in the truth. Most of
all, appealing to the way pursued by Jesus and the early
church cannot, in any way, justify persecutory actions. On the
basis of arguments like this, Christians have no need to
ground their doctrine of the social order on any other basis
than the theological one.[27]
   Productive tolerance is desirable and involves no compromise for Christian faith; rather, productive tolerance is
congruent with Christianity. It is rooted in an appeal to the

example of Christ and the early church, and in the belief that true faith is the gift of God which coercion cannot instil in the heart.[28] Having embraced believers baptism and the believers church and so insisted upon the priority of sincere and freely confessed faith, baptists cannot coherently draw any other conclusion concerning the state other than that it is obliged before God to maintain religious liberty. This is not to abandon the state to some supposed value-free neutrality; rather it is the expectation that the state should in this way serve the cause of true religion. In imitation of God's generous grace this involves doing good to all, irrespective of creed. At this point, Christians should live up to the highest values of their own confession by taking the way of Christ as their norm and guide. When they do not, their conversation partners have a right to challenge them for falling short. It is appropriate to be *intolerant* of attempts to undermine such toleration. In this entire area it also helps to have a positive theology of the religions, not in any way to deny the finality and uniqueness of Christ, but in seeing in them, whatever their flaws, the providential work of God in preserving meaning and community,[29] and some degree of preparation for the fullness of the truth which is in Christ.[30]

Free church Christians came to see the importance of religious plurality rather than uniformity and argued for the freedom of all people to follow their consciences. With the passage of time this has come to mean freedom for different religions to co-exist in the same society. However, this does not change the principle. Religious liberty is based upon the belief that people do not come to honest religious convictions by being pressured or persecuted but by discovering for themselves that which holds true in their own consciences. The Christian gospel cannot therefore be made credible by means of coercion but only by means of God's Spirit. It is God who takes the initiative in salvation, calling and drawing people by the Spirit as the message of Christ is communicated to them. No government or worldly power can do this and should not try; rather they should leave to God those things that supremely are God's and not interpose themselves where they do not belong. Their task is to preserve the peace in order that freedom to preach the gospel and for people to respond to it may take place without let or hindrance. If Christians ask for this freedom for themselves they are duty bound to allow it to others even when they profoundly disagree with them since they are called to 'do to others what you would have them do to you'.[31] However, this does not provide a mandate for abusive religion to go unchecked. Where specific forms of religion, Christian or otherwise, can be shown to be destructive of social or personal well-being it is appropriate for those powers which are given for the preservation of the human good to call them to account.

Tolerance in the Church

So we come to the practice of tolerance within the church. To what extent is tolerance desirable and when does it lead to compromise? All movements are caught in a tension between identity and diversity. On the one hand, they need an identity otherwise they have no reason for existing. On the other, they need a constituency or they have no way of making an impact. But the greater the constituency the greater the diversity and the sharper the realisation that even within an overall framework of belief and practice it is still necessary to encompass a range of opinions. Encompassing or tolerating diversity is both a demand and a delight: a demand because we must learn how to disagree graciously; a delight because other perspectives enrich our own, sometimes by challenging them. Unrestricted diversity is of course chaos, but principled diversity is constructive. When it comes to openness to the new and the 'progressive' there have to be those beliefs which are established and affirmed in the light of which the new and progressive can be sifted and discerned. No Christian therefore can be indifferent to questions of fundamental orthodoxy, of normative Christianity. The question is: how and where do we draw the lines?

In doctrinal terms the church has long distinguished between dogma, doctrine and opinion. These three categories act as concentric circles with dogma being the innermost, doctrine the next and opinion the outermost. There is a core to Christian belief. These are the dogmas of the church, its core convictions about God in the light of Jesus Christ and about the drama of salvation. The Nicene-Constantinopolitan Creed is the primary symbol and confession of these beliefs and it is shared by more or less the whole church.[32] *Dogmas* are irreversible for to reverse them, to conclude that they are no longer true, would be to abolish the very community which confesses them.[33] *Doctrines* are constructs and beliefs which are deemed to be of the highest importance but where disagreement need not mean that we cannot recognise in each other fellow believers and church members. Disagreements about the form of Scripture, the nature of the atonement, baptism and Eucharist, or the second coming may be sharp and do indeed sometimes lead to the division of the church into denominations. But it is possible to recognise the apostolic faith in each other even across the disagreements. *Opinions* are personal judgments or interpretations about Christian belief or practice which come under the heading of 'the right of private judgment'. Here we are in the realm of conscientious but relative decisions.

Maintaining these distinctions between dogma, doctrine and opinion is absolutely essential when it comes to understanding tolerance. It has been said that for the 'Liberal' everything is opinion; for the 'Fundamentalist' everything is dogma. But if everything is opinion then we are faced with a massive loss of identity since there is nothing to define what we are and no core to our being as a Christian movement. If everything is dogma then we are faced with the multiplication of division since everything is escalated to the status of an absolute. It is no wonder then that Fundamentalist movements tend to fragment repeatedly as opinions and private judgments are arbitrarily exalted to normative status. And how do we distinguish what is dogma, doctrine or opinion? At this point, we are properly thrown back on the tradition of the church which has expressed its mind in the ecumenical creeds of the early centuries. The creeds reflect not human whims or sectional self-interest but the well-winnowed, tried and tested tradition of the whole church of Jesus Christ. This is the dogmatic core by which our Christian identity stands or falls and the old dictum still prevails: in essentials unity, in non-essentials diversity, in all things charity.

Here we make reference to Scripture. Issues of identity and tolerance are not new. Paul exhorts Timothy to, 'Hold fast to the standard of sound teaching that you have heard from me',[34] and tells Titus to, 'teach what is consistent with sound doctrine'.[35] There is clearly that 'faith which was once for all entrusted to the saints' for which we are to 'contend'.[36] These are references to the dogmatic core. Yet it is clear that the diversity of the first Christians was immense, so much so that Paul has to insist:

> Welcome those who are weak in faith, but not for the purpose of quarrelling over opinions. Some believe in eating anything, while the weak eat only vegetables. Those who eat must not despise those who abstain, and those who abstain must not pass judgment on those who eat; for God has welcomed them. Who are you to pass judgment on servants of another? It is before their own lord that they stand or fall. And they will be upheld, for the Lord is able to make them stand. Some judge one day to be better than another, while others judge all days to be alike. Let all be fully convinced in their own minds. Those who observe the day observe it in honour of the Lord. Also those who eat, eat in honour of the Lord, since they give thanks to God; while those who abstain, abstain in honour of the Lord and give thanks to God. We do not live to ourselves, and we do not die to ourselves. If we live, we live to the Lord, and if we die, we die to the Lord; so then, whether we live or whether we die, we are the Lord's. For to this end Christ died and lived again, so that he might be lord of both the dead and the living. Why do you pass judgment on your brother or sister? For we will all stand before the judgment seat of God.[37]

Within the shared faith of the first Christian churches in Jesus as Messiah there was still evidently a wide range of belief, conscientious decision and practice. It is striking here that Paul does not attempt to legislate for people's opinions or to impose a uniformity of belief or practice. He is content to let people live to God, satisfied that to live before the face of God in good conscience is enough.[38] What counts is living in honour of God. Paul commends here both trust and tolerance: trust in people's sincere intent and tolerance of the differing opinions at which they might arrive in matters that do not belong to the core of faith. To tolerate is not, of course, to approve. But if Christians truly wish to maintain the unity of the body, and not to desire this is a grievous sin, it is to tolerance that we are called.

It might be objected that to tolerate heresy is to tolerate sin. The issue is what constitutes heresy and how we discern it. This is not for us individually to decide, but for the church in continuity with its creeds and its tradition. Heresy is deviation from the dogmatic core of the church. To be sure, denominational movements add to that core and wish to maintain their own doctrines which serve to define the core-beliefs of a distinct movement within the church, such as believers baptism and the autonomy of the local church. Yet it is possible to do this without denying that others who do their doctrine differently are Christians – they are just not baptists. Lacking a *magisterium*, an authoritative teaching office, evangelicals have a tendency to erect subsidiary doctrines and even opinions as tests of orthodoxy and fellowship.[39] Those who do not match these criteria are off the list of those with whom fellowship is sought. Here we come perilously close to making interpretative opinion a test of orthodoxy and being intolerant in such a way as to violate the body of Christ. Rather, variations here constitute not grounds for separation and division but for the exercise of productive tolerance within an overall firm commitment to Christian dogma.

To summarise: tolerance of each other for the Lord's sake is a Christian virtue. It honours the body of Christ and enables diverse people to live together within the framework of a common faith. Without a doubt it has its limits. None of us can ever say that no issues will ever be so important to us as to require in conscience that we dissent. To go on being tolerant is a precarious venture, but we should not imagine that we have reached the limits swiftly or prematurely. To tolerate each other across large differences of opinion and judgment feels at times like the unlikely requirement that 'the wolf and the lamb will feed together'.[40] It demands much grace, but it is growth in grace which is the stuff of the Christian pilgrimage and which opens up unheard of possibilities of constructive growth. To refuse the challenge of tolerance is to miss opportunities filled with potential. The virtues which are learned and practised in this way in the Christian community then become those which can set the tone for the wider community and seek their reflection in the wider communities in which we live and work.

Notes

[1] Michael R. Watts, *The Dissenters: From the Reformation to the French Revolution* (Oxford: Clarendon Press, 1978), 2.

[2] A.D. Lindsay, *The Churches and Democracy* (London: Epworth Press, 1934), 14, 24, 26, 31–32.

[3] Franklin H. Littell, 'The Work of the Holy Spirit in Group Decisions', *Mennonite Quarterly Review* 34.2 (1960), 83.

[4] The argument in the next two sections draws on Nigel G. Wright, 'Disestablishment – Loss for the Church or the Country? A Dissenting Perspective', *Journal of European Baptist Studies* 4.3 (May 2004), 22–32.

[5] Jürgen Moltmann, *The Spirit of Life: A Universal Affirmation* (London: SCM Press, 1992), 107.

[6] *Encyclopaedia Britannica: Micropaedia Volume 2* (Fifteenth Edition, Chicago: 1992), 976–78.

[7] Article 'Alexandre Vinet' in Hans von Campenhausen et al. (eds.), *Die Religion in Geschichte und Gegenwart* Volume 6 (Tübingen: J.C.B. Mohr, 1962), 1405.

[8] Duffy, *Saints and Sinners*, 282, 295, 310–11.

[9] John Coffey, *Persecution and Toleration in Protestant England 1558–1689* (Edinburgh: Longman, 2000).

[10] Coffey, *Persecution and Toleration*, 22–23.

[11] In this chapter, I use the words 'toleration' and 'tolerance' almost interchangeably, but toleration usually carries the overtone of a formal civil and political arrangement and tolerance has a more personal nuance to it.

[12] Coffey, *Persecution and Toleration*, 3.

[13] 'On the New Forcers of Conscience under the Long Parliament' (1646).

[14] David Fergusson points out that in Reformed Scotland toleration was resisted: 'Believing toleration to be corrosive of the moral and spiritual identity of a covenanting community, they continued to cite Old Testament precedents for compulsion in matters of religion. In doing so they maintained the Augustinian tradition of "compelling them to come in".' He also argues that the very same impulse that has given to the Reformed tradition a noble concern for the civil order and has resulted, for instance, in improvement of health, education and relief of poverty, led it from time to time into persecutory actions, not excluding the burning of 'heretics': 'The Reformed Tradition and Tolerance', in Raymond Plant (ed.), *Public Theology for the 21st Century: Essays in Honour of Duncan B. Forrester* (London: T&T Clark, 2004), 107, 111–12.

[15] Coffey, *Persecution and Toleration*, 55.

[16] Zechariah 4:6.

[17] *A Short Declaration of the Mistery of Iniquity* (1612), in McBeth, *A Sourcebook for Baptist Heritage*, 70.

[18] Despite my best efforts, I have yet to locate this phrase in Lawrence's work.

[19] The use of these terms is problematic. A 'state church' would normally be understood as one which is supported and maintained by the state with the clergy, for instance, being employed and paid as civil servants. This would be the case with the Lutheran Church in Denmark. Other churches, particularly in Germany, see themselves as 'people's churches' or *Volkskirchen;* in these cases although self-governing the churches are supported by a special 'church tax' levied by the government while maintaining a definite independence from state authority. Often the Roman Catholic Church, while always guarding its own independence, will negotiate a detailed 'concordat' in individual countries regulating state relations over such matters as church schools. In England, which lacks a single written constitution, the relation of the Church of England to the state is largely one of historical precedent modified in certain respects through agreements reached with government from time to time. There was a time when the House of Commons was understood to represent the laity of the Church and so to have legislative powers over certain aspects of its life. This time is now past but remnants of it remain. The Church of England denies that it is a state church and so the term 'established church' is more appropriate. As the Presbyterian

Church of Scotland is self-governing it denies that it is an established church and prefers the designation 'national church'. The best modern defence of the establishment of the Church of England is Paul Avis, *Church, State and Establishment* (London: SPCK, 2001).

[20] Simon Chan, *Spiritual Theology: A Systematic Study of the Christian Life* (Downers Grove, IL: InterVarsity Press, 1998), 51.

[21] I believe these words are original to Clifford Longley, the Roman Catholic former religious editor of *The Daily Telegraph*.

[22] These themes will be dealt with more systematically in the next chapter.

[23] 'On Heretics and Those Who Burn Them' (1524), in H. Wayne Pipkin and John H. Yoder (eds.), *Balthasar Hubmaier: Theologian of Anabaptism* (Scottdale, PA: Herald Press, 1989), 58–66. The editors describe this as 'the first text of the Reformation directed specifically to the topic of the liberty of dissent', ibid, 58.

[24] In the introduction to Christopher Dawson, *The Gods of Revolution* (New York; Minerva, 1972/1978), x, as cited by Mark Noll, *Turning Points: Decisive Moments in the History of Christianity* (Leicester: Inter-Varsity Press, 1997), 251.

[25] David Fergusson, 'The Reformed Tradition and Tolerance', 109–10 citing David Tracy, *The Analogical Imagination* (London, SCM Press, 1981), 13.

[26] Moltmann, *Church in the Power of the Spirit*, 155–57.

[27] Fergusson, 'Reformed Faith and Tolerance', 113–19. Fergusson points out that these arguments were put forward cogently by Sebastian Castellio, a former colleague of John Calvin who came into conflict with him not least about the burning of Michael Servetus for heresy in 1553.

[28] Fergusson, 'Reformed Faith and Tolerance', 110–11; also Coffey, *Persecution and Toleration*, chapter 3.

[29] Grenz, *Renewing the Center*, chapter 8, 'Evangelical Theology and the Religions'.

[30] Fergusson, 'Reformed Faith and Tolerance', 118.

[31] Matthew 7:12.

[32] World Council of Churches, *Confessing the One Faith: An Ecumenical Explication of the Apostolic Faith as it is Confessed in the Nicene-Constantinopolitan Creed (381)*. Faith and Order Paper No. 153 (Geneva; WCC Publications, 1991).

[33] 'A dogmatic choice is one by which the church so decisively determines her own future that if the choice is wrongly made, the community determined by that choice is no longer in fact the

community of the gospel; thus no church thereafter exists to reverse the decision.' Robert W. Jenson, *Systematic Theology Volume 1: The Triune God* (New York and Oxford: Oxford University Press, 1997), 17.

[34] 2 Timothy 1:13.

[35] Titus 2:1.

[36] Jude 3.

[37] Romans 14:1–10.

[38] John Henry Cardinal Newman tellingly described conscience as 'the aboriginal Vicar of Christ': 'Letter to the Duke of Norfolk', *Certain Difficulties felt by Anglicans in Catholic Teaching* Volume 2 (London: Longmanns Green, 1885), 248.

[39] We are familiar with some of these in the form of scriptural inerrancy, penal substitution, eternal torment and the premillennial return of Christ. For my understanding of these distinctives and their relation to evangelical identity see my *The Radical Evangelical: Finding a Place to Stand* (London: SPCK, 1996).

[40] Isaiah 65:25.

11. The Free State

Understanding the Social and Political Order

Introduction

A constant assertion of this book has been that what is believed about the church has implications for what is to be believed about the social order and the state. The counterpart of a free church is a free state. Our attention now turns to the task of understanding the place and role of the state in God's purpose. The argument that follows draws upon many of the individual points made in this book and puts them together in a constructive whole. It acts therefore as an overall summary of the basic arguments, leaving us free in the last chapter to look towards the future.

It is true that the church of Jesus Christ has been able to survive and sometimes to thrive under political systems for which it has little sympathy. Yet the denunciation of 'sacred power' in the church, that pattern of domination by some over others rather than a shared participation in the communion of the Triune God, must be deemed to go hand in hand with the rejection of repressive power within the state; for this reason, Baptist Christians have consistently allied themselves with the concern for religious liberty, considered to be the most important of all liberties and the foundation of all the rest, and for the recognition of human rights to protect people against arbitrary and unjust uses of power. There is an historical correlation between the baptist way of being the church and the development of liberal democracy which, whatever its undoubted faults, has shown itself to be the political system which can contribute most to growth in human dignity and progress. No political systems can be equated with the kingdom of God since, like individuals, they all fall short of the glory of God; but short of the coming kingdom, liberal democracy represents the least worst of the humanly derived systems on offer.

In this chapter the task is to set out a theology of the state, building upon what has been affirmed in the previous chapters.[1] In doing this we face certain questions, one of which is that the word 'state' never occurs in the Scriptures. According to Max Weber, 'a state is a human community that (successfully) claims the monopoly of the legitimate use of physical force within a given territory'.[2] In biblical times this almost invariably took the form of a ruler or series of rulers who exercised direct and personal rule. In more bureaucratic times it has come to be a complex of office holders and their administrations to whom power is entrusted, sometimes by virtue of election, at others by virtue of conquest. The 'state' can clearly take many forms but its defining quality is a monopoly of the exercise of physical force. The New Testament language of principalities and powers features as part of this discussion insofar as these terms refer to earthly rulers and potentates.[3] In this chapter we are concerned to understand the function under God of these powers, the ways in which the church might relate to them, and the thorny question of what bearing all of this might have upon the use of force which is an apparently inevitable part of the practice of the state.

A Classical Text

A key text in this discussion is also a problematic one. Romans 13:1–7 asserts:

Let every person be subject to the governing authorities; for there is no authority except from God, and those authorities that exist have been instituted by God. Therefore whoever resists authority resists what God has appointed, and those who resist will incur judgment. For rulers are not a terror to good conduct, but to bad. Do you wish to have no fear of the authority? Then do what is good, and you will have its approval; for it is God's servant for your good. But if you do what is wrong, you should be afraid, for the authority does not bear the sword in vain! It is the servant of God to execute wrath on the wrongdoer. Therefore one must be subject, not only because of wrath but also because of conscience. For the same reason you also pay taxes, for the authorities are God's servant, busy with this very thing. Pay to all what is due to them – taxes to whom taxes are due, revenue to whom revenue is due, respect to whom respect is due, honour to whom honour is due.

On the face of it, this looks like a glowing endorsement of authority not just in Rome but in all places at all times. Some translations have preferred to speak of the authorities as 'ordained' of God, giving rise to a common parallel in some circles between church and state, each with its ordained ministers in its own sphere and each invested by God with equal dignity. This positive assessment of worldly power gives rise to the logic of a fruitful partnership between two equal powers often expressed by the official 'establishment' of one religious tradition as the state or national church. On this basis, establishment 'represents an entirely proper engage-ment with the God-ordained institution of the state'.[4]

While clear in calling Christians to a respectful attitude to the 'powers that be', Romans 13 is also highly ironic. The very imperial, pagan government that Paul here casts in a positive light, possibly to counteract negative attitudes among the early Christians, would within a few years engage in the first of several major persecutions of the church which would claim the lives in Rome of both Peter and Paul. So much for not being a terror to good conduct! Light can be shed on how to read Romans 13 by a closer understanding of its historical context.

In Rome the authorities had only two fundamental tasks. The first was to punish wrongdoing, and the second to praise benefactors, those who made large donations for public benefit. Paul therefore exhorts the Christians, on the one hand, to avoid wrongdoing, which would bring them into trouble with the first function, and, on the other, to 'do good', probably meaning where possible to do acts of benefaction, to attract praise.[5] In both ways Christians show themselves to be good citizens and commend the 'Way'. Rather than giving large theological prescriptions at this point Paul is giving sensible direction for the local context, at a time incidentally when Rome was still enjoying peace and stability, the larger principle being that Christians should commend their faith through good citizenship wherever they are.[6]

If Paul here casts the state's role under the providence of God constructively, showing what at its best the state might accomplish, then other biblical passages, most of all Revelation 13, paint it in rapacious and demonic colours. It is clear that the New Testament witness to the state is not 'monolithic or unambiguous'.[7] Ambivalence towards the state is the order of the day. The 'powers' are simultaneously to be regarded as created by God, fallen away from their true purpose yet capable of being redeemed, although not in their entirety until the final coming of God's kingdom.[8] We can never think about them without holding these thoughts together in our minds, and when we fail to achieve this we see things wrongly. The ambivalence we entertain towards the state is evident in biblical attitudes in Old and New Testaments. It was characteristic of the church before Constantine and in movements such as Anabaptism which recognised the necessity of government while rejecting its invasive and violent excesses and its consequent discontinuity with divine or ecclesial action. To overlook the fallenness of the powers and to enter into alliance with them, as is the case with established religion, is to become implicated and involved in their corruption. But cynically to overlook their createdness is to despise what God has made. To discount the possibility of their redemption is to deny the saving work of

Christ. The possibility of redemption enables recovery of creation's intended ontology (its essential and created being) and points to an area of greater continuity with divine, redemptive action. We cannot therefore close off the possibility that the powers may find themselves fulfilling beneficial purposes. Here then is the element of ambivalence when we regard the state, an inescapable tension between any political allegiance and discipleship. To stress the createdness of the powers at the expense of their fallenness leads us to naivety and potentially to enslavement to them. This is the element of truth in those conservative positions which would separate the spiritual and the political dimensions and claim that religion and politics do not mix. To stress their fallenness at the expense of their createdness might lead us to negate the necessary good they can do. Only in maintaining the ambivalence do we judge with sound judgment. Our contention is, however, that first of all we must recognise the fallen nature of the powers and their severe inability in doing good. Only thus are we freed from illusion to recognise within them the ontology of God's creation and the relative possibilities of restoration.

The Trinitarian Vision of the Church

Certain elements in Christianity – its monotheism, its use of military imagery, the language of sovereignty and its universal claims – made it viable as an imperial religion, the one God with the one Lord supposedly giving support and comfort to the one Emperor. Yet, properly understood, these themes are subject to constant reinterpretation through the crucified Messiah who is the revelation of the one God so that, with closer acquaintance, Christianity has often proven to be an awkward and ambiguous partner for the powerful. The language of suffering, self-sacrifice and the cross is not the most congenial for under-girding a vision of national glory. This awkwardness of the Christian God is all the greater once the doctrine of the Trinity with its severely qualified understanding of the unity of God as communion rather than singularity is taken into account. A communion of co-equal divine persons begins to sound suspiciously like a democracy. Since the doctrine of the Trinity is the fountainhead of all Christian theology, including of the church, this is where our constructive thinking about both church and social order ought to begin. The God whose being is in independence from the world has yet opened himself to it so that it exists in dependence upon and interaction with Father, Son and Holy Spirit. There are no autonomous realms of reality separate from Christ's lordship: Jesus Christ can speak to every aspect of life, even to the life of the state. Within this awareness of God's action as Trinity it becomes possible to give an account of the whole of reality and to discern the action of God in first creating, then preserving and finally redeeming the world. In particular, the doctrine of the Trinity is the source of the theology of mission and constitutes a claim upon all creation. Christian mission flows from the prior mission and self-giving of God through Christ in the Spirit. Christian faith cannot therefore be dissolved into general religious consciousness. God's universal and loving mission has taken form in a particular human being, in particular events and in a particular community – but with universal intent. The humble mode of God's self-revelation in Christ indicates that the mission is pursued by the declaration of truth not the quest for power, by persuasion and regeneration not imposition.

The church is that community of believers which participates by the Spirit in the fellowship and mission of the Triune God. Through the Son and by the Spirit believers are drawn into the communion of God's own being and become partakers of the divine nature. The word preached evokes response and participation in the Spirit. Inevitably, therefore, the church is a confessing or believers church constituted by the Spirit from those gathered into communion. As God's being has stability and form, so the church has stability of relationships and takes form as a community of equally valued persons each giving and receiving, each serving and being served within the body of Christ. The church is an *icon* of the Trinity. But the being of God is dynamic. God moves outwards to embrace the world God has made. This is the *missio Dei*, the mission of God, and to be gathered into God's being is to share that mission. The church is therefore a missionary, messianic community sharing in the earthly mission of the Messiah and the manner of its fulfilment. Only in this way can the church be the agent of God's redemption. Yet the church is not so much the *agent* of mission as its *locus*, the community where God is most clearly at work. Without claiming masterful control of history it is the place where the powers of the kingdom are present as the Spirit's first fruits. It rehearses and re-enacts the story which has given it birth. It shapes and forms its members so that Christ is formed within them. Its central concern is the disclosure through its life as the new humanity of the meaning of history in which individuals find their personal meaning. The church is only authorised to represent the reign of God in the way Jesus did, challenging the powers of evil and bearing in its own life the cost of the challenge.

As I have sought to argue throughout this book, this missionary and messianic concept of the church requires a free church ecclesiology. Existence as a freely choosing and disciplined community is the authentic form of the church's life. This requires the reformation of existing ecclesial bodies and the renewal of congregational life in a decentralised direction in which power is commonly owned by the church's members. Only so can the church adequately act as an evangelistic, socially transforming community which confronts the patterns of control and domination of the political community. This does not imply the rejection of power relations since the management of power is an inevitable aspect of all corporate existence, but it does require their refashioning along alternative lines – the proper use of power. Salvation has an inevitably ecclesial character since it takes form in a community and so it has from the beginning been a form of political existence. But this is an *alternative* political existence in which believers march to the beat of a different drum. Where this is lost sight of the church's potential as a transformative community is diminished.

The Social Order and the State

As with the church, the social order must also be seen within the context of Trinitarian action in creation, preservation and redemption and these may helpfully be seen as three 'orders' in which God is at work in the world. Father, Son and Spirit have brought creation into being, are now active in preserving what has been made from the destructive powers of sin and evil, and are all the more active within creation drawing it towards the consummation of all things in which creation will be set free from its suffering, sin and decay. To redeem the world and bring creation to its fulfilment it must in the meantime be preserved and the state is a providential gift of God as part of the world's preservation from anarchy. Life, created by God, is lived in the framework of God's gracious upholding of existence. Social existence belongs intrinsically to creation and reflects the divine image and community. It is not good for humans to be 'alone'.[9] Human personhood depends upon community since it is through relationships that persons are formed. By the grace of God, and against the force of human sin which is destructive of it, such community is preserved for the sake of humane existence. This belongs to the order of preservation. God's saving activity, revealed through Christ and the Spirit, is directed through the church towards the recovery of God's peace, of *shalom*. The cultural mandate, the requirement to build culture and develop the shared potential of human beings, is to be taken seriously as an aspect of the restoration of all human experience to its intended goals. Creation is to be respected and celebrated and the redeemed life includes a deeper penetration into its intrinsic meaning and worth. This includes its social dimensions, its institutional constellations and the particularities of ethnic identity. Theology is concerned for the recovery and fulfilment of God's intended creation from beneath the distortions of human fallenness.

As part of this, the 'state' as we currently know it and which we have defined as the centralised agency disposing of the monopoly of force within a given territory, is a temporary expedient which God ordains or allows as a means of restraining chaos and anarchy while the world waits to be redeemed. This is a doctrine of a limited state. The state belongs to the order of preservation and cannot be the means of final redemption and for that reason cannot claim divine honours or messianic significance. All human realities are relativised in the light of the transcendent Lord and ultimate loyalty is due only to him. The state belongs to this world and to this age. This is the effect of the declaration in Romans 13:4 that rulers are 'God's servant to do you good', not objects of ultimate concern and devotion. The state is best understood as a 'permissive ordinance' since within a fallen world it will always be a temporary and imperfect measure meant to substitute in the present age as part of God's preserving work for God's kingdom which is yet to come and which alone can safeguard a perfect balance of justice and compassion. Israelite kingship is the ambiguous model for this, a permissive ordinance of divine accommodation to human unwillingness to submit to divine kingship which nonetheless was taken up into the divine purpose. It remained a flawed and intrinsically unstable instrument employing domination and exploitation.[10]

There is, of course, no state 'as such', no metaphysical entity of independent existence outside the people who compose it. Actual states are rooted in and develop from the human capacity for corporate and co-operative organisation and are the particular forms assumed under the conditions of sin and fall from this potential. They are malleable, capable of reconfiguration in differing forms. Despite the role assigned to them by God the state and all systems of human government are intrinsically flawed, although providentially overruled. Indeed, all systems of government, however stable and peaceful in the present, in some form have their historical origin in violence and the lust for power and are ultimately maintained by violence. Being 'constellated' from human potential they are themselves inherently fallen and like individual human beings are capable both of much good and of much evil. For this reason, although free churches insist that all states are called to do the will of God and are glad when they can give overt acknowledgement to their creator, those same free churches are suspicious of any 'establishment' of religion, any binding partnership between church and state. Because states remain intrinsically fallen structures they are likely to seek to control religion for their own purposes, to bend it to their will, to use it to give legitimation to their own actions. At this point, free church Christians depart from those in other traditions who are enthusiastic about state-sponsored religion. While fully agreeing that all human systems need to be guided by moral and theological codes that enable them to serve humanity constructively, they refuse to be so tied to the state that they lose their own freedom of action and become subordinate to the interests of the powerful.

It is significant in this regard to the Christian that the Roman state perceived Jesus as a political offender and insurrectionist, and crucified him.[11] A faith which has the cross at its heart cannot take a naive attitude towards political authorities but will be aware of the discontinuity between divine and state action: states rarely do the will of God and often act in ways utterly contrary to it. It is to the credit of Anabaptism that this discontinuity was recognised. Christianity is an eschatological faith with a future hope that subverts present pretensions. Free church Christians share the conviction that everything in heaven and earth owes allegiance to the Christ through whom all things were made. They fully affirm that creation can never be integrated and whole until all things yield to Christ's lordship. They hope for the day when this will be reality. In this sense, they have a 'Christendom' vision: but it is a vision of God's future not of our present. Their objection is not to the vision but to any premature attempt to realise the vision before its time has come. When this has been done in the past it has led to the attempt to impose by force what can only be accomplished by grace. By all means the church should seek to influence the social order, but only by means of persuasion and appeal since this is the way of the cross and the cross determines all. But the cross which judges human states also indicates that they are providentially determined. Against their will they are required to do God's will to the extent that a limited justice and peace are maintained.

The limited, temporal role of the state involves the maintenance of justice, peace and freedom. Whatever the state does it will do imperfectly. It is inevitably tainted by the self-interest of the powerful, yet it is the providentially ordered framework within which human beings may live out their lives peacefully, freely and fairly. As a fallen structure it will only ever deliver a limited justice, peace and freedom and does even this by the grace of God. But only God's kingdom can bring about the full reality. At this point an important distinction is to be made between *policing* and *making war*. Policing is directed to the maintenance of order and upholding of the peace and can be directed with precision against evildoers. It aims to thwart and restrain wrongdoing. The state's judicial function regulates and channels public anger against those who offend and to achieve this it needs to be effective and just. Policing serves also to safeguard community values. By contrast, war is undertaken between nations and by its very nature destroys the peace and afflicts the innocent. The New Testament in general and Romans 13 in particular do not mandate such action and so it poses greater problems for the Christian conscience. Questions remain about the legitimacy of the defence of the civil order on which internal peace depends and an impartial international policing function between nations in conflict.

In matters of religion the state is called to be fair and just and to respect plurality. To act in this way reflects Christian values. No state or society can be value-neutral but the value of *impartiality*, not to be 'a respecter of persons', is a fundamental biblical requirement of rulers, and love for neighbour, stranger and enemy are all enjoined upon believers. In this way the state provides the historical framework within which religious faiths might argue and persuade. The maintenance of religious liberty is therefore a duty of the state and is arguably the liberty from which all others derive. True faith cannot be coerced. The impartial state, theologically understood and by contrast with its justification by political liberalism, is not the product of neutrality towards the Christian faith, but of the free church religious vision which includes tolerance and respect for others as aspects of what a godly and Christ-influenced social order ought to be like. Although religious liberty was resisted for many years by the Roman Catholic Church on the grounds that 'error has no rights' we have noted how even the Roman Catholic Church now affirms this value. We have also noticed a parallel version of sacred power in some Protestant traditions which looked to the state to enforce godliness. By contrast, free church Christianity entertains a different social vision of reliance upon persuasion to achieve this goal. It supports *plurality* without endorsing *pluralism* in the sense that all religions are deemed to be equally true. It hopes for a 'principled pluralism',[12] a 'covenantalism' or 'chartered pluralism'[13] as a way of holding together social unity and diversity. It recognises that the social order must be informed by moral values but also believes that these should arise from within and not be imposed from without.

The doctrine of election, which stresses the freedom of divine grace in drawing sinners to faith, implies that faith in Christ is not a matter of human legislation but of free divine action. To anticipate the divine decision is a form of presumption. Constantinianism created a hybrid of Christianity and coercive power which is a denial of the essential aspects of the freedom of God and the freedom of humanity. Persecution of religion and the privileging of any one religion to the despite of others are both alike to be rejected. But state impartiality towards religion does not of necessity imply indifference. Religious traditions and living faiths shape lives and foster personal and civic virtues in a manner essential to the social order. Politics is a function of culture and culture has religion at its heart. So the effort to secure tolerance by denying the reality of religion is bizarre. We do not deny the need for societies to derive their fundamental values from a religious source but we do insist that impartiality is itself a positive religious value and not some kind of 'halting between opinions'. It is entirely consistent that Christianity both seek to propagate itself and evangelise culture and that it refuse to do this through imposition but only through persuasion. It is equally coherent that those who hold strong religious convictions themselves should act towards others in ways in which that they themselves would wish to be treated, with respect and tolerance.

Having drawn attention to the fallen nature of the state and so of its continual tendency to become oppressive we need also to assert that within the fallen structures of human states is a created 'ontology' awaiting redemption. This is a crucial balancing statement. However much the state has become a vehicle for the domination of some by others, there is at its root that which is essential for human life in community. In that the purpose and goal of creation is *covenant* and that humans are ontologically capable of harmonious relationship with God and each other, symbiosis, community and co-operation are essential elements of their existence. Christian action towards the state therefore is directed towards qualifying its nature as domination in the direction of covenant so that God's original purpose for it comes to fulfilment and the organs of state become increasingly the means of a fruitful life together in community. This task is only ever fragmentarily accomplished but it is better that it be accomplished in part rather than not at all.

The Relationship of Church and Social Order

How in the light of this discussion does the church relate to the social order? First, it is essential to maintain the church–world distinction. The language of 'church and state' already implies a distinction and a potential conflict between two centres of loyalty. From the beginning, Christianity, whatever the variations, has insisted that there is a dialogue between church and rulers. This acted as a stimulus towards a more open society. Yet Constantinianism confused the distinction between two radically different realms and overestimated the fallen state's capacity to be congruous or continuous with the redeeming activity of God. It thus imported into the church a form of imperialism at variance with the church's fundamental commitment to the way of Christ. God's rule over the church is by means of the indwelling Spirit but over the state it is permissive and by providential overruling. The order of providence and that of redemption are to be distinguished from each other, even if the former exists for the sake of the latter. The church's task is to seek first God's kingdom and apply itself to conformity to God in Christ through the Spirit. Rightly undertaken this is a political service in that it relativises the importance of the state and enables it to assume its appropriate place as a servant rather than a lord. The church must concern itself therefore with its primary duty and although it can accomplish a variety of things within the social order it must not seek them apart from this duty.

Of equal importance is the recognition that the cause of Christ will never be advanced by means of worldly power or binding alliances with the state. This was the Constantinian error and it stands in direct contrast to the way of cross and resurrection embraced by Jesus. Worldly power is beguiling and attractive and in each generation its temptations need to be faced and resisted anew. The temptation is to seek power ostensibly in order to do good things. Yet the fallenness of the powers needs to be taken into account. Those who seek to bend the powers to their will eventually find themselves being bent. In this sense, Christians are 'anarchists';[14] they are suspicious of worldly power and do not believe that God's redeeming purposes are achieved by seeking to control the system of domination and use it for supposedly good ends. The goodness of the ends becomes lost in the manner of their achievement. In keeping with Jesus' mission, the church *as church* is to remain detached from partisan power struggles and to concern itself with truth rather than propaganda. For it to fulfil its task a distance of church from state is necessary which is jeopardised by establishment, implicit concordat or holy alliance. This implies that the church should reject any unqualified form of alignment with political and governmental authorities nor should it be taken captive by partisan programmes. Its transcendent dimensions make mandatory a critical distancing from all temporal movements. This is the 'separation of church and state' and is, as we have noted, a fundamental free church axiom. It stands in contrast to the idea of an established church or a state religion. Its rationale lies in the perception that because the powers are fallen, any formal alignment of the church with them is bound to be corrupting and the distinction between church and world eroded. The powers of state are tempted to use religion for narrow political ends, to legitimate their own status or policies. The church is tempted to pursue its ends by the illegitimate means of power, privilege and imposition. This is an unholy alliance and a wrong understanding of mission. It is a form of sectarianism since it identifies the church with national, localised identities rather than allowing it to be the new humanity which transcends all earthly loyalties. It also suffers from the illusion of establishing 'premature absolutes'[15] within the always provisional circumstances of humanity, emphasising a premature universality rather than the church's continuing humanity. Because it is faith in the crucified and looks for the coming of 'the kingdom of our God and of his Christ'[16] to replace the kingdoms of this world, Christianity makes an inherently unstable and unpredictable state religion.

Sociologically speaking of course there can be no *absolute* separation of church and state since all institutions benefit from the stability of other institutions. An established church, its advocates argue, obviates a merely private religion and maintains the tradition of social responsibility. The most persuasive argument in its favour within the English context is that, provided it undergoes some reform to obviate Erastianism (the exercise of ecclesiastical discipline by the civil authority) and fulfils increasingly an ecumenical and representative function within a religiously plural society, a weak establishment such as now exists maintains sufficient distance from the state to be a symbol of a transcendent dimension in a way which checks the monistic tendencies of the secular.[17] Paradoxically, this could serve precisely the opposite, critical purpose from the monism which has been the weakness of establishment in the past.

The disestablishment of religion does not, of course, imply the separation of church from society. Christians live in society and follow the example of their Lord in so doing. They are concerned to affirm the accountability of all aspects of human existence and culture to him, to witness to his meaning for the public square and to see public affairs shaped, as much as is feasible in the present age, by Christian perspectives. They seek to ensure that the state remains properly secular (avoiding idolatry), impartial in matters of religion (while respecting the place and importance of religious faith among its citizens) and committed to justice, peace and freedom. The existence of such a state is a blessing and its absence or distortion a potential tragedy. However, the state is a permissive ordinance, a temporary substitute in a world of unbelief for the kingdom of God which the world has yet to receive. While Christians are determined by faith in God and their opinions are informed by their faith and values, in the political realm they are bound to argue for solutions and remedies which operate with what is humanly possible for a given society at a given time. They will operate with a constellation of engagement models and aspects of these will be investigated in the next chapter.

The church recognises the fallenness of all political powers and their limitations. All come under judgment. It guards itself against delusion and false hope and refuses to locate final hope for humanity in any human ideology or political system but only in the Messiah. Its *detachment* is, in fact, a form of *engagement* freeing it to distinguish between relative goods. Because the powers are rooted in created reality they are however capable of redemptive improvement and the Christian duty is to seek for this. This is done by:

- *Faithfully being the church.* In remaining true to their vocation Christians collectively resist encroachments and develop values which can be offered in time to the public arena. The justice, peace and freedom which are the responsibility of the state receive definition and are protected from distortion, in part, through the witness of the church. From within its own life the church is able to offer ways of relating in social organisms which may be translated into the wider community. This is particularly so in the common ownership and exercise of power distinctive of the free church and in the practice of reconciling forgiveness. Messianic communities have innovative potential for all humanity.

- *Participating constructively in the social order and the intermediate structures of society.* The maintenance of liberty depends on 'intermediate structures' as buffers between the state and the unbridled use of power on the one hand and the unaccountable market on the other. They offer maximum opportunity for involvement and allow the values of the church to be translated into the wider community in the development of a moral consensus and practice out of which social legislation ultimately grows. Civic society and culture provide space for voluntary human association in ways which enable both government and market to function less coercively.

- *Political participation.* The power of government to affect the whole of a society means that redemptive change must in time impact this dimension, not, however, by imposition but by regeneration. If the church *as church* needs to maintain a critical distance between itself and the state, it is nonetheless fully open to Christian individuals to immerse themselves in the political process and make an impact upon it. While the church as a gathered community seeks to model the life of Christ and so to be like a light to the nations, Christian individuals scattered throughout society, including in its political councils, are in a position to bring to bear a steady and invisible influence upon it, like salt.[18] Instructive here is the career of Elijah: even while Elijah, the official spokesperson for the Lord, engaged in prophetic opposition to the corrupt King Ahab from outside the political system, the equally devout Obadiah, in charge of Ahab's palace, was very much inside the system and was in a position to mitigate Jezebel's cruelties in his role.[19] Concern to make an impact should not be considered an arrogant 'seizing of the levers of power' but as the proper use of God-given power and opportunity. The state exists as the outer limit and framework of society and is a legitimate sphere of involvement to the degree that it entails no basic compromise of Christian principle. Christian involvement in this sphere can be seen both negatively and positively: negatively in opposing those things which corrupt and damage, positively in encouraging those things which make for improvement and goodness in society. But the crucial distinction is in the critical distance maintained by the church as a community for the sake of its corporate witness, and the influential involvement of individuals as an influence for good.

Each of these above spheres makes vital contributions to political life. They are to be seen interactively with the impulses of the Spirit arising primarily and repeatedly within the church without being confined to it. The church does not receive the Spirit as a static possession but only dynamically so within the missionary dialogue with the world, a dialogue which is full of surprises and holds open the possibilities of change for both church and world. The legislation of social change and the nurture of just and humane institutions is a necessary task but can only happen because of the wider process of cultural formation. For this reason, the political sphere is no more an arena of social responsibility than others. It is one among many avenues of social change, although it is to be recognised that the breakdown or corruption of the organs of state can wreak great havoc. Excessive dependence upon political action as the principal thrust against social evil neglects the fact that the political is dependent upon vital forces nurtured elsewhere. Private, public and political realms are interrelated and interdependent. The evangelisation of culture can produce major paradigm shifts in the public consensus which ultimately have power to shape official, political and economic structures.

The Church and Violence

It needs to be asserted unambiguously that Christians are called to a non-violent life in imitation of Christ. God's redemptive purposes are not achieved through violence. It is an understatement to say that violence, particularly state sponsored violence, is an extensive problem and the involvement of the church in it as a consequence of its involvement in worldly power has done untold harm to the cause of Christ. Within the fallen world system it is inevitably the case that certain actions are deemed *necessary* for the preservation of the system. As systems carry with them their own logic and rationality, within the terms of such rationality they may indeed be necessary. However, Christians who live by faith in the God of resurrection are not bound by human necessity or the false rationality of fallen systems. This freedom is made known in Christ. The call to peacemaking is not a call to 'legalistic' obedience but to proclamation of and witness to the gospel. The issue concerns whether violence is a way of carrying out the witness.

Although Jesus' death was an example of willing self-sacrifice we doubt that this can be used to legitimate passive non-resistance. Jesus practised a third way between violence and resignation to injustice: non-violent resistance. This was an active form of resistance which did not mirror the evil of the evildoer but sought creative ways of awakening a conscious-ness of injustice. The instances he gave, including turning the other cheek and going the extra mile, contained prophetic actions and humour. Evil is certainly to be resisted, but not by recycling the injustices involved.[20] By their nature Jesus' actions are not repeatable. Non-violence is not therefore a new law, but a new freedom from the vicious circle of necessity. Without claiming there can never be exceptions we *can* say that non-violence and active peacemaking are at the heart of the gospel and of the church's task. Only the rejection of violence in principle, the recognition that it does not bring resolution, creates the pressure to develop creative alternatives. The church should never legitimise the violence of war, but it is also wise not to judge those who take up violence out of desperation.

Quite rightly, any discussion of the role of the state needs to address the question of whether, in the light of the non-violent, redemptive way of Jesus, it can ever be right for individual Christians to serve either in the police service or the military. If the state is given to preserve society it must be asserted that the state holds the monopoly of force; but its use remains always morally ambiguous and questionable. Here we encounter the paradox to which our past references to Anabaptism call attention. Some Anabaptists took the view that since the state was largely about the use of force and they were about following Christ, Christians could not be called into the service of the state. Baptists tended to argue differently.[21] Yes, the state was given to restrain violence and preserve society and this was a necessary function in a fallen world. Christians could therefore be called into the service of such a state even in those offices which required the use of force since this was to co-operate with God in his preserving work even if God's redeeming work could only be fulfilled through the preaching of the gospel. How then might this square with the non-violent example of Jesus?

The normativeness of Jesus for the Christian is applied to these preserving functions not as their necessary rejection but as their modification. The manner, but not the fact, of their exercise will be modified in the light of Christ. The state monopoly of force is itself a measure to bring violence under control and must be in each case justified and accountable. If it is known that the state disposes of this function effectively and fairly then it removes the pressure to 'take the law into one's own hands' and perpetuate violence within society. The policing function is therefore aimed to reduce violence not perpetuate it. In that this function is mandated by God as a concession to the fallen human condition it becomes a possible sphere of individual Christian obedience, especially so when non-violent restraint is the norm. Even so, some lethal force may prove necessary in the policing function as a limited and reluctant concession within an overall commitment to non-violence which police services at their best achieve. However, we resist the logic that extends a concession at one point into a legitimation of violence at any point. If violence is evil primarily because it usurps the divine prerogative over life, this limited divine permission changes its moral nature, as is shown by the divine command to Israel in particular circumstances. The judicial use of force is not morally the same as the random use of violence. It will always remain a questionable, boundary area in which accountable action will be required, not sinless perfection. We believe that there is once more a tenable distinction at this point between individual, conscientious Christian action and the peaceful way embodied in the Christian community as a whole. It is never the church's calling to give religious legitimation to killing. However, individual Christians must make their own conscientious decisions about how they are to work and contribute within society and some will be able to accept for themselves what others find impossible.[22]

The position here espoused understands the state's use of force to be a possible sphere of Christian action but within the overall belief that it is the duty of the Christian to work for the reduction and minimisation of all forms of violence and coercion. A Trinitarian vision of the social order envisages its formation to correspond wherever possible with the divine purpose. This includes qualifying the powers of state in the light of God's purpose of redemption. Fallen society will never fully correspond with the kingdom of God but a realistic strategy aims to lessen its violence. The distinction between war and policing is one such step. That between force and violence, although questionable, discriminates between socially authorised protection of the innocent and morally illegitimate violence. Advocating the use of non-lethal force and non-violent restraint wherever possible captures both the need to maintain order and the imperative to leave open for the offender space for repentance and amendment. The demands of the order of preservation can to a degree be co-ordinated with that of redemption.

In all of these discussions, the resurrection of Jesus Christ is both the sign of hope for the world and the assurance that risky imitation of Christ's way has ultimately redemptive power. In the Trinitarian activity of God, the life, death and resurrection of Christ are the means of redemption. This is the ground of a universal Christian hope and is the point and means of reconciliation. In so far as Christian action in the Spirit corresponds to the self-giving way of Jesus it participates in his ministry of reconciliation. The resurrection is the sign that in the providence of God such action is never wasted, whatever its short term cost. The church shares in the redeeming work of Christ to the extent that, inspired by him, it risks its life.

Notes

1 This chapter is a (hopefully) simplified argument following the line of the twenty-one theses on church and state which I develop in *Disavowing Constantine*, chapter 9.

2 Max Weber, 'Politics as a Vocation', in H.H. Gerth and C.W. Mills (eds.), *From Max Weber: Essays in Sociology* (London and Boston: Routledge & Kegan Paul, 1948), 78.

3 1 Corinthians 2:8; Ephesians 2:1; 3:10; 6:12.

4 Paul Avis, 'Establishment and the Mission of a National Church', *Theology* 103.811 (2000), 11.

5 Compare this with 1 Peter 2:14.

6 Bruce W. Winter, *Seek the Welfare of the City: Christians as Benefactors and Citizens* (Carlisle: Paternoster, 1994), 26–40.

7 Avis, *Church, State and Establishment*, 39.

8 Walter Wink, *Engaging the Powers: Discernment and Resistance in a World of Domination* (Minneapolis: Fortress Press, 1992), 3–10. See also Nigel G. Wright, *Power and Discipleship: Towards a Baptist Theology of the State* (Oxford: Whitley Publications, 1996).

9 Genesis 2:18.

10 1 Samuel 8:11–22.

11 Jürgen Moltmann, *The Crucified God: The Cross of Christ as the Foundation and Criticism of Christian Theology* (London: SCM Press, 1974), 136–45.

12 John Coffey, 'How Should Evangelicals Think about Politics? Roger Williams and the case for principled pluralism', *Evangelical Quarterly* 69.56 (January, 1997), 39–62.

[13] The terms are used by Os Guinness in 'Tribespeople, Idiots or Citizens? Religious Liberty and the Reforging of the American Public Philosophy', *Spectrum* 23.1 (1991), 40.

[14] Vernard Eller, *Christian Anarchy: Jesus' Primacy over the Powers* (Grand Rapids: Eerdmans, 1987).

[15] S.C. Mott, *Biblical Ethics and Social Change* (Oxford: Oxford University Press, 1982), 191–92.

[16] Revelation 11:15.

[17] Adrian Hastings, 'Church and State in a Pluralist Society', *Theology* 95.765 (1992), 170.

[18] Matthew 5:13.

[19] 1 Kings 18:7–16.

[20] Wink, *Engaging the Powers*, 175–82.

[21] For a fuller discussion of this see Wright, 'Baptist and Anabaptist Attitudes to the State', 349–57.

[22] Romans 14:1–12.

12. Paradigms for Engagement

The Shape of the Future

Introduction

Much of this book has been concerned with history. But knowing where we have come from is really about charting a course for the future. It would be entirely wrong to view the issues raised in this book as merely rehearsing things past: we are seeking perspectives on what is to come. Any discussion of the church needs to be set against that future vision of 'a great multitude which no one could count, from every nation, from all tribes and peoples and languages, standing before the throne and before the Lamb'.[1] This is a vision of the ultimately free church in an ultimately free state! We are on the way to its realisation, but it is not yet. Properly understood, the baptist way of being the church is inherently dynamic. It is not about the sublime recapitulation of truths once for all delivered but about an ongoing process of change under the rule of Christ and under the Word of God in a process, as the Reformers saw, of continual reformation. The church is always in the process of being reformed.

John Smyth and Thomas Helwys, the founders of the first two Baptist churches, were previously part of a Separatist congregation which began its life in Gainsborough in around 1606. The members of this church had a covenant in which, 'As the Lord's free people, they joined themselves by a covenant of the Lord into a church estate, in the fellowship of the gospel, to walk in all his ways, made known or to be made known unto them.' W.T. Whitley commented on this that, 'There was a fine touch of modesty and expectancy here; they did not think that they had reached finality, but they were ready to live up to all the light to be vouchsafed.'[2] Most significantly, this covenant was directed towards the future and it committed this group, and the movement that flowed from it, to an open-ended lifestyle by which they expected both to *learn* more about the ways of God and to *change* more in response to what they learnt. This open-endedness was well expressed by the saying of John Robinson, who was the pastor of the linked congregation at Scrooby Manor, in his final sermon to the Pilgrim Fathers, whom he also served as pastor, 'The Lord has yet more light and truth to break forth from his word.'[3]

It may be said then that the baptist tradition is inherently progressive in that it expects to learn and to change. To be true to the tradition is to be orientated towards the future and to be aware of a pilgrimage in which we will both learn new ways and adapt old ways to the new circumstances in which we live. This open flexibility is one reason why the baptist way of being church has proven to be highly effective in the mission of the church. It also has the capacity to adapt itself to future needs. This chapter is about these adaptations and identifies three areas for reflection: the task of church renewal and church planting, the ecumenical imperative of working towards a united church and the engagement of the church with its social and political environment. Each of these areas is complex and the intention here is not to offer swift solutions but to explore typologies or paradigms by means of which to think through the responses which are required in each case.

A Typology for New Ways of Being Church

Whereas globally the church continues to grow remarkably, in the Western world there is a widespread sense that the distance between the churches and the cultures in which they are set is growing wider, rendering the church less accessible to contemporary people. This has led to a search for new ways of being church which both take account of the shifts in culture we have experienced and minimise the unnecessary cultural barriers towards entering the church.[4] In all practice of religion, faith, ethnicity and culture have a tendency to coalesce. The baptist movements have generally been successful in distinguishing between ethnicity and faith, and in denying that faith is a component of ethnic identity. They have not always been so successful at distinguishing between culture and faith, confusing the essence of their principles with particular cultural forms. Christian faith is capable of endless cultural expressions. Granted that the gospel must itself be a 'stumbling block',[5] how do we minimise the unnecessary cultural obstacles that human beings put in the way of belonging to the church? At this point, the baptist conviction that church life is essentially simple allows a wide range of possibilities.

It is now widely recognised that the Western church is just as much in a missionary context as any other part of the world, the difference being that the prevailing 'religion' or ideology which dominates the West is now secular humanism. On this basis, strategies for evangelism and church planting in other places ought to illuminate the possibilities for mission in the West. As one example, John Travis developed a typology of strategies for church planting in Muslim cultures around a spectrum of possibilities for Christ-centred communities.[6]

- C1 represents the transplant of a church from one country to another in which everything is exactly the same as the country of origin including the language. Such a church would be attractive to expatriates and possibly also to members of the host community who are well acquainted with and sympathetic to that culture and its language.
- C2 is the same as C1 except that it uses the local language and so becomes accessible to a wider circle. It avoids Islamic vocabulary but translates its religious language into the host language in a way which makes clear its distinctiveness.

- C3 is like C2 but in addition uses local music styles, dress, art and other elements of the host culture which are deemed not to have Islamic religious overtones but to be essentially cultural. C1–C3 believers all identify themselves as 'Christians'.

- C4 is like C3 but goes further in adopting indifferent or biblically permissible religious practices such as praying prostrate, praying towards Jerusalem, washing before prayer and before handling the Bible, abstaining from pork and from alcohol or from keeping dogs as pets, using some Islamic terms and some items of clothing popular among Muslims. The point here is to emphasise continuity with their own cultural heritage and to avoid the cultural and ethnic overtones associated with 'Christian'. The Muslim community, however, does not see them as fellow Muslims.

- C5 believers are as C4 except for self-identity in that they call themselves 'Muslim followers of Isa' as Hebrew Christians might call themselves 'messianic Jews'. They attempt to remain 'maximally Muslim' even while rejecting those aspects of Islam which conflict with Scripture. Their desire is to remain in the Muslim community for as long as possible in order to 'win Muslims as a Muslim'.[7] Deviance from Muslim theology may lead in time to their being excluded from that community but short of that a whole mosque might begin to follow Jesus. Clearly, both C4 and C5 could only be carried forward by believers from Muslim backgrounds and would represent a radical indigenisation of Christian faith.

- C6 believers are essentially 'secret believers' who have not gone public on their faith.[8] Strictly, this category should not figure on the spectrum since we are not here talking about Christ-centred *communities*. The category serves as a reminder of what is happening beyond the church, but what follows here refers to the options available from C1 to C5.

This typology would by no means command universal assent among mission thinkers but it is illuminating in demonstrating a broad understanding of mission strategy. C4 and C5 remain experimental categories whose potential may not yet have been clearly demonstrated, although parallel strategies among Jewish people have proven to be effective. If in Acts 15 the crucial debate concerned how people might become believers in Jesus while remaining culturally Gentile rather than Jewish, the strategy in contemporary Jewish evangelism has become, how may Jewish people become followers of Jesus without becoming Gentiles? By derivation, how may Muslims become followers of Jesus without becoming detached from their religious and social culture in ways that are not demanded by the gospel? By another step of derivation, the spectrum might be seen to apply to mission in the secular West which is on a par with Islamic environments for its resistance to the gospel. How may contemporary 'secular' people embrace Christ without being required to cross unnecessary cultural barriers? It should be possible to strip out of church life those elements which have accrued to it, and yet are not strictly essential, for the sake of concentrating on what really does matter, the presence of Christ at the centre of one's own spiritual community.

In chapter 1 we noted a somewhat different spectrum in identifying traditional, contemporary and postmodern (sometimes called 'emerging') ways of being church, but this can be seen to correspond to the categories in C1–C5. The C1–C5 spectrum acknowledges that each point on the spectrum may be a valid strategy. Those at either end should not therefore accuse each other of either irrelevance or assimilation.[9] In particular, it is a mistake to believe that to survive, all churches must transition to the postmodern approach; rather, all churches are under a challenge to be spiritually dynamic, whatever their preferred cultural style. People are different and respond to varying approaches; there is enough room in mission for many different strategies. Churches which are defiantly traditional in their approach and make no concessions to cultural relevance can nonetheless make an impact upon their communities. Others are unlikely to be attracted to such churches, or having been part of them, may come to find them unable to meet their needs over the long haul. Churches which have developed a contemporary style tend to be those which attract most attention. Postmodern churches are largely still experimental. In secular terms, the C5 approach asks how much of church life is strictly necessary to be church and how much simply reflects a particular culture, and then imagines other possibilities.[10]

As churches explore their mission the C1–C5 spectrum transposed to the engagement with secular culture offers insights into strategy. What is essential is the recognition that there is an 'ecclesial minimum', which in previous chapters we have sought to identify. Although the minimum offers the possibility of great flexibility, when it is dispensed with we are no longer talking about the church of Christ. Strategists need to be clear therefore about what is absolutely essential and what is culturally relative and the point at which a mission project can be said to crystallise into the kind of ordered community that can be called a church. Human communities come in many forms. They can be 'thin' in the sense that what holds people together is a limited range of interest. By contrast, being church in the free church tradition needs to be a 'thick' experience in which people interact at a variety of points and in so doing build identity, and shape those who belong.[11] These communities are inherently more demanding since it is less easy to opt out when demands are made. However, it ought to be possible to deliver thick communities across the whole of the C1–C5 spectrum. It is also possible to imagine the values of the free church being faithfully expressed in any and all of these strategies.

A Typology for Ecumenical Engagement

In the introduction to this book I made a daring claim. I invited readers to read the history of the church not within the traditional framework of Orthodox, Catholic and Protestant but as representing two fundamental tendencies in church order,[12] the catholic and the baptist which could be seen as the twin foci of an ellipse. These, seen in the broadest terms, are the two basic tendencies of the church. The catholic tendency (which in this scenario includes the Orthodox and many Protestants) views the authenticity of the church as deriving from its historical origins in Christ and prizes continuity. The baptist tendency (which might include Catholics such as the liberation theologians as well as Protestants) finds it in the vitality of the local congregation and prizes freedom. Each has its besetting sin: the catholic is attracted to 'sacred power' and the baptist reaction to this leads it into fragmented sectarianism. Yet these sins can be mirrored in each other: when catholics make exclusive claims to being the church they have become sectarian; when baptists become prey to personalities and domination they are seduced by sacred power. At the same time, each broad tradition has what the other needs: the baptists need the connectedness and the continuity exhibited by catholics at their best which enable them to see themselves as part of one church of Christ; the catholics need the spiritual vitality and the ownership of the church's life by the whole people of God which baptists demonstrate at their best. A hopeful, if very long-term, vision of the future holds that such a rapprochement between the two tendencies might just be a possibility. Rather than view the two forms of inclusive institution and believing community as mutually exclusive, held in tension they might be viewed as the *yin* and the *yang* of the church, opposite but complementary forces which mitigate each other's risks.[13] The preconditions for this would be the decisive rejection by catholics of sacred power, while maintaining the proper commitment to connectedness, and for baptists of sectarianism, while reaffirming their commitment to spiritual freedom. For baptists this opens up the question of dialogue with the catholic tradition in the shape of its main representative, the Roman Catholic Church, a task which some might consider unthinkable and others impossible. As a way of addressing the relevant issues, we engage in conversation at this point with current attempts of the Catholic Church to open up a new dialogue.[14]

In 1995 Pope John Paul II issued his now famous encyclical *Ut unum sint: That They May All Be One: Commitment to Ecumenism*.[15] In the midst of a spiritual and tender reflection on the unity of the church and in particular the role of the papacy in promoting it as a 'minister of unity',[16] he made the following highly personal statement:

> As Bishop of Rome I am fully aware, as I have reaffirmed in the present Encyclical Letter, that Christ ardently desires the full and visible communion of all those Communities in which, by virtue of God's faithfulness, his Spirit dwells. I am convinced that I have a particular responsibility in this regard, above all in acknowledging the ecumenical aspirations of the majority of the Christian communities and in heeding the request made of me to find a way of exercising the primacy which, while in no way renouncing what is essential to its mission, is nonetheless open to a new situation.[17]

He goes on to issue to other 'Churches and ecclesial communities' the following far-reaching invitation:

> This is an immense task, which we cannot refuse and which I cannot carry out by myself. Could not the real but imperfect communion existing between us persuade Church leaders and their theologians to engage with me in a patient and fraternal dialogue on this subject, a dialogue in which, leaving useless controversies behind, we could listen to one another, keeping before us only the will of Christ for his Church and allowing ourselves to be deeply moved by his plea "that they may all be one … so that the world may believe that you have sent me" (Jn. 17:21)?[18]

It is difficult to read this invitation with goodwill without wishing to respond. At the same time, it would be unwise to overlook the multiplicity of issues it raises and, on the face of it, the unlikelihood of clear and deliverable outcomes within an imaginable time-scale. This is especially so for people like baptists for whom the papacy and its association with 'despotic absolutism'[19] has been the embodiment of everything they dislike about the Roman way.[20] However, precisely because of these things the invitation of John Paul II offers the opportunity to examine a crunch issue in ecumenical understanding.

Mapping the territory

In general, John Paul II's invitation has received a warm welcome and response, as has his wider commitment to ecumenical relations. The responses have been set out in summary form in a Working Paper.[21] While it soon becomes abundantly clear that objections to the papacy are alive and well, there also seems to be sufficient willingness in the following mainstream responses to offer alternative ways of thinking or to seek for win-win solutions for the sake of progress.

1. The scriptural foundation of the papacy

Not surprisingly, Catholic interpretation of biblical texts continues to be contested and the concern is expressed that later institutional developments in the church are read back into the New Testament.[22] A clear difficulty is experienced by some in finding in these texts or elsewhere a justification of the role of the Bishop of Rome. Whereas some identify an open 'Petrine function' to be exercised as a ministry of unity, Peter was not the only person to exercise this in the New Testament. Paul must be included here, and the identification of that function as a matter of necessity with the Bishop of Rome can, from this perspective, only be assumed on extra-biblical grounds. A case might be made for a ministry of universal *episkope* (oversight) serving the unity of the churches, just as Peter was told to 'strengthen his brethren',[23] but again the exercise of that function by the Bishop of Rome is not in itself biblically required. Conceivably, there are other ways of achieving this goal.

2. The concept of 'divine right'

Because the Catholic Church considers the primacy of the Bishop of Rome a matter of 'divine right', she sees it as belonging to the essential and irrevocable structure of the church. Protestants by contrast have seen the papacy as a humanly created rather than divinely ordained institution. But even so various possibilities remain open. Either it could be seen in principle as part of God's will for the church but with its *institutional form* being capable of considerable adaptation (a Lutheran suggestion); or it could be interpreted as a *providential ordering* within human history, even if not specifically mandated in Scripture (an Anglican suggestion). Both these approaches might allow for a general acceptance of the 'theological essence' of primacy while allowing for reservations concerning its actual historical style or shape. This is where as a matter of fact most of the offence has been caused within Christian history. Suitably adapted therefore the papacy could gain a much wider acceptance.[24]

3. The concept of 'universal jurisdiction'

Closely allied to the former point is the claim of the papacy enunciated at Vatican I to immediate jurisdiction over all churches and their bishops, a claim which has been vigorously and strongly opposed by all non-Catholic churches. At this point, the papacy as it has been practised has been a cause for division not unity. Here we perhaps see in its sharpest relief the proposed shift from understanding the papacy not as a power *over* but as a ministry of unity *towards* the universal church. The claim of the papacy to universal jurisdiction was denounced especially by Orthodox Churches as the overweening self-exaltation of the Western Patriarch. It was both centralising in tendency and, in practice, negated rather than strengthened the authority even of Catholic bishops within their dioceses. A way forward proposed by some churches could involve an appropriate balance between the personal, collegial and communal dimensions of spiritual oversight with the Bishop of Rome holding a primacy of honour within a pattern of complementary forms of oversight. Even such a primacy of honour would require appropriate levels of authority and power in reaching its assigned goal of, for instance, initiating and proposing. But, primarily, the Pope is a servant of the servants of God.

4. Papal infallibility

This doctrine constituted the most difficult and controversial aspect of Vatican I viewed in ecumenical perspective and it was fiercely rejected by all non-Catholics because it gave to the

Pope a teaching authority apparently apart from the consensus of the faithful.[25] It is the whole church which is entrusted with the task of guarding the fundamental teachings of the faith and the Pope in his teaching office is a spokesman for this consensus, as well, of course, as a significant influence in the conciliar processes through which it is formulated. As part of a complementary and participative process the Pope could be understood to have a universal teaching office.

It will be clear from the above themes that many of the respondents have already assumed a number of understandings which are foreign to baptists, not least some kind of episcopal understanding of the ordering of the church. Equally, it should be clear that many of the objections held by baptists are not theirs exclusively. The themes outlined help us to move our attention to the response made by the Baptist Union of Great Britain (BUGB).

The response of the Baptist Union of Great Britain

The Baptist Union Council agreed a response to *Ut unum sint* in April 1997 and appears to have been the only Baptist body to do so formally.[26] In the broken state of the church, even that part called baptist, the statement of the BUGB is as close as at least one group of Baptists is likely to come to a common mind. Specifically it welcomes in the Encyclical the following:

- Its careful grounding in the inspired Scriptures.
- Its willing recognition as Christians of all who have been justified by faith and incorporated into Christ through baptism.[27]
- Its sense of inner repentance and the need for personal and communal conversion.[28]
- The call to continual reformation.[29]
- The importance of doctrine as an expression of the content of faith.[30]

However, Baptist understandings of the nature of leadership and ministry in the church, which have had little room even for episcopacy, make it hard for them to conceive of any acceptable form of universal primacy. While unity within the whole church is certainly a desirable goal it would not be assumed that primacy is a necessary means of achieving this. This is not to say that there is a lack of openness in considering how such a ministry might serve to accomplish this goal. The final issue would concern the kind of leadership and ministry offered by the Bishop of Rome and the ways in which power and authority are used. If he can truly develop this ministry as a ministry of love, as a servant of the servants of God within the collegiality of his fellow bishops, then this may well be a significant contribution to the unity of the church. British Baptists do not assume that the Bishop of Rome or any other leader of a world communion should occupy as of right or perpetuity the position of first among equals. If the Spirit were to lead in the direction of a 'collegiality of spiritual leaders' there is no reason why this should be attached permanently to any of the historic centres of world Christianity. However, the position and influence of the Bishop of Rome is such that nothing of a constructive nature would be likely to come about without his leadership within this process. Certainly for the sake of mission the unity of the church is not an issue that can be avoided.

A wider European response

The response of the Baptist Union of Great Britain is both negative and positive – negative in that it warns of the difficulties inherent in gaining a positive attitude to the Petrine office from Baptists but positive in that it welcomes the idea of a ministry of unity and sees its potential. A more uniformly negative note is struck by the German Baptist theologian Erich Geldbach.

Geldbach begins by pointing to the writings of John Smyth, the first English Baptist, as an example of how far Baptist theology is in its origins from the Roman Catholic tradition. The two faith communities were very greatly removed from each other.[31] As an agent of Antichrist, the pope was responsible (in Smyth's view) for all the wrong teachings and practices of the Roman Church and those other churches which had not adequately broken with her. Baptists have seen the church in local terms and have shown little interest at all in the unity of the wider church, paying lip service only to the image of the church as the body of Christ, with its implications of organic relationships, and being content to split whenever difficulties have suggested it may be the easier option.[32] The Roman Church was feared, not without reason, as an incorrigibly totalitarian religious and potentially political system. Such fears were only exacerbated by the catalogue of false beliefs (as they were seen) promulgated by Vatican I claiming that the Pope's authoritative teaching was infallible *ex sese*[33] and that he had universal and judicial primacy over the whole church. In Geldbach's judgment,

> Baptists did not follow a prejudice, but reached a clear theological verdict supported by hard evidence that for the Church of Christ to function properly and credibly a papal office was unnecessary. It was contradictory to the simplicity of the apostolic age, and its claim to universal primacy and infallibility was counterproductive both to the Gospel of Christ and freedom-loving humankind.[34]

For Baptists the life of the church is to do with community expressed primarily in local congregations as believers in Jesus Christ meet freely for worship, fellowship, instruction and participation in God's mission. By extension, it is expressed in the interdependence of associations, conventions and unions of churches and it is essential for them that this is *not* expressed in such legally binding structures as would threaten the freedom of believers or of local congregations. By contrast, for the Roman Catholic position communion finds embodiment in the institutional bonds which unite congregations into dioceses presided over by bishops who in turn unite dioceses into the whole church which is presided over by the Bishop of Rome. Here we encounter a significant distinction since what makes for fellowship in the Roman conception, being bound into an institutional system, would threaten, for the Baptist, precisely that which makes it of value, the fact that it is freely chosen in the first place and freely sustained thereafter.[35] We shall see that this distinction is significant for the way in which the Pope's ministry of unity is understood.

If Geldbach finds reason to question the underlying concept of communion that is at stake in conversations between Baptists and Catholics, a further European writer raises similar and related concerns about the concept of *unity* that is at play in describing the Bishop of Rome as a 'minister of unity'. Miroslav Volf, a Croatian Pentecostal and therefore a baptist in the terms of this book, writes intentionally from a free church perspective and acknowledges in his writings a clear debt to John Smyth, the first English Baptist.[36] He finds significance in the fact that there is no 'office of unity' in the New Testament itself and that this idea first emerged as the specific task of the bishop in the letters of Ignatius in the second century.[37] This raises the question of whether the New Testament understanding of the church's unity corresponds with that of the later church. Volf argues that there is a significant difference in the way unity is understood and that his own proposal makes for a more Trinitarian emphasis. While responding to *Ut unum sint*, his argument takes its starting point from the crucial earlier document produced by Vatican I and entitled *Pastor aeternus*.[38] In this we read,

> So then, just as he sent apostles, whom he chose out of the world (see John 15:19), even as he had been sent by the Father (see John 20:21), in like manner it was his will that in his church there should be shepherds and teachers until the end of time (Matt 28:20). In order, then, that the episcopal office should be one and undivided and that, by the union of the clergy, the whole multitude of believers should be held together in the unity of faith and communion, he set blessed Peter over the rest of the apostles and instituted in him the permanent principle of both unities and their visible foundation.[39]

The logic here is clear enough. The oneness of believers requires for its visible ground the oneness of the episcopate which itself requires the single person of Peter as 'a lasting principle and visible foundation' of its unity. One Pope is the precondition of a united episcopacy, just as the one bishop is the foundation of the unity of the clergy and so of all the believers. The unity of the church is grounded in the *singularity* of its primary minister. The one temporal shepherd corresponds with the one eternal shepherd. This logic is developed by Joseph Cardinal Ratzinger who despite pointing out explicitly that the correspondence of the church to the Trinity points away from 'the exercise of the primacy by a single human being' and towards the notion of a 'communal primacy', confounds this train of thought by recapitulating the logic of singularity contained in *Pastor aeternus*. The unity of Christians is held together 'by persons responsible for this unity and is represented once again in a personalized form in Peter'.[40]

Volf finds in this a monistic approach to the unity of the church. It is *Christologically* grounded; but this falls short of being *Trinitarian*. Here Volf's argument touches upon precisely that verse cited in *Ut unum sint* in the midst of the Pope's invitation and appeal to fraternal and patient dialogue. Volf makes much of words that are actually omitted in the text of John 17:21 as produced in the Encyclical: 'As you, Father, are in me and I am in you, may they also be in us.' Volf's focus alights upon the 'as' in, '*As* you Father are in me and I am in you.' *How* are Christ and the Father one in the life of the divine Trinity? The question of the nature of the divine unity then becomes derivatively a question about the church's unity. The Trinitarian unity is of equally divine persons in mutual self-giving, the unity of mutual indwelling and love. So, 'Ultimately, it is this perfect divine love between equal divine persons that provides the model for the relations between the members of the church.'[41] This is a significantly different model of unity from that proposed by *Pastor aeternus* or Cardinal Ratzinger. Unity is grounded not in singularity, as in the bishop or the Pope as representatives of the one God, but in the 'self-giving love of the many'.[42] It is relational not monistic.

Where does this lead in relation to any understanding of primacy? As with Cardinal Ratzinger's first instinct it leads away from a primacy of singularity towards something communal. Communality is in keeping with the models of unity put forward in the New Testament which are more faithful to the Trinitarian insights out of which the later doctrine of the Trinity was to emerge. Thus there is no ministry of unity as such in the New Testament since that unity is brought about through the indwelling of God's Spirit within every person who is in Christ. Ordained ministers must indeed attend to the unity of the whole but this is only one dimension of their ministry and the responsibility for unity lies with the people of God as a whole.[43] In keeping with this Volf recalls that Heribert Mühlen, a Catholic theologian, proposed a 'trinitarianisation' of the papal office, while clarifying that he did not imply by this the establishing of a triumvirate.[44] A communal primacy is implied in Trinitarian doctrine. It is only in the practice of self-giving love modelled on the life of the self-giving God who loves a sinful world that any form of primacy approaches what it should be.[45]

Some modest proposals

It should already be clear that to discuss and debate these issues is itself to make progress on them. What else might, however, constructively be said? Here I offer some lines of inquiry and development that impinge upon both parties to the discussion.

1. Baptists, along with other Protestants, need to recognise and acknowledge that the habitual tendency to fragment which is a feature of ecclesiological localism is a scandal and a sin. This is not to say that there have never been times when dissent and disruption were theologically justified by the church-dividing magnitude of the issues at stake. It is to say that when this becomes a habit it is grievous failure. The converse of this repentance is the recognition that the body of Christ is universal and that the aspiration of the catholic tradition to maintain the unity of that body is right in principle.

2. Catholics need to recognise that when concern for the unity of the body is expressed by means of a singularity of oversight, divine law or a common jurisdiction, this is

likely to be perceived by baptists as having potential for oppression and the denial of freedom to consciences and to congregations. This is the practice of sacred power and to them it both contradicts the way of Christ and is counter-productive. This is not to say that there is not a legitimate exercise of doctrinal and moral discipline within and between congregations but that the line between godly discipline and institutional self-seeking can be a fine one. Baptists live out their lives in ordered congregations, but this order is not perceived as proceeding *hierarchically* with authority always flowing down from above. Rather, Christ's authority at work in ministers whom he sends is recognised and accorded from below, from among the people, whose task is to do more than reiterate the Amen.

3. Baptists need to give renewed consideration to the balance within and between the communal, collegial and personal dimensions of church government and oversight. They accept that within the primary communal discipline and oversight of the congregation the collegial oversight of elders and deacons works with and alongside the personal oversight of pastors and others for the enrichment of all. Each dimension of oversight adds to the overall well-being of congregations. But if they apply in the local congregation should not these dimensions also be applicable for associations, conventions or unions of churches and does it not therefore point in the direction of episcopal ministries? In other words, if on a regional or national level churches are called to watch over each other communally should there not also be within this a greater recognition of collegial and personal oversight as variations and applications of communal oversight? And if this is so, might there not also be appropriately at the international level, in ways which do not compromise the freedom of unions, associations and local congregations, expressions both of collegial and personal oversight?[46] Finding ways to be organically connected to each other requires the ministry of persons who can carry the trust, respect and affection of the many but in a way entirely dependent upon spiritual and moral authority. The recognition and valuing of those who

can fulfil these roles and act as joints between different parts of the body of Christ should receive more attention than it ever has done from Baptists.

4. Catholics may recognise that given baptist understandings of unity which focus on relationships before institution or organisation, it is already possible for the Pope to act as a minister of unity towards such churches or ecclesial communities as may be open to this. Where the Catholic Church, the largest Christian communion in the world, chooses to use its immense influence and power to affirm other Christian communities, to support them in their mission and to accord them esteem, the benefits could be considerable. Evangelical Christians, such as baptists are, will respond to the kind of lead which gives a high priority to evangelisation, mission and engagement with the non-Christian world. For Baptists, evangelisation has always been the mainspring of concern for unity.[47] Unity and mission are inextricably linked, but often shared mission can stimulate an increased sense of unity and common endeavour.[48]

5. The Trinitarian reflections we have encountered suggest the possibility of a communal or collegial approach to universal primacy. The recognition that there may be a Petrine *function* does not carry with it the implication that this be an exercise in singularity. The function may be fulfilled communally. It has not been established on biblical or theological grounds that the Bishop of Rome or any other person defined geographically must in perpetuity and of necessity be part of this function. However, pragmatically, given that we are the heirs of a considerable history, it seems impossible for any kind of primacy to be possible without the support and participation of the Bishop of Rome and, indeed, of other historic Christian leaders.

6. It may be that the investigations of this chapter concerning differing understandings of unity point to the fact that catholics and baptists represent after all two incompatible systems. However, at the very least, in response to the Pope's appeal, there is a case for rapprochement rooted in mutual respect and a commonly confessed apostolic faith,

and for seeing where this might take us. I have sought to identify historic weaknesses in both traditions: the tendency, as baptists might see it, for the catholic approach to become a stifling and suppressive system of control and the undeniable baptist reproduction of divisions. Both weaknesses are the dark side of the positive strengths of these ways of being church: the catholic concern for the unity of the universal body of Christ through continuity and connectedness; the baptist concern for the vitality and freedom of the local congregation. We each need what the other can bring.

If rapprochement is to happen its preconditions are that we recognise in each other not only the apostolic faith but also properly ecclesial status. Volf has commented:

> Should, for example, a Catholic or Orthodox diocese whose members are inclined more to superstition than to faith and who identify with the church more for nationalistic reasons – should such a diocese be viewed as a church, while a Baptist congregation that has preserved its faith through the crucible of persecution *not* be considered such? Would not an understanding of ecclesiality that leads to such a conclusion take us to the brink of absurdity? Equally untenable is the early, though still widespread Free Church position that denies ecclesiality to the episcopal churches.[49]

Recognition that both traditions are church is indispensable. So is the insight that for the only future we may currently foresee and from the baptist side at least, the recognition that may be accorded to the Bishop of Rome is likely to be one of honour and not of jurisdiction or power. However, if both the catholic and baptist foci in that ellipse we call Christianity could see the ways in which they could enrich each other, and draw from each other the good things that they bring, without sacrificing what really matters to either side, then it would become possible to imagine a new kind of unity within the body of Christ, the spiritual potential of which would be immense.

A Typology for Engagement with the Social and Political Environment

The church exists for the sake of God, but also for the world which God created and loves. In this section the concern is with the relationship between the public and the private in the practice of Christian discipleship and therefore with the 'social teaching' of the Christian churches. In chapter 2 we drew attention to the way in which Ernst Troeltsch, after surveying the history of Christian social thinking, concluded that there were to be found within it three broad types which he distinguished as the church-type, the sect-type and mysticism.[50] Each type could appeal to Scripture for justification and only together did they exhaust the breadth of New Testament teaching. As noted, the church-type was characterised by *universality* and the contrasting sect-type by *intensity*. Mysticism was characterised by *inwardness* and focused on the realm of private spiritual experience without laying any particular claims to a communal identity or to the public realm other than the freedom to ignore it and go its own way.

There can be no denying that this has been an enormously influential and valuable approach and Troeltsch's work has classical status. A similar thing might be said about H. Richard Niebuhr's seminal work entitled *Christ and Culture*.[51] Here again Niebuhr worked with ideal types, five in number, of the ways in which Christ has been deemed to relate to created but fallen human culture throughout Christian history. The *Christ against Culture* type, which Niebuhr saw illustrated by the various Anabaptist movements deriving from the sixteenth century, but particularly by the Amish of North America, sets fidelity to Christ over against accommodation to the culture in an intensification of Troeltsch's sectarian-type. This is a retreat from the public into the private. The *Christ of Culture* type accommodates to culture to the point where no conflict between the two is experienced and so could be exemplified by Liberal Protestantism. This is a merging of the private with the public so that the church becomes a religious echo of public culture. The *Christ above Culture* type is seen by Niebuhr as the centre ground occupied historically by the church according to which Christ makes sense not only of the church's story but of the whole of creation which finds its true nature in the Logos from whom all things derive their rationality. Yet public culture is called to a fulfilment in the Christ who is most clearly known in the church and so judges culture at the same time as elevating it. *Christ and Culture in Paradox*, illustrated chiefly by Lutheranism, detects a kind of dualism between Christ and culture so that any relation between them is more likely to be derived through conflict and dialectic rather than a smooth cohesion. Finally, Niebuhr is working towards what seems to be his preferred type which is *Christ the Transformer of Culture*, illustrated he believes by names in Christian history such as Augustine, Calvin and F.D. Maurice. Christ redeems and transforms the public culture.

Typologies are illuminating but also misleading in that they invite people to pigeonhole movements and groups according to a set of preconceived identities. They therefore need to be used with wisdom and sensitivity. What follows is an alternative attempt to identify the possible relationships of the church to its social and political environment, to map the territory of the public and the private. It is hoped therefore to work towards a degree of clarity and so follows a dialectic of thesis, antithesis and synthesis: First, both *participating and possessing*; secondly, *neither participating nor possessing*; finally, *participating without possessing*.

Both participating and possessing

In these perspectives, the Christian church lays claim not only to participating in the public realm but also to possessing it in the sense that it lays down the truths and the ideology which under-gird, determine and shape that realm. The church is viewed as the proper determining force in the public as in the private realms. Yet under this general heading there are distinctions to be made about how this is done and what its implications might be. In this first set of descriptions, epistemological optimism is the order of the day: God's truth can be known through reason and revelation and can be authoritatively interpreted by the church. This truth should be applied to the public realm since it is beneficial for all: it is the truth of God. Where therefore the church has the influence to do so it should not hesitate to lay claim to the public realm and seek to determine it. After all, if the church does not do this then someone else or something else, less benign and less in accord with the truth, will do so in its place. In the success story of the church's rise from obscure Jewish sect to imperial religion over just three centuries, the church did acquire the power to claim the public realm as its own. Within this overall heading I differentiate three approaches.

The first is *theocracy*. Theocracy looks for the immediate rule of God on earth through the powers that be, and although I shall argue that it remains an uncharacteristic approach within Christianity, there is no doubt that it has been present. It may take two forms, occurring either when the religious function-ary assumes the mantle of secular power or, more commonly, when the secular ruler is deemed to be chosen of God, is invested with the divine right to rule and is given authority over the church as well as over temporal affairs. The technical term for this is 'Caesaro-papism', and it is to be applied chiefly to the Byzantine Emperors over the Eastern Church from the sixth to the tenth centuries. If there is a 'problem' of the public and the private then according to theocracy it is easily solved: any distinction between the two is abolished. What is publicly confessed by the ruler is to become the private faith of the subject: *cuio regio eius religio*.

Slightly distinguished from theocracy is *Constantinian Christendom*, for although the first Christian Roman Emperor certainly wished to use the Christian religion as a means of legitimating his own rule, and was followed in this by some of his successors, not least Theodosius I, the Western Church by and large fell short of full-blown theocracy. Belief in the public truth of Christianity did indeed insist that both private and public life should come under the divine lordship expressed in Christ. But Western theologians in the tradition of Augustine would be less likely to give unhesitating legitimation to imperial power. There are, after all, two cities and the City of

Man is not the same as the City of God. The latter as an other-worldly and future reality calls the former into question and exposes its self-seeking and rapacious powers. Augustine launched a remarkably robust critique of imperial power: kingdoms without justice are like criminal gangs.[52] Characteristically and significantly, the West retained the language of church *and* state, the two not being entirely the same but a tension existing from time to time between them despite the fact that they worked together in partnership. The church does indeed claim to supply the public truth that makes sense of the state within a comprehensive theology; but the church's truth would lead it to criticise the state from time to time rather than to confirm it and to expose the claim that something was the will of God simply because the king or emperor claimed it. The church retained a degree of independence from the state and for much of its history was helped in this in that it was a supra-national body not immediately captive to national interests. There are Old Testament examples enough for such prophetic confrontation and for resisting the insistence that the temple is the king's sanctuary, rather than the Lord's.[53] Nonetheless, this is *Christendom* in that the church's truth possesses, interprets and determines the public realm. And it is *Constantinian* Christendom in that the partnership between church and state led to the willingness of the church to enforce its truth as public truth through the use of the state's coercive powers, seeing this first of all as an appropriate exercise of discipline towards erring and straying Christians, like the Donatists, but with the passage of time applying such force also to unbelievers.

But just here is the third possibility of *non-Constantinian Christendom*. The term 'Christendom' is often used in an undifferentiated way which overlooks the complexity of the phenomenon. We have seen that within the church's tradition there have been those who rejected coercion to enforce religious conformity. The free church tradition unhooked religious belief from state power so as to permit freedom of conscience and toleration of religious diversity. It did this for well-articulated theological reasons. Public religion therefore was not to be imposed upon private conscience. The first advocates of this, although they foresaw a freedom not just for dissenting Christians but for other faiths as well, did not view their proposals as a surrender of the possession of the public realm by Christian truth. Instead, they believed that faithfulness to Christ pointed in the direction not of a state that would coerce consciences but of a *truly* Christian one that would protect tender consciences and foster religious liberty. This tradition advocated the separation of church and state to distinguish more clearly between the coercive powers of the magistrate and the persuasive power of the gospel and its advocates, but it was still within a vision of Christendom in which Christian truth was determinative for the public realm. The theologically articulated free church, free state tradition fits into this category.

So far then, I have reviewed various ways in which the Christian faith was embraced as both private and public truth. What was believed privately by Christians counted also as the truth which dominated the public arena, and what was accepted as the public religion was either enforced or, in its more tolerant free church form, encouraged and facilitated within the private realm. Manifestly this situation no longer prevails. We have moved in the West from a once publicly Christian world in which *unbelief*, where it was held at all, was held in private, to a publicly Christian world in which *belief*, where it is held at all, is held in private. This brings us then to the position antithetical to that we have just examined.

Not participating and not possessing

If the rise of the Christian faith to fulfil the role of public truth is astonishing, it is equally amazing to chart that process by which it was displaced. This is generally attributed to the secularising effects of the post-Enlightenment period, the outcome of which was the gradual removal of Christian faith from its public role to the realm of private belief and a few vestigial and arcane cultural artefacts. If the concern of the advocates of non-Constantinian Christendom was that the public religious ideology should not be imposed within the private world of the religious conscience, the antithetical concern of post-Enlightenment secularism has been that private religious conscience should not be allowed to lay claim to the public realm which was to be the domain instead of a supposedly neutral 'reason'. Christian faith therefore did not only not possess the public realm, it was only to be taken seriously if it was prepared to submerge its identity, lay aside its own forms of moralising and reasoning and participate in the public arena by accommodating itself to the methodology of secular reasoning. An appeal to God was deemed not to 'count' in the public discourse and when such appeals were made they sounded at best at odds with the way that discourse was carried through and at worst like an irrational attempt to hijack the dialogical process. Religious reasoning was playing outside the rules of the game which were now determined from elsewhere. Extreme versions of this in the modern world have been the possession of the public realm by the avowedly anti-Christian ideologies of communism and fascism.

The real focus in this section concerns what I identify here as *Hard Secularism.* Hard secularism is more than a political theory. It is a metaphysics and takes its lead from scientism, which is more than a method of gaining knowledge and understanding: it is a materialistic, atheistic worldview hostile to religion which it sees as a force for superstition and which it is only prepared to tolerate insofar as it does not have significant social or political effects upon public existence or other people. Privatisation of religion is, according to this account, a containment strategy since faith is perversely persistent and proceeding against it only strengthens it. The most effective strategy therefore is to ignore it, to hold it as of no significance, to draw attention wherever possible to its decline and its marginality. Active faith and belief is 'fundamentalism' and religious practice is 'cultic'. Although by no means in the same league as other ideologies, hard secularism would possess the public realm as its own territory. Consequently, private faith is not allowed to possess the public realm, nor to participate in it on its own terms but only on those which are laid down for it by secularism itself.

It is time to move to the third area of exploration.

Participating without possessing

I sought previously to differentiate between theocracy, Constantinian Christendom and non-Constantinian Christendom as differing visions of the way in which Christian faith can be affirmed as public as well as private truth. In the third of these options Christian faith bears witness to truth that is both public and private, but envisages adherence to that truth being gained and maintained through voluntary means alone. The Christendom vision of the whole of society as subject to the Lordship of Christ was never of itself wrong. In this I find myself in agreement with a comment by Gerald W. Schlabach on the most trenchant contemporary Christian critic of Christendom thinking, Stanley Hauerwas. Schlabach, a Mennonite and so reputedly 'sectarian' theologian, comments:

> Hauerwas has discovered a dirty little secret – Anabaptists who reject historic Christendom may not actually be rejecting the vision of Christendom as a society in which all of life is integrated under the Lordship of Christ. On this reading, Christendom may actually be a vision of shalom, and our argument with Constantinianisms is not over the vision so much as the sinful effort to grasp at its fullness through violence, before its eschatological time. Hauerwas is quite consistent once you see that he does want to create a Christian society (*polis*, *societas*) – a community and way of life shaped fully by Christian convictions. He rejects Constantianism because 'the world' cannot be this society and we only distract ourselves from building a truly Christian society by trying to make our nation into that society, rather than be content with living as a community-in-exile.[54]

The Christendom vision which affirms both the public and the private truth of Christ is not wrong but the means to that vision's achievement may be. Since the gospel works by persuasion not by coercion the church must content itself with the rising and the falling of its influence in any given society and culture since to employ other means than this would be to impose its truth prematurely and oppressively upon others. Participation in the public realm can never be foregone since this would be to deny the public truth of Christ to which the church bears witness, but the witness is sustained with a view to the eschatological fulfilment of Christ's reign. Of the positions I have explored, non-Constantinian Christendom represents the nearest approximation to what I describe, reflecting the belief that the groundings of a healthy, tolerant and free society are more securely rooted in this theological soil than in reductionist secularism or some alien totalitarianism. But we now live after any kind of Christendom – the titles of a host of books suggest this perception is widely shared.[55] There is a further item of the landscape to note and this is *Soft Secularism*.

As different meanings of the term 'Christendom' needed to be differentiated, so with 'secularism'. As there is a difference between *science* as a method of inquiry and *scientism* as an all-encompassing metaphysics requiring its own leap of faith, so we are wise to distinguish between the *hard secularism* which is essentially an atheistic worldview and the *soft secularism* which is a political strategy designed to hold together religiously and ideologically diverse societies. The 'secular' is here portrayed as a common meeting ground for people of all faiths. Understood in these terms, soft secularism may value the public contribution of religious communities and happily admit their insights into the public arena for a fair hearing while maintaining a clear and constitutional distance between any organ of religion and the means of coercion and compulsion. There is therefore religious participation without religious possession of the organs of government and social control.

Ostensibly, this is not far from the insights of non-Constantinian Christendom which may in part have paved the way for its emergence. Soft secularism can value the public role of religion while believing, for historical reasons rooted not least in the religious conflicts of previous centuries, that religion itself is corrupted when what should be a matter of voluntary commitment becomes wedded to political power. Soft secularism is a political strategy for maintaining a proper distinction at this point not in the belief that religion should be excluded from the public arena but that it is helpful neither to religion nor to the political realm for their association to be too close. In this sense there is insight in the rubric that religion and politics do not mix; there is equal truth in saying that politics is about morality and morality is closely associated with religion. When it comes to the distinctive property of the state, which is the power to coerce and enforce, religion and politics do indeed inhabit different realms: the ideal and the possible, the final and the relative, the eternal and the temporal, the compulsory and the voluntary. Faith groups should have access to public debate and political bodies in recognition of their contribution to the moral formation of citizens, their involvement in local communities and the social capital they generate. The 'politics of recognition' at these points is simply good politics.[56] It is important that religious voices be heard in the public realm in a spirit of tolerance and not suppressed or dismissed. It is also important that fairness and equality of treatment be the goal of any secular agency.

Soft secularism may be the best model for social existence currently on offer or potentially realisable.[57] At the very least it is a conversation partner with which Christians can do business and with which there are many points of similarity. Christians might prefer to 'possess' the public realm more comprehensively, but there is no real choice in many Western nations short of a massive Christian revival which changes the whole climate of debate. The biblical narrative gives evidence of many different configurations of the public and the private in the relationships between God's people and the wider world. It is possible to be faithful to God in all of them. We may believe that a firm theological foundation better preserves those public virtues which make for the common good. But we do not need to possess the public realm to participate in it. Religious and spiritual truths are at their most potent when they are offered modestly as witness from below rather than requirement from above. But Christian faith can never forsake its public testimony or concerns. Participate we must in order to be true to our ultimate hopes and visions and so that, informed by an ultimate future which puts all things in context, we might seek the welfare of the earthly city in which we are in exile.

Final Words

The concerns of this chapter have been to do with the transmission of the Christian faith, the growth of the churches, the unity of the whole church of Jesus Christ, and the witness of that church within human civil and political communities. This is the uncharted territory of the church's future mission. The wisdom of that perspective which proclaims the free church in a free state is necessary for our onward journey to provide coherence in the challenges which await us. This book has been dedicated to making those insights clear and making them known. The nature of the free church contribution will develop and change, but a firm understanding of the theology that lies behind it is essential in ensuring that such change is constructive. My contention is that both in the growth of churches of the baptist kind and in their impact upon the catholic tradition to which they stand in some contrast the energy of the free church tradition in the future will be undiminished. However, the best hope is for a new kind of understanding between these two great impulses within Christianity, one which is mutually enriching and, shorn of both sacred power and sectarianism and reflecting more completely the life of the Triune God, prepares the way for a church which is closer to the one for which Jesus prayed.

Notes

1 Revelation 7:9.
2 W.T. Whitley, *A History of British Baptists* (London: Charles Griffin & Co., 1923), 20.
3 See on this *http://www.mlp.org/sermon.html*. George Rawson's famous hymn, 'We limit not the truth of God' uses these words in its refrain: *Baptist Praise and Worship* (London: Oxford University Press, 1992), No. 107.

4 For instance the Church of England Report *Mission-Shaped Church: Church planting and fresh expressions of church in a changing context* (London: Church House Publishing, 2004).

5 1 Corinthians 1:23; 1 Peter 2:8.

6 John Travis, 'The C1 to C6 Spectrum: A Practical Tool for Defining Six-Types of "Christ-centred Communities" ('C') Found in the Muslim Context', *Evangelical Missions Quarterly* (October, 1998), 407–408. I am grateful to David Kerrigan for drawing my attention to this article.

7 1 Corinthians 9:19–23.

8 John 19:38.

9 Joshua Massey, 'His Ways are Not Our Ways', in *Evangelical Missions Quarterly* (April, 1999), 197.

10 Stuart Murray and Anne Wilkinson-Hayes, *Hope from the Margins: New ways of being church* (Cambridge: Grove Books, 2000); Alan Jamieson, *A Churchless Faith: Faith journeys beyond the church* (London: SPCK, 2002).

11 For the distinction between thin and thick communities I am grateful to Dr Parush Parushev of the International Baptist Seminary, Prague.

12 It is church order which is in view here. In fundamental theology baptists are catholic in that they share the confession of faith of the whole church.

13 Martin E. Marty, 'Baptistification takes over', *Christianity Today* (2 September 1983), 33, 36.

14 Some of what follows here is drawn from Nigel G. Wright, 'The Petrine Ministry: Baptist Reflections', in *Pro Ecclesia: A Journal of Catholic and Evangelical Theology* XIII.4. (Autumn 2004), 451–65.

15 Catholic Church, *Ut unum sint: That They May All Be One: Commitment to Ecumenism* (London: Catholic Truth Society, 1995).

16 Catholic Church, *Ut unum sint*, Paragraph 88.

17 Catholic Church, *Ut unum sint*, Paragraph 95.

18 Catholic Church, *Ut unum sint*, Paragraph 96.

19 Küng, *Church*, 450. On a more positive note Küng also says: 'If a pope really does exist for the Church and if he really fulfils his task of selfless pastoral service to the whole Church, then through him great things can be achieved and evils be avoided', 454.

20 It is noteworthy that the Baptist World Alliance was the only world communion to decline the invitation to send observers to the Second Vatican Council: See Ken Manley, *The Baptist World Alliance and Inter-Church Relationships* (Baptist Heritage and Identity booklet No. 1; Falls Church, VA: Baptist World Alliance,

2003), 15. At the same time, especially among English Baptists there has often been a deep sense of the church's catholicity, represented by such ecumenical statesmen as J.H. Shakespeare (1857–1928) and E.A. Payne (1902–1980), both having served as General Secretaries of the Baptist Union of Great Britain.

21 Pontifical Council for Promoting Christian Unity, 'Petrine Ministry: A Working Paper' (June 2002).

22 Matthew 16:16f. and John 21:15f., in particular.

23 Luke 22:32.

24 Leon Joseph Cardinal Suenens was to the point here: 'When I was young, the Church was presented to us as a hierarchical society: it was described as "juridically perfect", having within itself all the powers necessary to insure and promote its own existence. This view reflected an image of the Church which was closely modelled on civil, even military society: there was a descending hierarchy, a uniformity which was considered as an ideal, and a tight discipline which extended to the smallest detail...The second Vatican Council emphasized the Church as the people of God on pilgrimage, at the service of the world...This was to stress the priority of baptism and the radical equality of the children of God, and automatically implies a reform of the concept of the Church which we today call "pyramidical", thus situating ministry within the heart and at the service of the whole ecclesiastical body. The perspective became more evangelical and less juridical without, however, repudiating the role of the hierarchy': *A New Pentecost?* (New York: Seabury Press, 1975), 1–2.

25 Significantly, both the promulgation of the doctrine of the Immaculate Conception by Pius IX in 1854, and so before Vatican I, and of the doctrine of the Assumption in 1950 by Pius XII were formally speaking on the Pope's sole authority. There was, of course, prior consultation on both these issues. See Duffy, *Saints and Sinners*, 292, 352.

26 *One in Christ: Ecumenical Notes and Documentation* No. 4 (1999), 360–65.

27 Catholic Church, *Ut unum sint*, Paragraph 13.

28 Catholic Church, *Ut unum sint*, Paragraph 15.

29 Catholic Church, *Ut unum sint*, Paragraph 16.

30 Catholic Church, *Ut unum sint*, Paragraph 18.

31 Erich Geldbach, 'The Petrine Ministry and the Unity of the Church: A Baptist Perspective', in James F. Puglisi (ed.), *Petrine Ministry and the Unity of the Church* (Collegeville, MN: The Liturgical Press, 1999), 157.

32 Geldbach, 'Petrine Ministry', 158, 162, 164; 'When in doubt, let's split.'

33 On his own authority without the need for confirmation by the councils or consensus of the church.

34 Geldbach, 'Petrine Ministry', 161.

35 Geldbach, 'Petrine Ministry', 162.

36 See especially Volf, *After our Likeness*, 127–58.

. 37 M. Volf, 'Trinity, Unity, Primacy: On the Trinitarian nature of unity and Its Implications for the Question of Primacy', in Puglisi (ed.), *Petrine Ministry* , 181.

38 Vatican I, First Dogmatic Constitution on the Church of Christ, *Pastor aeternus*, in N.P. Tanner (ed.), *Decrees of the Ecumenical Councils, vol II: Trent to Vatican II* (London/Washington, DC: Sheed & Ward/Georgetown University Press, 1990).

39 Cited by Volf, 'Trinity, Unity and Primacy', 173–74.

40 Volf, 'Trinity, Unity and Primacy', 176 citing for this discussion Joseph Ratzinger in, *Church, Ecumenism and Politics: New Essays in Ecclesiology* (New York/Slough: Crossroads/St Paul's, 1988), 31–36.

41 Volf, 'Trinity, Unity and Primacy', 179.

42 Volf, 'Trinity, Unity and Primacy', 180.

43 Volf, 'Trinity, Unity and Primacy', 181.

44 Volf, 'Trinity, Unity and Primacy', 182, citing H. Mühlen, *Entsakralisierung: Ein epochales Schlagwort in seiner Bedeutung für die Zukunft der christlichen Kirchen* (Paderborn: F. Schöning, 1971), 257.

45 Volf, 'Trinity, Unity and Primacy', 183.

46 In relation to the Baptist international movement, the Baptist World Alliance, Denton Lotz once expressed this as a vision for, 'An *ecclesial* function. To sensitize Baptists Worldwide to the *ecclesial* function of the BWA and as such to see a direct line of spiritual and moral authority flowing from the local congregation to the association, state convention, national body and finally to the Baptist World Alliance – and from the BWA back again to the local congregation.' BWA General Council Agenda Book, Dresden, July 1999, 93 cited by Manley, *Baptist World Alliance*, 43. The statement is noteworthy for its dynamic vision expressed in mutuality.

47 Denton Lotz in the Foreword to Manley, *Baptist World Alliance*, 3.

48 In this regard, the kind of lead offered in Encyclicals such as *Evangelization in the Modern World* (London: Catholic Truth Society, 1990), is welcome and constructive.

49 Volf, *After our Likeness*, 133–34.

50 Troeltsch, *Social Teaching* Volume II, 993.

51 H.R. Niebuhr, *Christ and Culture* (New York/London: Harper & Row, 1951, 1975).

52 Augustine, *City of God* (London: Penguin, 1972), 139.

53 Amos 7:12–13.

54 Cited by Hauerwas himself without reference in *After Christendom? How the Church is to behave if freedom, justice and a Christian nation are bad ideas* (2nd edn.; Nashville: Abingdon, 1991) 7–8.

55 In addition to that by Hauerwas see David Smith, *Mission After Christendom* (London: Darton, Longman & Todd, 2003); Douglas John Hall, *The End of Christendom and the Future of Christianity* (Valley Forge. PA: Trinity Press International, 1997); Stuart Murray, *Post-Christendom : Church and Mission in a Strange New World* (Carlisle: Paternoster, 2004); Wright, *Disavowing Constantine.*

56 I am largely indebted for the term 'soft secularism' and the immediate points made here to Professor David Fergusson of Edinburgh University who included them in a presentation to the Evangelical Alliance Commission on Faith and Nation, 26 September 2003.

57 It can be seen here that soft secularism is very akin to what is often called political pluralism. Pluralism also could be seen in both 'hard' and 'soft' categories: hard pluralism is that form which insists that all ideologies and religions are but relative expressions of truth and so denies any claim to 'exclusive', 'final' or 'normative' truth. As has previously been pointed out, this is nothing other than a hidden claim to possess for itself the kind of truth that it denies to others. It is therefore 'hard' because it is (secretly) 'intolerant'. Soft pluralism is the variety which allows all claims to truth a fair hearing and accepts that there will be outright contradictions and some positions are preferable to others. Sometimes this is simply called 'plurality' and at other times 'authentic pluralism' in that it more authentically allows people genuine and contradictory differences.

Bibliography

Archbishops' Council, *Statistics: A Tool for Mission* (London: Church House Publishing, 2000)

Augustine, *City of God* (London: Penguin, 1972)

—, *On Original Sin*, chapters 3–4: *Nicene and Post-Nicene Fathers* Volume 5 (New York: Christian Literature Company, 1887)

Avis, Paul, 'Establishment and the Mission of a National Church', *Theology* 103.811 (2000), 3–12

—, *Church, State and Establishment* (London: SPCK, 2001)

Baillie, Donald M., *The Theology of the Sacraments* (London: Faber & Faber, 1957)

Bainton, Roland H., 'The Left Wing of the Reformation', in *Studies on the Reformation* (London: Hodder & Stoughton, 1964), 119–29

The Baptist Confession of Faith of 1689: A Faith to Confess (Haywards Heath: Carey Publications, 1975)

Baptist Union of Great Britain, *Patterns and Prayers for Christian Worship* (Oxford: Oxford University Press, 1991)

Barth, Karl, *Church Dogmatics: The Doctrine of Reconciliation*, Volume IV/2 (Edinburgh: T&T Clark, 1958)

Beasley-Murray, George R., *Baptism in the New Testament* (London: Macmillan, 1962)

—, *Baptism Today and Tomorrow* (London: Macmillan, 1966)

Beasley-Murray, Paul, *Radical Believers: The Baptist Way of Being the Church* (Didcot: Baptist Union of Great Britain, 1992)

Bettenson, H.R. (ed.), *Documents of the Christian Church* (Oxford: Oxford University Press, 1967)

Boff, Leonardo, *Ecclesiogenesis: The Base Communities Reinvent the Church* (Glasgow: Collins, 1982)

—, *Trinity and Society* (Tunbridge Wells; Burns & Oates, 1988)

Bradshaw, Timothy, *The Olive Branch: An Evangelical Anglican Doctrine of the Church* (Carlisle: Paternoster, 1992)

Calvin, John, *The First Epistle of Paul to the Corinthians* (Edinburgh: Saint Andrew Press, 1960)

—, *Institutes of the Christian Religion* Book IV, chapter 14:1 (ed. John T. McNeil; Philadelphia: Westminster, 1960)

Campenhausen, Hans von, et al. (eds.), *Die Religion in Geschichte und Gegenwart* Volume 6 (Tübingen: J.C.B. Mohr, 1962)

Chan, Simon, *Spiritual Theology: A Systematic Study of the Christian Life* (Downers Grove, IL: InterVarsity Press, 1998)

Church of England, *Mission-Shaped Church: Church planting and fresh expressions of church in a changing context* (London: Church House Publishing, 2004)

—, *The Alternative Service Book* (London: Hodder & Stoughton, 1980)

Clark, Neville, 'The fulness of the church of God' in Alec Gilmore (ed.), *The Pattern of the Church: A Baptist View* (London: Lutterworth Press, 1963), 79–113

—, *Preaching in Context: Word, Worship and the People of God* (Bury St Edmunds: Kevin Mayhew, 1991)

—, *Pastoral Care in Context; Vision of God and Service of God* (Bury St Edmunds: Kevin Mayhew, 1992)

Coffey, John, 'How Should Evangelicals Think about Politics? Roger Williams and the case for principled pluralism', *Evangelical Quarterly* 69.56 (January, 1997), 39–62

—, *Persecution and Toleration in Protestant England 1558–1689* (Edinburgh: Longman, 2000)

Congar, Yves, *Ecclesiogenesis: The base communities reinvent the church* (Glasgow: Collins, 1982)

Cook, Henry, *What Baptists Stand For* (London: Kingsgate Press 1947, 1964)

Creighton, Louise, *Life and Letters of Mandell Creighton* Volume 1 (Longmanns, Green & Co., 1904)

Cross, Anthony R., 'Faith-Baptism: The Key to an Evangelical Baptismal Sacramentalism', *Journal of European Baptist Studies* 4.3 (May, 2004), 5–21

Dakin, Arthur, *The Baptist View of the Church and Ministry* (London: Baptist Union, 1944)

Davis, Kenneth R., *Anabaptism and Asceticism: A Study in Intellectual Origins* (Scottdale, PA: Herald Press, 1974)

Doctrine and Worship Committee , Baptist Union of Great Britain, *Forms of Ministry among Baptists: Towards an Understanding of Spiritual Leadership* (Didcot, Baptist Union, 1994)

—, Baptist Union of Great Britain, *Believing and Being Baptized: Baptism, So-called Re-baptism and the Children of the Church* (Didcot: Baptist Union, 1996)

Duffy, Eamon, *Saints and Sinners: A History of the Popes* (New Haven and London: Yale University Press, 1997, 2001)

Dulles, Avery, *Models of the Church: A Critical Assessment of the Church in all its Aspects* (Dublin: Gill and Macmillan, 1976)

Dunn, James D.G., *Baptism in the Holy Spirit* (London: SCM Press, 1970)

—, *Unity and Diversity in the New Testament* (London: SCM Press, 1977, 1990)

Durnbaugh, Donald F., *The Believers' Church: The History and Character of Radical Protestantism* (London: Macmillan, 1968)

Eller, Vernard, *Christian Anarchy: Jesus' Primacy over the Powers* (Grand Rapids: Eerdmans, 1987)

Estep, William R., *The Anabaptist Story* (Grand Rapids: Eerdmans, 1975)

Fahrer, Walfred J., *Building on the Rock: A Biblical Vision of Being Church Together from an Anabaptist-Mennonite Perspective* (Scottdale, PA: Herald Press, 1995)

Fergusson, David, 'The Reformed Tradition and Tolerance', in Raymond Plant (ed.), *Public Theology for the 21ˢᵗ Century: Essays in Honour of Duncan B. Forrester* (London: T&T Clark, 2004)

Fiddes, Paul S., *Participating in God: A Pastoral Doctrine of the Trinity* (London: Darton, Longman & Todd, 2000)

—, 'Baptism and the Process of Christian Initiation', *The Ecumenical Review* 54 (2002), 48–68

—, *Tracks and Traces: Baptist Identity in Church and Theology* (Carlisle: Paternoster Press, 2003)

Flemington, W.F., *The New Testament Doctrine of Baptism* (London: SPCK, 1948)

Flew, R. Newton, *Jesus and his Church: A Study of the Idea of the Ecclesia in the New Testament* (London: Epworth Press, 1938)

Geldbach, Erich, 'The Petrine Ministry and the Unity of the Church: A Baptist Perspective', in James F. Puglisi (ed.), *Petrine Ministry and the Unity of the Church* (Collegeville, Minnesota: The Liturgical Press, 1999), 153–69

Giles, Kevin, *What on Earth is the Church? A Biblical and Theological Inquiry* (London: SPCK, 1995)

Giles, R.S., 'The Church as a Counter-Culture Before Constantine' (M.Litt Dissertation, University of Newcastle-upon-Tyne, 1987)

Gilmore, A. (ed.), *The Pattern of the Church: A Baptist View* (London: Lutterworth, 1963)

Green, Michael, *Baptism: Its Purpose, Practice and Power* (London: Hodder & Stoughton, 1986)

Grenz, Stanley J., *The Baptist Congregation: A Guide to Baptist Belief and Practice* (Vancouver, British Columbia: Regent College Publishing 1985, 1998)

—, *Renewing the Center: Evangelical Theology in a Post-Theological Era* (Grand Rapids: Baker Academic, 2000)

Guinness, Os, 'Tribespeople, Idiots or Citizens? Religious Liberty and the Reforging of the American Public Philosophy', *Spectrum* 23.1 (1991), 29–50

Gunton, Colin E., *The Promise of Trinitarian Theology* (Edinburgh: T&T Clark, 1991)

Gunton, Colin E. and Hardy, Daniel W. (eds.), *On Being the Church: Essays on the Christian Community* (Edinburgh: T&T Clark, 1989)

Hall, Douglas John, *The End of Christendom and the Future of Christianity* (Valley Forge. PA: Trinity Press International, 1997)

Hasler, August Bernard, *How the Pope Became Infallible: Pius IX and the Politics of Persuasion* (New York: Doubleday, 1981)

Hastings, Adrian, 'Church and State in a Pluralist Society', *Theology* 95.765 (1992), 165–76

Hauerwas, Stanley, *After Christendom? How the Church is to behave if freedom, justice and a Christian nation are bad ideas* (2nd edn.; Nashville: Abingdon, 1991)

Hayden, Roger (ed.), *Baptist Union Documents 1948-1977* (London: Baptist Historical Society, 1980)

Hollenweger, Walter J., *The Pentecostals* (London: SCM Press, 1972)

Hooker, Richard, *Laws of Ecclesiastical Polity*, Vol. III.i.7–8, in John Keble (ed.), *Richard Hooker: Works*, Vol. 1 (Oxford: Oxford University Press, 1845)

Hopkins, Mark, *Nonconformity's Romantic Generation: Evangelical and Liberal Theologies in Victorian England* (Carlisle: Paternoster, 2004)

Hughes, David Michael, 'The Ethical use of Power: A Discussion with the Christian Perspectives of Reinhold Niebuhr, John Howard Yoder and Richard J. Barnet' (PhD Dissertation, Southern Baptist Theological Seminary, 1984)

Jamieson, Alan, *A Churchless Faith: Faith journeys beyond the church* (London: SPCK, 2002)

Jenson, Robert W., *Systematic Theology Volume 1: The Triune God* (New York and Oxford: Oxford University Press, 1997)

Jeschke, Marlin, *Believers Baptism for the Children of the Church* (Scottdale, PA: Herald Press, 1983)

Jewett, Paul K., *Infant Baptism and the Covenant of Grace* (Grand Rapids: Eerdmans, 1988)

Johnson, Luke T., *Decision-Making in the Church: A Biblical Model* (Philadelphia: Fortress Press, 1983)

Jones, Keith G., *A Believing Church: Learning from some contemporary Anabaptist and Baptist Perspectives* (Didcot: Baptist Union of Great Britain, 1998)

Klaassen, Walter, *Anabaptism: Neither Catholic nor Protestant* (Waterloo, Ontario: Conrad Press, 1973)

Kuhrt, Gordon, *An Introduction to Christian Ministry* (London; Church House Publishing, 2000)

Küng, Hans, *The Church* (London: Burns & Oates, 1968)

Lightfoot, J.B., *St. Paul's Epistle to the Philippians* (London: Macmillan, 1913)

Lindsay, A.D., *The Churches and Democracy* (London: Epworth Press, 1934)

Littell, Franklin H., 'The Work of the Holy Spirit in Group Decisions', *Mennonite Quarterly Review* 34.2 (1960), 75–96

—, *The Origins of Sectarian Protestantism: A Study of the Anabaptist View of the Church* (London/New York: Macmillan, 1964)

Lumpkin, William L., *Baptist Confessions of Faith* (Valley Forge: Judson Press, 1969)

MacLaren, Brian, *A New Kind of Christian: A Tale of Two Friends on a Spiritual Journey* (San Francisco: Jossey-Bass, 2001)

Manley, Kenneth R., 'Origins of the Baptists: The Case for Development from Puritanism-Separatism', in William H. Brackney (ed.), *Faith, Life and Witness: The Papers of the Study and Research Division of the Baptist World Alliance – 1986–1990* (Birmingham, AL: Samford University Press, 1990), 56–69

—, *The Baptist World Alliance and Inter-Church Relationships* (Baptist Heritage and Identity booklet No. 1; Falls Church, VA: Baptist World Alliance, 2003)

Marcel, Pierre, *The Biblical Doctrine of Infant Baptism* (London: James Clarke, 1953)

Martin, Ralph P., *The Family and the Fellowship: The New Testament Images of the Church* (Carlisle: Paternoster Press, 1979)

Marty, Martin E., 'Baptistification takes over', *Christianity Today* (2 September 1983), 32–36

Massey, Joshua, 'His Ways are Not Our Ways', in *Evangelical Missions Quarterly*, (April, 1999), 188–97

McBeth, Leon H., *A Sourcebook for Baptist Heritage* (Nashville: Broadman Press, 1990)

McClendon Jr, James William, *Systematic Theology Volume 1: Ethics* (Nashville, TN: Abingdon, 1986)

McFadyen, Alistair, *Bound to Sin: Abuse, Holocaust and the Christian Doctrine of Sin* (Cambridge: Cambridge University Press, 2000)

Migliore, Daniel L., *Faith Seeking Understanding: An Introduction to Christian Theology* (Grand Rapids: Eerdmans, 1991)

Minear, Paul S., *Images of the Church in the New Testament* (Philadelphia: Westminster Press 1960)

Moltmann, Jürgen, *The Crucified God: The Cross of Christ as the Foundation and Criticism of Christian Theology* (London: SCM Press, 1974)

—, *The Church in the Power of the Spirit: A Contribution to Messianic Ecclesiology* (London: SCM Press, 1977, 1992)

—, *The Spirit of Life: A Universal Affirmation* (London: SCM Press, 1992)

Mott, S.C., *Biblical Ethics and Social Change* (Oxford: Oxford University Press, 1982)

Murray, Stuart, *Post-Christendom: Church and Mission in a Strange New World* (Carlisle: Paternoster, 2004)

— (ed.), *Translocal Ministry: Equipping the Churches for Mission* (Didcot: Baptist Union, 2004)

Murray, Stuart and Anne Wilkinson-Hayes, *Hope from the Margins: New ways of being church* (Cambridge: Grove Books, 2000)

Myers, Ched, *Binding the Strong Man: A Political Reading of Mark's Story of Jesus* (Maryknoll, NY: Orbis Books, 1998)

Newbigin, Lesslie, *The Household of God: Lectures on the Nature of the Church* (London: SCM, 1953)

Newman, John Henry, *Certain Difficulties felt by Anglicans in Catholic Teaching* Volume 2 (London: Longmanns Green, 1885)

Nicholson, John F.V., 'The Office of Messenger amongst English Baptists in the seventeenth and eighteenth centuries', *Baptist Quarterly* 17 (1957–58), 206–25

Niebuhr, H.R., *Christ and Culture* (New York/London: Harper & Row, 1951, 1975)

Noll, Mark, *Turning Points: Decisive Moments in the History of Christianity* (Leicester: Inter-Varsity Press, 1997)

Norman, J.G.G., 'The Relevance and Vitality of the Sect-Idea', *Baptist Quarterly* 26.6 (1979), 248–58

Owen, John, 'The True Nature of a Gospel Church and its Government', in William H. Gould (ed.), *The Works of John Owen*, Volume XVI (Edinburgh: Banner of Truth Trust, 1968), 11–208

Parker, G. Keith (ed.), *Baptist Confessions in Europe: History and Confessions of Faith* (Nashville, Tennessee: Broadman Press, 1982)

Pawson, J. David, *The Normal Christian Birth; How to give new believers a proper start in life* (London: Hodder & Stoughton, 1989)

Payne, Ernest A., *The Fellowship of Believers: Baptist Thought and Practice Yesterday and Today* (London: Carey Kingsgate Press, 1944)

Payne, E.A., 'Contacts between Mennonites and Baptists', *Foundations* 4.1 (1961), 3–19

Pipkin, H. Wayne and Yoder, John H. (eds.), *Balthasar Hubmaier: Theologian of Anabaptism* (Scottdale, PA: Herald Press, 1989)

Pontifical Council for Promoting Christian Unity, 'Petrine Ministry: A Working Paper' (June 2002)

Robinson, H. Wheeler, *Baptist Principles* (London: Kingsgate Press 1945)

Roman Catholic Church, *Evangelization in the Modern World* (London: Catholic Truth Society, 1990)

—, *Catechism of the Catholic Church* (London: Geoffrey Chapman, 1994)

—, *Ut unum sint: That They May All Be One: Commitment to Ecumenism* (London: Catholic Truth Society, 1995)

Schweizer, Eduard, *Church Order in the New Testament* (London: SCM Press, 1961)

Smith, David, *Mission After Christendom* (London: Darton, Longman & Todd, 2003)

Spurgeon, C.H., *Infant Salvation: A Sympathetic Word to Bereaved Parents* (London; Passmore and Alabaster, no date)

—, *The Metropolitan Tabernacle Pulpit* Volume 24 (Passadena TX: Pilgrim Publications, 1972)

Suenens, Leon Joseph Cardinal, *A New Pentecost?* (New York: Seabury Press, 1975)

Tanner, N.P. (ed.), *Decrees of the Ecumenical Council, Volume II: Trent to Vatican II* (London/Washington, DC: Sheed & Ward/Georgetown University Press, 1990)

Toews, John E., 'Rethinking the Meaning of Ordination: Towards a Biblical Theology of Leadership Affirmation', *The Conrad Grebel Review* 22.1 (Winter, 2004), 2–25

Tracy, David, *The Analogical Imagination* (London, SCM Press, 1981)

Travis, John, 'The C1 to C6 Spectrum: A Practical Tool for Defining Six-Types of "Christ-centred Communities" ('C') Found in the Muslim Context', *Evangelical Missions Quarterly* (October, 1998), 406–11

Troeltsch, Ernst, *The Social Teaching of the Christian Churches* Volume I (London: George Allen & Unwin, 1932)

Verduin, Leonard, *The Reformers and their Stepchildren* (Exeter: Paternoster, 1966)

Volf, Miroslav, *After Our Likeness: The Church as the Image of the Trinity* (Grand Rapids and Cambridge: Eerdmans, 1998)

—, 'Trinity, Unity, Primacy: On the Trinitarian Nature of Unity and its Implications for the Question of Primacy', in James F. Puglisi (ed.), *Petrine Ministry and the Unity of the Church* (Collegeville, Minnesota: The Liturgical Press, 1999), 171–84

Watts, Michael R., *The Dissenters: From the Reformation to the French Revolution* (Oxford: Clarendon Press, 1978)

Weber, Max, 'Politics as a Vocation', in H.H. Gerth and C.W. Mills (eds.), *From Max Weber: Essays in Sociology* (London and Boston: Routledge & Kegan Paul, 1948)

West, W.M.S., *Baptist Principles* (London: Baptist Union, 1960)

—, 'The Child and the Church: A Baptist Perspective', in William H. Brackney and Paul S. Fiddes (eds.), *Pilgrim Pathways: Essays in Baptist History in Honour of B.R. White* (Macon, GA: Mercer University Press, 1999)

Westerhoff, John, *Bringing up Children in the Christian Faith* (Minneapolis: Winston Press, 1980)

White, B.R., *The English Separatist Tradition* (Oxford: Oxford University Press, 1971)

—, *Authority: A Baptist View* (London: Baptist Publications, 1976)

White, B.R. (ed.), *Association Records of the Particular Baptists of England, Wales and Ireland to 1660: Part 3. The Abingdon Association* (London: Baptist Historical Society, 1974)

Whitley, W.T., *A History of British Baptists* (London: Charles Griffin & Co., 1923)

Whitley, W.T. (ed.), *The Works of John Smyth* (Cambridge: Cambridge University Press, 1915)

Williams, George H., *The Radical Reformation* (Philadelphia: Westminster Press 1962)

Williams, George H., and Mergal, Angel M., *Spiritual and Anabaptist Writers* (Philadelphia: Westminster Press, 1962)

Wink, Walter, *Engaging the Powers: Discernment and Resistance in a World of Domination* (Minneapolis: Fortress Press, 1992)

Winter, Bruce W., *Seek the Welfare of the City: Christians as Benefactors and Citizens* (Carlisle: Paternoster, 1994)

World Council of Churches, *Baptism, Eucharist and Ministry*, Faith and Order Paper No. 111 (Geneva: WCC, 1982)

—, *Confessing the One Faith: An Ecumenical Explication of the Apostolic Faith as it is Confessed in the Nicene-Constantinopolitan Creed (381).* Faith and Order Paper No. 153 (Geneva: WCC Publications, 1991)

Wright, Christopher J.H., *Living as the People of God: The relevance of Old Testament ethics* (Leicester: Inter-Varsity Press, 1983)

Wright, Nigel G., *The Radical Kingdom: Restoration in Theory and in Practice* (Eastbourne: Kingsway, 1986)

—, *Challenge to Change: A Radical Agenda for Baptists* (Eastbourne: Kingsway, 1991)

—, '"The Sword": An Example of Anabaptist Diversity', *Baptist Quarterly* 36.6 (1996), 264–79

—, 'Baptist and Anabaptist Attitudes to the State: A Contrast', *Baptist Quarterly* 36.7 (1996), 349–57

—, *Power and Discipleship: Towards a Baptist Theology of the State* (Oxford: Whitley Publications, 1996)

—, *The Radical Evangelical: Finding a Place to Stand* (London: SPCK, 1996)

—, *Disavowing Constantine: Mission, Church and the Social Order in the Theologies of John Howard Yoder and Jürgen Moltmann* (Carlisle: Paternoster 2000)

—, *New Baptists New Agenda* (Carlisle: Paternoster 2002)

—, 'Religious Abuse: The Precarious Potential of Religious Believing', *Journal of European Baptist Studies*, 3.2 (January 2003), 5–14

—, 'Disestablishment – Loss for the Church or the Country? A Dissenting Perspective', *Journal of European Baptist Studies* 4.3 (May, 2004), 22–32

—, 'The Petrine Ministry: Baptist Reflections', in *Pro Ecclesia: A Journal of Catholic and Evangelical Theology*, XIII.4 (Autumn, 2004), 451–65

Yoder, John Howard, *Body Politics: Five Practices of the Christian Community before the Watching World* (Nashville, TN: Discipleship Resources, 1992)

New Baptists, New Agenda

Nigel G. Wright

There are at present 80 million Baptists in the world; yet what does it mean to be a Baptist, and how are present belief systems being transmitted to the next generation? *New Baptists, New Agenda* forms a valid and timely contribution to the growing debate about the health, shape and future of the Baptist church. It considers the steady changes that have taken place among Baptists in the last decade – changes of mood, style, practice and structure, and encourages us to align these current movements and questions with God's upward and future call. Nigel G. Wright shows that productive, faithful and creative Christian living is possible and necessary if Baptists are to respond to the shifting cultural paradigms of the time.

1-84227-157-1

Studies in Baptist History and Thought

Series Editors:
Anthony R. Cross, Curtis W. Freeman, Stephen R. Holmes,
Elizabeth Newman, Philip E. Thompson

Please note that these titles are not always published in sequence.

The Gospel in the World (SBHT vol. 1)
International Baptist Studies
David Bebbington (ed.)

1-84227-118-0

More Than a Symbol (SBHT vol. 2)
The British Baptist Recovery of Baptismal Sacramentalism
Stanley K. Fowler

1-84227-052-4

Baptism and the Baptists (SBHT vol. 3)
Theology and Practice in Twentieth-Century Britain
Anthony R. Cross

0-85364-959-6

The Making of a Modern Denomination (SBHT vol. 4)
*John Howard Shakespeare and the English Baptists
1898–1924*
Peter Shepherd

1-84227-046-X

Baptist Sacramentalism (SBHT vol. 5)
Anthony R. Cross and Philip E. Thompson (eds)

1-84227-119-9

'At the Pure Fountain of Thy Word' (SBHT vol. 6)
Andrew Fuller as an Apologist
Michael A.G. Haykin (ed.)

1-84227-171-7

Calvinism, Communion and the Baptists (SBHT vol. 7)
A Study of English Calvinistic Baptists from the Late 1600s to the Early 1800s
Peter Naylor

1-84227-142-3

Offering Christ to the World (SBHT vol. 8)
Andrew Fuller and the Revival of English Particular Baptist Life
Peter J. Morden

1-84227-141-5

The Search for a Common Identity (SBHT vol. 9)
The Origins of the Baptist Union of Scotland 1800–1870
Brian Talbot

1-84227-123-7

Edification and Beauty (SBHT vol. 17)
The Practical Ecclesiology of the English Particular Baptists,
1675–1705
James M. Renihan

1-84227-251-9

Baptist Identities (SBHT vol. 19)
International Studies from the Seventeenth to the Twentieth
Centuries
Ian M. Randall, Toivo Pilli and Anthony R. Cross (eds)

1-84227-215-2